Scots Folk Singers and their Sources

Scottish Cultural Review of Language and Literature

Series Editors

Rhona Brown (*University of Glasgow*)
John Corbett (*bnu-hkbu United International College*)
Sarah Dunnigan (*University of Edinburgh*)
Ronnie Young (*University of Glasgow*)

Associate Editor

James McGonigal (*University of Glasgow*)

VOLUME 31

The titles published in this series are listed at *brill.com/scrl*

Scots Folk Singers and their Sources

A Study of Two Major Scottish Song Collections

By

Caroline Macafee

BRILL
RODOPI

LEIDEN | BOSTON

Cover illustration: Joe Edwards, Harvest Time, mid-late 20th century. Reproduced with permission from the Estate of Joe Edwards; Image National Museums Scotland.

Library of Congress Cataloging-in-Publication Data

Names: Macafee, Caroline, author.
Title: Scots folk singers and their sources : a study of two major Scottish song collections / Caroline Macafee.
Description: Leiden ; Boston : Brill | Rodopi, 2021. | Series: Scottish cultural review of language and literature, 1571–0734 ; vol. 31 | Includes bibliographical references and index. |
Identifiers: LCCN 2021015514 (print) | LCCN 2021015515 (ebook) | ISBN 9789004464407 (hardback) | ISBN 9789004464414 (ebook)
Subjects: LCSH: Folk songs, Scots—Scotland—Sources. | Folk songs, English—Scotland—Sources. | Folk songs, Scots—Scotland—History and criticism. | Folk songs, English—Scotland—History and criticism. | Scots—Music—History and criticism. | Scottish Travellers (Nomadic people)—Music—History and criticism. | Music—Social aspects—Scotland—History. | Folk singers—Scotland. | Greig-Duncan folk song collection. | School of Scottish Studies Archives (Edinburgh)
Classification: LCC ML3655 .M25 2021 (print) | LCC ML3655 (ebook) | DDC 782.42162/9163—dc23
LC record available at https://lccn.loc.gov/2021015514
LC ebook record available at https://lccn.loc.gov/2021015515

Typeface for the Latin, Greek, and Cyrillic scripts: "Brill". See and download: brill.com/brill-typeface.

ISSN 1571-0734
ISBN 978-90-04-46440-7 (hardback)
ISBN 978-90-04-46441-4 (e-book)

Copyright 2021 by Koninklijke Brill NV, Leiden, The Netherlands.
Koninklijke Brill NV incorporates the imprints Brill, Brill Nijhoff, Brill Hotei, Brill Sense, Brill Schöningh, Brill Fink, Brill mentis, Vandenhoeck & Ruprecht, Böhlau Verlag and V&R Unipress.
All rights reserved. No part of this publication may be reproduced, translated, stored in a retrieval system, or transmitted in any form or by any means, electronic, mechanical, photocopying, recording or otherwise, without prior written permission from the publisher. Requests for re-use and/or translations must be addressed to Koninklijke Brill NV via brill.com or copyright.com.

This book is printed on acid-free paper and produced in a sustainable manner.

Contents

Preface IX
List of Figures and Tables XII
Abbreviations XVII

1 **Introduction** 1
   1.1 Origins of the Study 1
   1.2 A Note on Tables and Figures 4
   1.3 Estimated Dates of Birth 5
   1.4 Social Background 8
   1.5 Self-Reported Data 10
   1.6 The Benefits of a Quantitative Approach 18

2 **Weighing the Catch** 21
   2.1 The Data Sources 21
   2.2 Selecting the Data 22
   2.3 Approaches to the Data: Transmission 25
   2.4 Approaches to the Data: Chronology 26
   2.5 Ballad Fragments: Definition 28
   2.6 Outline of the Contributors, and a Note on the Reliability of Estimated Dates 30

3 **Did Greig and Duncan Neglect the Travellers?** 39
   3.1 The Fog of Euphemism 39
   3.2 The Supposed Neglect 42
   3.3 Travellers in *Greig-Duncan* 43
   3.4 A Very Small Fraction of the Population 45
   3.5 Traveller Songs 47
   3.6 The Traveller and G-D Repertoires: Two Exercises in Comparison 50
   3.7 The Traveller Mystique 52

4 **Song Transmission** 54
   4.1 Historical Stages of Song Transmission 54
   4.2 Outline of the Data and a Note on Selection 58
   4.3 Categories of Song Transmission Information 61
   4.4 Inter-Personal Transmission 63

        4.4.1 *The Predominance of General Population Males as Non-family Sources* 63
        4.4.2 *The Relative Lack of Non-family Transmission from the Travellers to the General Population* 65
        4.4.3 *The Female Preference for Family and Female Sources* 66
        4.4.4 *The Male General Population and Male* G-D *Preference for Non-family Sources* 67
        4.4.5 *The Traveller Preference (Both Sexes) for Family Sources* 67
        4.4.6 *Same-Sex and Opposite-Sex Transmission Pairs within the Family* 68
  4.5 The Travellers Embedded in a Literate Society 71

5 The Reticence of Female Singers 75
  5.1 Older and Younger Women 75
  5.2 (Older) Women and the Child Ballads 77
        5.2.1 *The Established Association between Women and the Big Ballads* 77
        5.2.2 *The Contribution of Females in the Child Ballad Data* 78
        5.2.3 *Decline in the Female Contribution over Time* 80
  5.3 Sex and Age Patterns in Non-family Song Transmission 86
        5.3.1 *Sources and Recipients in Non-family Transmission* 86
        5.3.2 *The Ages of Source Individuals* 87
  5.4 Domestic and Non-domestic Spheres 91

6 The Devolution of the Child Ballads to the Travellers 95
  6.1 The 'Child Ballad' – a Valid Concept? 95
  6.2 Combining the G-D and SSSA Data – a Valid Approach? 96
  6.3 Decline in Child Ballad Contributors and Contributions 98
  6.4 G-D as a Baseline 99
  6.5 Age Gap between Contributors and Sources 101
  6.6 Narrowing Ballad Repertoire 103
  6.7 Transmission is Increasingly Family-Dominated 107
  6.8 Greater Retention amongst the Travellers 109
  6.9 The Cultural Context of Ballad Singing 112
  6.10 The Performance Context of Ballad Singing 115

7 Social Change and Education *versus* Tradition 117
  7.1 Demography of the Contributors 117
  7.2 The 1840s Birth Cohort 120
  7.3 Education and the Regional Culture of the North-East 123

CONTENTS

- 7.4 The Demographic Transition Model 126
- 7.5 Extended Family Song Transmission 130
- 7.6 Rural Society in Flux 132

8 The Missing Singers of the 1920s 138
- 8.1 A Bimodal Distribution 138
- 8.2 Is the 1920s Dip Merely a Coincidence? 139
- 8.3 Singing at Work and Play *versus* Recorded and Broadcast Music 142
- 8.4 The Decline of Traditional Singing amongst the Travellers 144
- 8.5 The Folk Revival 146

9 Conclusions 148
- 9.1 Issues and Themes 148
- 9.2 Summary of Main Findings 149
- 9.3 Group Portraits 151
    - 9.3.1 *Greig-Duncan* 151
    - 9.3.2 *The Travellers* 153
    - 9.3.3 *The General (Including Core) Population* 156
    - 9.3.4 *The Folk Revival Contributors* 158
- 9.4 Timeline 159
- 9.5 Directions for Future Research 163

Appendix A: Additional Tables 167
Appendix B: Notes on the Selection of *Greig-Duncan* Data 194
Bibliography 197
Index 210

Preface

The origins of this book are described below in the Introduction. While working for Tobar an Dualchais/Kist o Riches as a cataloguer, data editor and indexer, I became interested in quantifying the song transmission data that I could see were latent in the cataloguing database. Over several years, in the intervals between other work, I pursued this study. My intention was to publish a couple of very dry journal articles and leave it to scholars in the field to make what they would of them. Having been informed how boring this was (by a colleague who wishes to remain anonymous), I embarked on the long trek towards this book.

I am very much aware that I am outside my own discipline in this research, but I hope that where I am in error, scholars in Scottish Ethnology will at least find this work worth the effort of correcting it. I was both encouraged and rather dismayed to read a recent paper by Eldar Heide about folklore archives in Scandinavia, particularly the Norwegian Folklore Archives (Heide, 2018). He points out the new opportunities for research that are opened up by digitisation – but acknowledges, at the same time, that these opportunities come belatedly: there has been a paradigm shift in Ethnology since the 1970s, and research interests have moved away from the traditional materials preserved in such archives. So it is often academics from other disciplines who are interested in what the collections contain. The archives that Heide is concerned with do not, for the most part, consist of tape-recordings, but nevertheless the present research is in some ways the type of study that Heide describes: an exercise in the data mining of material now largely of historical interest.

Yet this study does pertain to an issue that has become rather submerged: the cultural identity of Lowland Scotland. The deserved praise and attention given to Traveller tradition bearers has been tending more and more to obscure and deflect the Lowland population's ownership of their own cultural tradition. Happily, however, the newly digitised material is being channelled into education by Tobar an Dualchais' outreach activities. The educational work of former Tobar an Dualchais Scots song cataloguers Steve Byrne and Chris Wright (https://localvoices.co.uk/) is also informed by it.

The School of Scottish Studies Archives and Tobar an Dualchais are keen to encourage scholars and the public to listen to the tape recordings, of which a large part is now available online. I certainly would not want to undermine this message. At the same time, the digitised cataloguing does have great research potential in its own right for the extraction of large amounts of data on particular topics, with audio available to clarify and expand the catalogue summaries. With this end in view, further indexing of the material is extremely desirable.

I was first introduced to the riches of the School of Scottish Studies Archives in 1973–74 as a first year student at the University of Edinburgh, taking the course then called 'Oral Literature and the Popular Tradition'. I had the privilege of being taught by Hamish Henderson, Ailie Munro, Alan Bruford, Peter Cooke, and other members of staff of the School at that time. I would like to express my gratitude to those teachers, mostly now no longer with us, who first opened my eyes to Scottish folk culture. I hope that the broad view of the Scots song collection that is presented here will reproduce for the reader the general impressions that the collectors would have formed as the recordings accumulated.

My much more recent debt is to my colleagues on Tobar an Dualchais between 2007 and 2012, with whom it was such a pleasure to work, and from whom I learned so much. The present study would not be possible without the expertise and dedication of Steve Byrne and Chris Wright, who worked mightily to complete the addition of classifications to the Scots song part of the database, and in Chris' case also indexing, as we approached the end of the main phase of the project, with the funding running out. I am also indebted to Steve for helping me find some obscure references. I would also like to thank Andy Hunter for passing on to me, through a mutual friend, his typescript of Bell Robertson's correspondence relating to her contributions to *The Greig-Duncan Folk Song Collection*. This made it easier to gain a perspective on this important contributor, as otherwise the material is scattered through the notes to individual songs in the published collection. I have another very large debt to a colleague who does not wish to be publicly acknowledged, but who helped me enormously, especially by asking questions, directing me to published sources, suggesting that the study be extended to *The Greig-Duncan Folk Song Collection*, and saving me from egregious errors. Any remaining errors are, of course, entirely my own responsibility.

I very much appreciate the input of two anonymous peer reviewers, whose detailed comments helped me to pull the book into its final shape, and gave me the encouragement I needed for that final effort. One suggested that it would have been better to have conducted one large multivariate analysis, such as a cluster analysis, rather than the plethora of smaller analyses actually presented. However, my feeling from the outset was that the data would not support statistical (as opposed to merely quantitative) analysis. Even if inferential statistical analysis was used, a multivariate analysis – leaving aside the problems of combining discrete and continuous variables – would produce entities that would either be very difficult to interpret (as well as difficult to distinguish from artefacts, since the data involve too much estimation to justify significance tests) or would correspond to patterns easily demonstrated by simpler methods. I have therefore retained my original approach, which attempts to bolster the various simple analyses of often incomplete data by approaching the data from a number of different angles.

I am grateful to the editor of *Scottish Language*, Prof. Robert Millar, for permission to reproduce parts of Macafee (2019), and to Profs. Simon Burnett and Dorothy Williams for permission to reproduce parts of a paper (Burnett *et al.*, 2017) written jointly with them. I am also grateful to Prof. Williams, and to the Robert Gordon University, for permitting me to work on this topic while temporarily employed by the university in 2013–14. An unusual interdisciplinary exchange of ideas gave rise to the paper. In the present work, I have reproduced only the parts that relate directly to folk song, but the structure of the analysis was only arrived at through the theoretical framework provided by my co-authors. I am very grateful also to Mairead MacDonald, then Director of Tobar an Dualchais, for making it possible for me to carry out the present research. The rights in the material continue to subsist with the School of Scottish Studies Archives and the individuals recorded, and I am very grateful to the Archives for permission to cite and quote specific information not presently online, and to the Archives Curator, Dr Cathlin Macaulay, and the Archivist, Kirsty Stewart, for their assistance. I am indebted to Dr Linda Williamson for permission to refer to the contributions of her late husband, Duncan Williamson.

The path to publication has been smoothed by the prompt and efficient input of the editor at Brill, Christa Stevens, and the judicious and supportive help of the commissioning editor, Dr Rhona Brown. Finally, my thanks to my husband, Alan Anderson, and our daughter Sophia for their patience and understanding as I followed this obsession, and for their intelligent conversations about it as it slowly took shape. My special thanks to Alan for finding and buying me a set of the out-of-print eight-volume *Greig-Duncan Folk Song Collection*, which is as rare as hen's teeth.

Figures and Tables

Figures

1.1 Male SSSA recipients in family transmission as a percentage of all SSSA male recipients, by half decade of first recording   12
1.2 Female SSSA recipients in family transmission as a percentage of all SSSA female recipients, by half decade of first recording   13
2.1 Numbers of SSSA contributors with Child ballad repertoires of different sizes   28
2.2 Numbers of SSSA contributors by half decade of first recording   31
2.3 Median ages of SSSA contributors (known dates of birth only)   32
2.4 Median ages of SSSA contributors (known and estimated dates of birth)   32
2.5 Numbers of Child ballad contributors by decade of birth: core population   33
2.6 Numbers of Child ballad contributors by decade of birth: Travellers   34
2.7 Numbers of Child ballad contributors by decade of birth: Revival   34
2.8 Numbers of Child ballad contributors by decade of birth: all SSSA   35
2.9 Numbers of SSSA contributors by decade of birth (known dates of birth only)   35
2.10 Numbers of SSSA contributors by decade of birth (known and estimated dates of birth)   36
2.11 Cumulated percentages of SSSA contributors by decade of birth   36
2.12 Numbers of G-D contributors by decade of birth (known dates of birth only)   37
2.13 Numbers of G-D contributors by decade of birth (known and estimated dates of birth)   38
4.1 Numbers of SSSA recipients by decade of birth   60
4.2 Numbers of G-D recipients by decade of birth   60
4.3 Percentages of male- and female-sourced SSSA and G-D non-family transmission pairs   64
4.4 Percentages of SSSA non-family transmission pairs sourced from each group   64
4.5 Percentages of SSSA non-family Child ballad transmission pairs sourced from each group   65
4.6 Percentages of recipient-source pairs in SSSA and G-D family transmission, by sex of source   68
4.7 Percentages of recipient-source pairs in SSSA and G-D nuclear family transmission, by sex of source   69

FIGURES AND TABLES   XIII

4.8   Percentages of recipient-source pairs in SSSA and G-D extended family
      transmission, by sex of source   69
4.9   Percentages of combined G-D and SSSA general population family transmission
      pairs that have male sources   70
4.10 Percentages of combined G-D and SSSA general population family transmission
      pairs that are same-sex   71
5.1   Numbers of female SSSA Child ballad contributors by half decade of
      first recording   76
5.2   Percentages of male- and female-sourced SSSA and G-D family Child ballad
      transmission pairs   79
5.3   Percentages of male- and female-sourced SSSA and G-D non-family Child ballad
      transmission pairs   79
5.4   Percentages of combined G-D and SSSA core population Child ballad
      contributors who are female, by decade of birth   81
5.5   Percentages of combined G-D and SSSA core population Child ballad sources
      who are female, by decade of birth   82
5.6   Numbers of SSSA Child ballad sources by decade of birth   83
5.7   Numbers of G-D Child ballad contributors by decade of birth   84
5.8   Numbers of G-D Child ballad sources by decade of birth   84
5.9   Percentages of SSSA Child ballad contributors with repertoires of different
      sizes   85
5.10 Percentages of male- and female-directed SSSA and G-D non-family
      transmission pairs   86
5.11 Percentages of SSSA non-family transmission pairs directed towards each
      group   87
5.12 Numbers of SSSA sources by decade of birth (known dates of birth only)   89
5.13 Numbers of SSSA sources by decade of birth (known and estimated dates
      of birth)   89
5.14 Numbers of G-D sources by decade of birth (known dates of birth only)   90
5.15 Numbers of G-D sources by decade of birth (known and estimated dates
      of birth)   90
6.1   Numbers of combined G-D and SSSA contributors compared with Child ballad
      contributors by decade of birth   99
6.2   Combined G-D and SSSA Child ballad contributors as a percentage of all
      contributors   100
6.3   SSSA and G-D Child ballad contributors as a percentage of all contributors   100
6.4   Percentages of SSSA and G-D recipient-source pairs in family transmission
      sourced to each generation   102

6.5 Percentages of SSSA and G-D Child ballad recipient-source pairs in family transmission sourced to each generation   102
6.6 Numbers of SSSA contributors with two or more whole Child ballads in the data, by half decade of first recording   104
6.7 Median ages of male SSSA Child ballad contributors by half decade of first recording   110
6.8 Median ages of female SSSA Child ballad contributors by half decade of first recording   111
7.1 'Some skills' in Scots: cities   125
7.2 'Some skills' in Scots: North-East v. Scots area overall   126
7.3 Percentages of SSSA and G-D family transmission pairs with nuclear and extended family sources   132
7.4 SSSA recipients in nuclear family song transmission as a percentage of all SSSA recipients, by decade of birth   133
7.5 SSSA recipients in extended family song transmission as a percentage of all SSSA recipients, by decade of birth   134
7.6 SSSA recipients in non-family song transmission as a percentage of all SSSA recipients, by decade of birth   134
7.7 SSSA Child ballad recipients in family song transmission as a percentage of all SSSA Child ballad recipients, by decade of birth   135
7.8 SSSA recipients for whom there is information that they acquired songs in childhood as a percentage of all SSSA recipients, by decade of birth   136
8.1 Hypothetical SSSA distribution of decades of birth   139
8.2 Numbers of SSSA recipients in family and non-family song transmission by decade of birth   141

Tables

1.1 Ratios of contributors to recipients   14
1.2 Numbers and percentages of Child ballad contributions overall and those with transmission information   15
2.1 SSSA Child ballad repertoire size   29
6.1 Geographical distribution of SSSA general population contributors and core population Child ballad contributors   97
6.2 Correlation coefficients between percentage participation in Child ballad transmission, and in family and non-family transmission   108
7.1 Social background of G-D contributors   118
7.2 Geographical background of G-D contributors   119

FIGURES AND TABLES   XV

7.3   Ratios of nuclear to extended family recipients for all recipients and for Child
      ballad recipients   131
9.1   Timeline   160
A1a   Status of date-of-birth information of contributors   167
A1b   Status of date-of-birth information of recipients   167
A1c   Status of date-of-birth information of sources   168
A1d   Status of date-of-birth information of Child ballad contributors   168
A2a   Numbers of instances of song transmission, by context of transmission   169
A2b   Percentages of instances of song transmission, by context of transmission   169
A2c   Numbers of instances of Child ballad transmission, by context of
      transmission   170
A2d   Percentages of instances of Child ballad transmission, by context
      of transmission   170
A2e   Numbers of family, non-family, and childhood transmission instances   171
A2f   Child ballad inter-personal transmission instances as percentages of all
      inter-personal transmission instances   172
A3a   Numbers and percentages of SSSA and G-D contributors and recipients as
      distributed across the demographic groups   172
A3b   Numbers and percentages of SSSA and G-D Child ballad contributors and
      recipients as distributed across the demographic groups   173
A3c   Numbers and percentages of SSSA and G-D childhood recipients as distributed
      across the demographic groups   174
A3d   Numbers and percentages of SSSA and G-D childhood Child ballad recipients as
      distributed across the demographic groups   175
A4a   Numbers and percentages of SSSA and G-D inter-personal sources as
      distributed across the demographic groups   176
A4b   Numbers and percentages of SSSA and G-D Child ballad inter-personal sources
      as distributed across the demographic groups   177
A5a   Percentages of SSSA contributors born before 1900 and before 1920 (known
      dates of birth only)   178
A5b   Percentages of SSSA contributors born before 1900 and before 1920 (known and
      estimated dates of birth)   178
A5c   Percentages of SSSA Child ballad contributors born before 1900 and 1920   179
A6a   Percentages of SSSA contributors born before 1920, by date of first recording
      (known dates of birth only)   179
A6b   Percentages of SSSA contributors born before 1920, by date of first recording
      (known and estimated dates of birth)   180
A6c   Percentages of SSSA contributors born before 1900, by date of first recording
      (known dates of birth only)   180

A6d Percentages of SSSA contributors born before 1900, by date of first recording (known and estimated dates of birth)   181
A6e Percentages of SSSA Child ballad contributors born before 1920 by date of first recording   181
A6f Percentages of SSSA Child ballad contributors born before 1900 by date of first recording   182
A7   Percentages of SSSA recipients in family transmission born before 1900 and before 1920   182
A8a Numbers and percentages of family and non-family recipient-source pairs   183
A8b Numbers and percentages of family and non-family Child ballad recipient-source pairs   183
A9a Recipients in family, non-family, and childhood transmission as a percentage of all recipients   184
A9b Recipients in family, non-family, and childhood Child ballad transmission, as a percentage of all Child ballad recipients   185
A10a Numbers and percentages of all contributors and Child ballad contributors that are male or female   185
A10b Numbers and percentages of all sources and Child ballad sources that are male or female   186
A11a Percentage change in numbers of Child ballads and Child ballad contributors between G-D and SSSA core population   186
A11b Percentage change in numbers of Child ballads and Child ballad contributors between G-D and SSSA Revival contributors   187
A11c Percentage change in numbers of Child ballads and Child ballad contributors between G-D and SSSA Travellers   187
A11d Percentage change in numbers of Child ballads and Child ballad contributors recorded between the 1950s and subsequent decades   188
A12 Median ages at time of first recording of SSSA contributors and Child ballad contributors   188
A13 Modal (peak) decade of birth of contributors, recipients and sources   189
A14a Percentages of SSSA sources born before 1880 and before 1900   189
A14b Percentages of SSSA non-family sources born before 1880 and before 1900   190
A15a Percentages of G-D sources born before 1800 and before 1840   190
A15b Percentages of G-D non-family sources born before 1800 and before 1840   191
A16a Numbers of family recipient-source pairs, broken down by relationship   191
A16b Numbers of family Child ballad recipient-source pairs, broken down by relationship   192

Abbreviations

core pop	(in figs. and tables) core population (i.e. general population minus Folk Revival)
d.o.b	date of birth
DOST	*A Dictionary of the Older Scottish Tongue*
FoC	'The formation of the collection' (Lyle, 2002a)
G-D	*The Greig-Duncan Folk Song Collection*
gen pop	(in figs. and tables) general population (i.e. not Travellers)
generation 0	the same generation
generation 1	the parental generation
generation 2	the grandparental generation
NSA	*The New (or Second) Statistical Account of Scotland*
OED	*The Oxford English Dictionary*
Rev	(in figs. and tables) Folk Revival
SND	*The Scottish National Dictionary*
SSSA	School of Scottish Studies Archives/School of Scottish Studies
TaD	Tobar an Dualchais/Kist o Riches
Trav	(in figs. and tables) Travellers

CHAPTER 1

Introduction

1.1   Origins of the Study

The present study has its origins in work that I did from 2007 to 2012 for Tobar an Dualchais/Kist o Riches (hereafter TaD), a project (still ongoing)[1] to digitise the tape-recorded ethnographic archives of the School of Scottish Studies at the University of Edinburgh (hereafter SSSA),[2] re-catalogue them within a structured database, and make them available online. For simplicity, I shall use the term *Scots song* in this work to refer to folk songs in Scots and English (as opposed to Gaelic). The cataloguing of the Scots song material in the archives was done by specialists, but in my capacities as a data editor and indexer, a large part of this passed in front of my eyes. Through my previous research in sociolinguistics, I was accustomed to working with data that were quantitative in nature, though not always sufficient in quantity or quality to be handled statistically. I began more and more to feel that the Scots song archive contained information of this kind, and that it was trying to tell me something.

Initially, I focussed on song transmission. How the singer acquired the song was a standard fieldwork question, and there was accordingly a large body of information across a couple of thousand tracks, dating from 1951 onwards and with good coverage of the relevant material up to the late 1970s. *Songs* are defined for the purposes of this study as song lyrics. This definition allows the inclusion of song lyrics transmitted in handwritten form, and recitations of lyrics that are otherwise usually sung. The transmission of tunes is a partly separate, and less well documented, issue that is not addressed in this work.

Towards the end of the main funding phase of the TaD project, it was possible to do a limited amount of indexing, and this was concentrated on the Scots song material, making it possible to search the cataloguing database for tracks tagged as 'song transmission'.[3] The relevant information for the present

---

[1] As of 2020.
[2] The School is now (2020) part of the Department of Celtic and Scottish Studies, but the Archives continue to have a separate identity within Information Services. The TaD project also includes two other Gaelic-language archives, John Lorne Campbell's Canna Collection (held by the National Trust for Scotland) and a series of BBC Radio Scotland broadcasts.
[3] The indexing is available only within the TaD cataloguing database, not the *Tobar an Dualchais/Kist o Riches* website. The database is not publicly available.

study was compiled from the track summaries.[4] I also compiled anonymised biographical details of the singers who provided transmission information, and, where relevant, the singers from whom they had learned their songs. The former will be referred to in this work as *recipients* and the latter as *sources*.[5] *Source*, in the sense it is used here, is not to be confused with *source singer*; this is an established term for the handful of influential singers, including Jeannie Robertson, Belle Stewart, and Jimmy MacBeath, who were brought before the public by Hamish Henderson and other song collectors, and provided inspiration and models for young singers in the Folk Revival of the 1950s and 1960s. Throughout this work, when reference is made to the (Folk) Revival, it is this period, sometimes called the second Folk Revival, that is meant (the first Folk Revival being the movement that included Francis James Child, Cecil Sharp, Gavin Greig, and Rev. James Duncan). Olson (2007a: 398–9) objects to the term 'Revival' as misleadingly implying the prior demise of the tradition, whereas in practice there is a continuity of regional song cultures, in which the Traditional Music and Song Association, in particular, is rooted, and which it continues to encourage through its festivals. However, the term 'Revival' is an established one, and will accordingly be used here.

In addition to giving information about their own song acquisition, recipients not infrequently add further details of how their sources themselves acquired the songs (e.g. a recipient who learned a song from her mother might also be able to say that her mother learned it from a broadside), giving a further body of recipient information at second hand.[6] The question arises, whether the population of *recipients* is representative of the Scots song *contributors* as a whole. I accordingly added anonymised details of the remaining contributors who did *not* provide such information.[7] As it turns out, the recipients are not entirely representative, with an over-representation of Travellers, and especially women Travellers, in proportion to the numbers recorded as contributors (see below, §1.5). The Travellers were, at the time when the SSSA began recording, a largely distinct population group leading – or having only recently given up – a characteristic lifestyle, which involved being itinerant as families for at least part of the year. An account of their numbers and *modus vivendi* is given below (§§3.1–3.4, §6.9). The number of Traveller contributors is itself out

---

4 Occasional reference was made to audio to clarify specific points, but the number of tracks, many not online and thus available only at the School in Edinburgh, was too large to listen to all of them within the scope of this study.
5 For numbers of recipients, see Table A1b; for numbers of sources, see Table A1c.
6 Some second-hand information, i.e. not from contributors on tape, also comes from the published sources mentioned below (§2.1).
7 For numbers of contributors, see Table A1a.

of all proportion to their small numbers in the Scottish population. The fact that they were still, in the 1950s, singing long narrative ballads for their own entertainment led to the SSSA focussing its collecting heavily on them – an emphasis that may, as Olson (2007a: 380) points out, have seriously distorted our view of the folk tradition. Munro (1991: 152) acknowledges this bias, as does Cooke (2007: 214).

The fieldworkers sought out people who were known locally as singers of traditional material, and generally recorded them in their own homes – or, in the case of Travellers who were on the road or engaged in fruit-picking, around their campfires – in the company of family members and others gathered for the sing-song. The fieldworker would try to get everyone present at a recording session to attempt a song, in order to discover any shy talents in the company. Hamish Henderson prided himself on being able to coax anyone to sing. For instance, he can be heard on a 1972 tape[8] teasing the elderly Margaret Reid (born in 1887), that he has got her on tape singing – he had succeeded in getting her to join in a little with her son, Charles Fiddes Reid. The SSSA collection thus includes a large number of contributors who were not notable as singers, but who were recorded because they were present, on the chance that they might also turn out to be singers. These recordings are, as it were, the accidental by-catch of the School's song fishing expeditions. Although there is often little biographical information about them, these contributors are nevertheless an interesting body of people. To continue the fishing metaphor, the by-catch gives us some idea of what was in the ocean along with the big fish who were specifically sought out.

The treatment in this work is therefore somewhat biased in the opposite direction to the usual focus on notable singers, as it includes individuals who contribute only a single song or even just a fragment. In the case of elderly individuals especially, a fragmentary rendition might be the result of memory loss, but in many cases, we can probably take it that they have been members of the audience for traditional song, on whom fragments have, as it were, rubbed off. Bryce Whyte, for instance, a Traveller born in 1914 and the husband of noted singer Betsy Whyte, declares that he is not interested in old songs,[9]

---

8 SA1972.212. Tracks are cited by their SSSA catalogue number, e.g. SA1972.212 is a tape recorded in 1972 and numbered 212. Most tapes also have track numbers, e.g. SA1952.22.A8, where A8 is track 8 on the A side. A second reference, e.g. TaD 76681, is to the same track re-catalogued by TaD. The relationship between the two sets of catalogue numbers is not always one-to-one. If the track is not available online at the time of writing, no TaD number is given.

9 SA1975.11, TaD 76681.

but he is nevertheless able to produce fragments of five Child ballads[10] (i.e. the ballads catalogued by Francis James Child in five volumes between 1882 and 1898). As Atkinson (2002: 7) points out, little attention has been paid to the listeners in the study of folk song, though MacColl and Seeger (1977: 20) offer some observations about Traveller audiences that they worked with, where non-singers, through hearing the same songs often, knew all the words. Such an audience are in a position to join in, offer prompts, and influence performers by expressing preferences for particular songs. Since many of the incidental contributors say something about how they learned a song, they also enlarge the data on song transmission and song sources. The sources are a somewhat more random selection of individuals than the recorded contributors, giving a useful basis for comparison.

The dates of birth (hereafter d.o.bs) of the contributors take us quite far back in time, but the point at which they peter out is rather tantalising. The number in the data with d.o.bs in the 1880s is quite large – 61 – but there are only 22 from the 1870s, and only two elderly women born even earlier. (These numbers include estimated d.o.bs – the basis of estimation is discussed below, §1.3, and the reliability of the estimates at §2.6.) A significant event that might be expected to have had some effect on the vitality and transmission of the folk tradition was the 1872 Education Act, which made education compulsory up to the age of thirteen. The SSSA data do not reach far enough back in time to allow a contrast between the generations reaching school age before and after the Act. The study was therefore expanded to include another major collection, the eight-volume *Greig-Duncan Folk Song Collection* (1981–2002), collected in manuscript form by Gavin Greig and Rev. James Duncan, almost entirely from North-East contributors, mainly between 1902 and 1911, and edited in eight volumes by Patrick Shuldham-Shaw, Emily Lyle and others. (It is referred to hereafter as G-D.) Some of the collection was taken down directly by Greig or Duncan from the singing of contributors; some was collected by intermediaries; and some was elicited by correspondence through Greig's articles in a local newspaper, the *Buchan Observer*.

1.2 A Note on Tables and Figures

The two collections yield two large sets of data, which can be sub-divided in a number of ways and interrogated in a number of ways. The resulting tables are

---

10   Child 10 'The Twa Sisters', 100 'Willie o Winsbury', 214 'The Dowie Dens of Yarrow', 279A 'The Jolly Beggar', and 293 'Jock o Hazeldean' (Sir Walter Scott's version).

INTRODUCTION

for the most part grouped together in Appendix A (references are to Table A1a, etc.), in order to facilitate comparison amongst them, and reference to them from different points in the book. One reason for including so many tables and figures is that the topics covered in this book do not exhaust what could be done with the results, and I wish to make these available as fully as possible for other scholars to draw upon.

The data sets are large enough to sub-divide in a variety of ways that are of relevance to the topics discussed in this book. The SSSA collectors' interest in the Child ballads makes it worthwhile to investigate this sub-set of the data separately, and to make comparisons with the overall data. The main type of information about song transmission relates to inter-personal transmission.[11] Within this, the data are sufficiently voluminous to allow the analysis of the sub-sets of *family* transmission – further sub-divided into *nuclear* and *extended* family transmission – and other inter-personal transmission, which is termed here *non-family* transmission.

Approaching the data from a number of different angles helps detect and adjust for any biases or anomalies. The collecting bias towards the Child ballads, and the consequent skewing of the SSSA collection towards the Travellers have already been mentioned (and will be explored in detail in Chapter 6). There are also some prolific individuals, such as Mrs Gillespie in G-D and Willie Mathieson in SSSA, who provide very full details of how they acquired their large repertoires. When we look at the whole body of examples of song transmission (referred to hereafter as *instances*), these data are skewed by the copious amount of information from such recipients. Counting the *recipients* instead of the *instances* provides an alternative perspective in which each individual is only a single data point.

1.3   Estimated Dates of Birth

The amount of biographical information about the G-D contributors is very variable: the contributors tended to be either well-known to the collectors or intermediaries, or, at the opposite extreme, not known personally, but corresponding by letter. The G-D editors have established dates of birth for a number of contributors and members of their families, aided by the notes of Greig's helper Mary Ann Crichton c. 1925. This information can be found in the biographical essays and in Lyle's (2002a) chapter on 'The formation of

---

11   See Table A2a for the numbers of song transmission instances under various headings, and Table A2b for percentages.

the collection' (hereafter FoC), all in vol. 8, with some additions in Campbell (2009).[12] However, just 21% of the 478 contributors in the G-D data have known d.o.bs.[13]

Likewise, the biographical data in SSSA are often very limited or non-existent. Known d.o.bs come from field notes (via the SSSA's original cataloguing or the published writings of fieldworkers), information on audio, and information obtained by TaD. The information is often in the form of the contributor's age at the time of recording, and may therefore err by a year.[14] Sometimes there is no date of birth for quite prolific singers, and conversely there is sometimes quite full biographical detail for those who recorded only fragments. Much depended on the circumstances at the time of recording, as well as the recent efforts of TaD to find the contributors or their surviving relatives, who might be able to provide such information. This is in no way a reflection upon the fieldworkers or their methods. The interviewer could only collect such personal details as he or she had the opportunity to ask for and as the person was willing to divulge in a particular context. Many recordings were made at informal singing sessions where it was not always possible to obtain even a name for each contributor. In other contexts too there were often individuals who happened to be present and who were invited to sing, and who remain anonymous or semi-anonymous. Some contributors specifically chose to be recorded anonymously. In the SSSA data for 1,159 contributors, 46% have known d.o.bs. The individuals who contribute Child ballads are better documented, no doubt because more attention was focussed on them, with 41% known d.o.bs out of 173 contributors in G-D, and 65% out of 308 in SSSA.[15] Unsurprisingly, much less is known about the song sources: only 6% of 515 individuals identified as sources in G-D, and 9% of 988 in SSSA, have known d.o.bs.[16]

Fortunately, various kinds of information can be used to obtain a rough estimate of a person's d.o.b or, where relevant, their age at the time of collecting or recording. The 'by-catch' are often spouses or relatives of the prominent contributors, as are many of the song sources, and their ages can accordingly be

---

12   Additionally, D. H. Edwards, in his 'Introductory paper' to George Kean's *Lilts of Life and Love*, gives Kean's date of birth as 1878 (Brechin: D. H. Edwards, Advertiser Office, 1900, p. xvii).

13   See Table A1a. The data used here omit some of the G-D contributors: for details see Appendix B below.

14   This is no doubt why the dates in Douglas and Miller eds. (1995) sometimes differ slightly from those obtained by TaD. It is also well known that in interview contexts people sometimes round their age to the nearest five or zero, so even 'known' dates may be approximate.

15   See Table A1d.

16   See Table A1c.

estimated in relation to their better-documented family members. The following assumptions are made: in the absence of any other information, a generation is taken to be on average thirty years;[17] siblings are allocated to the same decade; and it is assumed that forty is the latest age of giving birth, and that the age of retirement is sixty-five. Spouses are taken to be the same age as each other, although in practice husbands are often a few years older than wives; but since the figures are tabulated by decades, the results should be broadly right in most cases. There is more risk of error with this assumption in the G-D data. As Carter (1979: 104) observes, North-East farmers 'were often considerably older than their wives'. An example amongst the G-D contributors is Mr and Mrs Lyall, between whom there was an age difference of 29 years (see Neilson, 2002: 566).[18]

Children are taken to be ten (again, in the absence of any other information). If a person is described by someone as 'old', his or her age at that point in time is taken to be sixty, but if there is no chronological reference point, the assumption is made that the person is one generation (i.e. thirty years) older than the (adult) person supplying the information. Additionally, TaD cataloguers were encouraged to guess at the age of individuals on the basis of their voices, though not all did so. In order to utilise these observations without putting too much weight on them,[19] only comments about elderly or child voices have been used here.

It is only rarely that specific historical events are mentioned that anchor a person's d.o.b, but some indications can be drawn from their life experiences, including service in either of the two World Wars. Traditional farming methods (such as ploughing with horses, and farmservants' accommodation in bothies and chaumers) were dying out in the 1940s, so contributors who experienced these in their working lives are assumed to have a d.o.b no later than 1920, and this is taken as their estimated d.o.b. Similarly, the Shetland whaling industry ended in 1929, so a notional d.o.b of 1900 is assigned to anyone who participated in that industry. A person in adult employment, getting married, or

---

17   If there are known d.o.bs for two or more siblings, these are averaged when estimating other family members from them. Travellers tended to marry young (see below, §7.4), and it is sometimes necessary to assume a shorter generation time in order to fit three or four generations within the existing chronological reference points.
18   The data include a small number of G-D rural contributors whose estimated d.o.bs might be affected by this source of error: Mrs Rae of Burngrains, Alexander Fowlie, Mr Gordon, and Alexander Glennie (whose d.o.b is estimated on the basis of his brother-in-law).
19   Where actual d.o.bs have subsequently been obtained, the guesses do not turn out to be especially accurate.

going to war is assumed to be twenty. As the d.o.bs are tabulated in decades, all dates are rounded down.

In both collections a higher proportion of female than male d.o.bs can be estimated, because of family links to other contributors whose d.o.bs are known. In SSSA, 26% of female d.o.bs can be estimated, but only 17% of male d.o.bs; in G-D the figures are 29% for females, only 18% for males.[20] SSSA contributors about whom there is no information at all can be fitted into a loose chronology based on the date of recording. Unless there is information to the contrary, they are assumed to be adults (at least twenty) at the time of recording, so the d.o.b of someone recorded in the 1950s is taken as 'pre-1930', and so on. Since the G-D collection was mostly made over a much shorter period, the *termini ante quem* of the unknown dates very much cluster at the latter end of the time period, so this exercise would not be very informative for the G-D data.

Obviously, someone else using the same fragmentary information could, and probably would, make widely different estimates, but it is hoped that the numbers are large enough for the many sources of error to cancel each other out to some extent. Some space is taken below (§2.6) to compare patterns over time with known d.o.bs only, and with the addition of estimated d.o.bs. Thereafter the reader is asked to take it upon trust that adding the estimated d.o.bs does not substantially alter the patterns seen in the graphs, apart from smoothing them.

1.4 Social Background

There is also an element of estimation involved in categorising individuals by their background. The population can be sub-divided in various ways, but the importance attached to the Travellers – which has only increased with the passage of time – makes the division of the SSSA corpus into *Travellers* and others, the *general population*, an obvious one. However, in counting individuals in the data as Travellers it is sometimes necessary to rely on circumstantial evidence, for instance relatedness to identifiable Travellers, or simply the context of recording, such as a Traveller camp or the berryfields of Blairgowrie. The berryfields were where Hamish Henderson collected from Travellers working as seasonal fruit pickers, which he famously remarked was 'like holding a tin-can under the Niagara Falls' (1962, 1992: 102). The general population category is the default for individuals who are not known or judged likely to be Travellers.

---

[20] For numbers, see Table A1a.

The Child ballad contributors tend to be better documented, making it possible to split the *general population* into (*Folk*) *Revival* contributors, on the one hand, and the *core population*, on the other.[21] Munro (1996: 52) defines singers as 'revival' if they have learned most of their songs 'from recorded or printed sources, from other revival singers or from source singers' and defines them as 'source' 'if the songs had been handed down in the oral tradition, or learned in childhood'. Olson (2007a: 389) regards this distinction as a false and even divisive and damaging one, as it privileges oral transmission. We have not used oral transmission as a criterion here. The complicated relationship between literacy and oral transmission is discussed below (§4.1). Revival contributors are defined for the purposes of this study as those who typically perform for audiences in the Folk Revival milieu of folk clubs, festivals, etc., or who are recording artists, or otherwise associated mainly with the folk scene. This definition is far from perfect, since, as Olson (2007a: 400) points out, the singers principally recruited by the two collections also tended to be 'performers', or, as MacColl and Seeger (1977: 19) call them, 'Singers' with a capital S. The Revival is discussed in terms of birth cohorts in Chapter 8 below.

The Revival singers are identified here either by their biographies or by the context of recording. They were often recorded without biographical details at folk festivals and competitions, so there is less basis for estimating their d.o.bs where these are not known. The re-cataloguing in TaD has not always succeeded in matching names to tracks for the festival and competition recordings. It is possible that further research in the SSSA's own catalogues would yield more information than there is access to via TaD, but it seems extremely unlikely that the patterns discussed in this book would be contradicted by adding further biographical details.[22] Older singers who were brought forward as mentors and models ('source singers') for the Folk Revival are not counted here as Revival singers. The younger generations of singers who identify as Travellers by descent are counted as such, although they might typically give platform performances.

Since the SSSA data used here combine material from different communities around the Lowlands and Northern Isles, and different Traveller family circles, generalisations must be treated cautiously. It would be possible to focus on more narrowly defined groups, for instance North-Eastern contributors (with

---

21 For numbers, see Table A1d.
22 Some anonymous singers can be identified as unique individuals in context, and have been counted as such here. There is a small risk of duplication, as anonymous singers, especially those recorded at public events, might already be in the database unrecognised. However, since these fall into the 'unknown d.o.b' category, only limited use is made of this data in any case.

or without the Traveller component), or contributors from rural backgrounds, but the smaller numbers would mean more random fluctuations, which would make patterns in the data harder to discern. It is hoped that the present study will provide a large-scale, albeit roughly woven, backdrop against which future, more narrowly focussed, quantitative studies might be carried out.

1.5 Self-Reported Data

The final reason for interrogating the data in a number of different ways is to compensate for issues of reliability with regard to the information received by the song collectors. Folk song scholars have been reluctant to raise the question of reliability, although this is an issue that the social sciences must constantly grapple with. Thus Rieuwerts (1995) writes very circumspectly even about the case of long-deceased Margaret Laidlaw, James Hogg's mother, and the ballad 'Auld Maitland', whose antiquity scholars reject, but for which Margaret Laidlaw provided an elaborate provenance, apparently in an atmosphere of some hostility towards the collector, Sir Walter Scott. In one of the rare instances when a fieldworker was able to ask the putative source for confirmation, Linda Williamson asked Sandy Townsley about 'Thomas the Rhymer', which Duncan Williamson recalled as having learned from him,[23] but Sandy Townsley was 'not forthcoming' (L. Williamson, 2020).

Although the SSSA researchers may have regarded it as unethical to question the reliability of the information they collected, lest they should appear to cast doubt on the veracity of their sources, they did lay the groundwork for addressing this issue by asking the same questions again in repeat interviews, sometimes after an interval of several years. The main problem, of course, is that the information is subject to the distorting vagaries of memory, but there may also be an element of distortion through self-presentation. When singers interact with fieldworkers or with an audience, the immediate dynamic of the situation may call forth a version of the facts that is tailored to please the hearer or to burnish the image of the singer, rather than to serve the abstract pursuit of scientific knowledge. This is only a more formalised version of the quasi-theatrical performance that is involved in all social interaction, as Goffman describes it: '[W]hen an individual appears in the presence of others, there will usually be some reason for him to mobilize his activity so that it will convey an impression to others which it is in his interests to convey' (1959, 1969: 15).

---

23   SA1976.146.B2, TaD 76943.

INTRODUCTION

The value placed on oral tradition by song collectors did not go unnoticed by their sources. The English singer Harry Cox revealed shortly before his death that he possessed a large collection of printed song texts. Although many of the songs collected from him over a period of half a century were identical to printed versions, he had always maintained that he had acquired them by ear (Atkinson, 2002: 20–21). Similarly, Porter and Gower (1995: xxxv) claim that songs reached Jeannie Robertson by oral transmission, even when her texts are close to printed versions that she had in her possession (Olson, 2007a: 401 n. 5). Jeannie Robertson's daughter, Lizzie Higgins, revealed that she had learned 'MacCrimmon's Lament' from a book,[24] and taught it to her mother,[25] but Jeannie Robertson herself recalled only that she had learned it 'long, long ago aff o one o my people'.[26]

For those Traveller singers who became participants and source singers in the Folk Revival, offering the audience an oral provenance for their songs was part of their stage performance. The answer to the frequently-asked question about how a song was learned has become a standard trope for introducing a song. The first UK radio programmes of folk song – 'Country Magazine' in the 1940s and 'As I Roved Out' in the 1950s – had a format consisting of snippets of field recordings followed by studio singers rendering the songs. 'The collectors' field reports had to stress human interest – the colourful personalities of their informants, their amusing stories, the quaintness of the local environment, and so on' (Gregory, 2004: 223). This popularised ethnographic approach was continued by Ewan MacColl in his 'Radio Ballads' (from 1957 on). Verrier (2004) describes how the early programmes in the series started by presenting a song and then discussing it, but by the fourth programme the actuality was mostly given first, then the song, these introductions being similar to what would now be heard in a folk club. Douglas considers that Ewan MacColl was also instrumental in creating the image of Traveller source singers like Belle Stewart and her family. He 'encouraged them to exploit the more exotic features of their Traveller identity to create a public image' (Douglas, 2002: 127). Hamish Henderson likewise helped to create Jeannie Robertson's stage persona (Byrne, 2010: 286–7).

Over the period of SSSA recording, the percentage of Traveller recipients who mention family sources rises to 100% in the second half of the 1960s (males) or first half of the 1970s (females) and remains there (Figures 1.1 and 1.2), though it must be borne in mind that the numbers are very small when the

---

24   SA1970.78.A3, TaD 66015.
25   SA1970.78.A3.
26   SA1954.88.A3, TaD 41227.

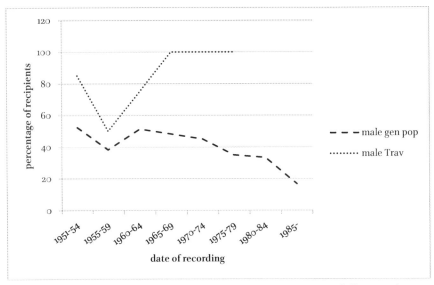

FIGURE 1.1 SSSA male recipients in family transmission as a percentage of all SSSA male recipients, by half decade of first recording
Note: figures based on 101 general population males and 42 male Travellers in family transmission. The number of tape-recorded ('first-hand') recipients is smaller than the total number of recipients.

data are broken down to this level. This tends to suggest that the Traveller contributors were becoming more sophisticated about what interested the fieldworkers, and were developing a regular way of presenting their songs. Over time, one can notice contributors who were repeatedly recorded by the SSSA anticipating the question and spontaneously introducing songs with an attribution to a source.

As mentioned above, a remarkably high number of female Travellers in the data have transmission information associated with them in relation to the number of this group recorded. For the general population, of both sexes, the contributors outnumber the recipients 2.2 to 1; for male Travellers 1.9 to 1, but for female Travellers only 1.7 to 1. This is even more pronounced when we consider the Child ballads: the figures for the general population remain much the same, but the ratio for male Travellers is 1.7 to 1 and for female Travellers only 1.2 to 1 (see Table 1.1).[27] At the time when the data for this study were assem-

---

27   The relationship between contributors and recipients is expressed in terms of ratios rather than percentages, as the set of recipients is not wholly a sub-set of the contributors. The differences in collection methods mean that the G-D material is not really comparable with the SSSA material, but G-D is included in Table 1.1 for the sake of completeness.

INTRODUCTION

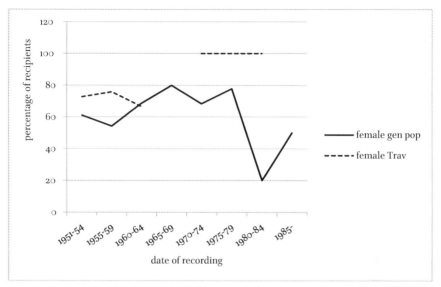

FIGURE 1.2 SSSA female recipients in family transmission as a percentage of all SSSA female recipients, by half decade of first recording
Note: figures based on 86 general population females and 56 female Travellers in family transmission. See also note to Figure 1.1.

bled it was possible to find 821 Child ballad contributions in the TaD database (including those not online). Of these, 379 included transmission information. Whereas the female Travellers contributed 24% of the ballad tracks, they contributed 32% of those with transmission information (see Table 1.2). This over-representation reflects the better documentation of the Traveller contributors in general, perhaps because the 'by-catch' in this population group produced fewer individuals who were not really singers – or at least not of the kind of material that was wanted. The differences are much smaller if we take only the better documented singers – i.e. contributors and first-hand recipients, in each case with known or estimated d.o.bs – in Table 1.1.

The female Travellers also form a disproportionately high percentage of the recipients in family transmission, i.e. those who source at least one song to a family member. Although they constitute only 14% of recipients, the female Travellers constitute 20% of *family* recipients. For the Child ballads, they constitute 22% of recipients, and 31% of family recipients. The figures are even higher in the *extended* (as opposed to *nuclear*) family category: 28% overall, and 40% for the Child ballads.[28] There are some limited, and perhaps not very

---

28   For numbers, see Tables A3a and A3b.

TABLE 1.1   Ratios of contributors to recipients overall and for the sub-set who contribute Child ballads, comparing results for all individuals with those for the better documented individuals (i.e. omitting those with unknown dates of birth, and second-hand recipients)

	Ratio of contributors to recipients		Ratio of contributors to first-hand recipients, known and estimated dates of birth only	
	All	Child ballads	All	Child ballads
Male core pop		1.5		1.2
Female core pop		1.8		1.4
Male Revival		5.6		2.1
Female Revival		3.2		1.8
Male Trav	1.9	1.7	1.8	1.3
Female Trav	1.7	1.2	1.7	1.2
Male gen pop	**2.2**	**2.1**	**1.9**	**1.4**
Female gen pop	**2.2**	**2.2**	**1.9**	**1.6**
ALL SSSA	2.1	1.9	1.9	1.4
Male G-D	2.4	2.8	1.6	1.4
Female G-D	1.8	1.9	1.9	1.4
ALL G-D	2.1	2.3	1.7	1.4

reliable, data on childhood[29] song learning. Here again, the female Travellers are somewhat over-represented at 19% of childhood recipients, and very much over-represented at 11 out of the 31 Child ballad childhood recipients (i.e. 35%).[30]

The association amongst the female Travellers, childhood transmission, and the Child ballads is correspondingly seen in terms of song transmission instances, with Child ballads comprising a very high proportion – 48 out of the 125 instances where childhood learning is mentioned by this group (i.e. 38%).[31] Male Travellers are similarly over-represented in these respects, though not to the same extent. It would be possible from these imbalances to obtain quite

---

29   'Childhood' is taken here to mean under the age of fourteen (see below, §2.2).
30   See Tables A3c and A3d.
31   See Tables A2e and A2f.

TABLE 1.2   Numbers and percentages of Child ballad contributions overall and those with transmission information, as distributed across the demographic groups. Note: where contributors record the same ballad more than once, this is counted as a single contribution. Variants recognised by the G-D editors or TaD cataloguers are counted as distinct ballads. Contributors may mention more than one source for a particular item, so the figures for items with transmission information are smaller than those for transmission instances in Table A2c.

	Child ballad contributions			
	All		With transmission information	
	n	%	n	%
Male core pop	202	25	96	25
Male Revival	94	11	20	5
Male gen pop	296	36	116	31
Male Trav	129	16	66	17
Female core pop	107	13	56	15
Female Revival	92	11	18	5
Female gen pop	199	24	74	20
Female Trav	197	24	123	32
SSSA TOTAL	821	100	379	100
Male G-D	248	40	69	24
Female G-D	378	60	224	76
G-D TOTAL	626	100	293	100

a distorted view of the song tradition, in the way that Olson (2007a: 380) suggests (see below, §6.9).

It can be hard to tell sometimes whether Travellers, in particular, mean their framing of their songs and stories to be taken entirely literally. For instance, Leitch, in his introduction to his interviews with Sandy Stewart, finds it necessary to express reservations as to whether all of the yarns told in the first person by his interviewee are in fact autobiographical (1988: xiii). Byrne judges that, as some source singers became famous within the folk scene and competition arose amongst them, 'some informants developed a propensity for creating or embellishing back stories about themselves and their songs, that were misleading to say the least' (2010: 287). Byrne (p. 285) also quotes Hamish Henderson himself admitting, in 1956, that there is an element of good-natured pretence going on: 'All folksong kids us on. And why not? Folksong after all is largely myth, so why expect practitioners to stick to facts when they are dealing with one of the great unrealities of life?' (Neat, 2009: 121).

To digress slightly, we can find a demonstrable example of this is the presentation of burker stories as recent family history. Burkers were murderers who preyed upon people on the margins of society to provide bodies for dissection in anatomy classes. The term comes from the notorious William Burke (of Burke and Hare), who was hanged in 1829. The case led to the passing of the Anatomy Act in 1832, which did away with grave-robbing and burking by giving licensed practitioners access to bodies unclaimed after death. Burking was a terrible episode in history that instilled fear and horror in the Travellers, which should not be minimised. However, it is clear that stories handed down about the burkers are made more effective by casting them as recent family history, even down to Stanley Robertson (born 1940).[32] For instance, Maggie Stewart from Banchory (born 1902) tells a version of a burker story of being trapped in a barn and finding traces of blood, taking warning from this, and escaping. She casts her father, as a young boy with his parents, as the protagonist.[33] John Stewart from Perthshire (born 1910) tells a very similar story with his father, as a child, as the protagonist.[34] Jock Stewart (born 1870) and Alec Stewart (born 1904) even tell burker stories in the first person.[35] There are many such examples where the person who supposedly escaped from burkers must have been born after 1832.[36]

Of necessity, the information provided by the contributors is taken at face value in this study. If more than one source is given for a particular song, each is treated here as a separate instance of song transmission. When asked about sources on separate occasions in the SSSA collection, contributors usually do give the same answers, but even when there is a contradiction, this could be more apparent than real: the person from whom the song was learned might not be the one from whom it was first heard; or it might have been learned from more than one person (indeed, it is not unusual for more than one person to be

---

32 SA1979.131.B3–B4, TaD 67417.
33 SA1954.93.B4, TaD 10220.
34 SA1979.36, TaD 65868.
35 SA1955.17.A2, TaD 11474; SA1969.195.A2, TaD 4314. These are not overtly told as fiction. There are also picaresque stories, involving escapes from burkers as well as other adventures, that are told in the first person but are presented as tall tales (e.g. SA1956.179.3–SA1956.180.1, TaD 14364; SA1978.165).
36 For instance, SA1954.96.B12; SA1974.245.B1c; SA1972.217.B3–B4; SA1953.237.B11a, TaD 2833; SA1961.40.B10; SA1978.160, TaD 55955; SA1955.65.A5–A7; SA1954.96.B12; SA1955.156.A10; SA1954.100.A6; SA1974.245.B1d; SA1981.87.1; SA1972.217.B9; SA1976.21.A11.

named as the source on the same track); it might have been learned piecemeal; or different versions or tunes might be involved. There are many examples of such complexities in the notes to songs in G-D. A song might be heard initially, then sought out, and the lyrics obtained in written form. It might be popular in the contributor's circle, and thus heard repeatedly without a conscious effort of learning, until one particular hearing that fixes it in the contributor's mind – or not: the data include song fragments. The attempt to oblige with an over-simplified answer may be the reason, together with lapses of memory, for occasional contradictory accounts. For instance, in 1956 Alec MacShannon thought he had learned 'Callieburn' from an old ploughman when he was fifteen, but by 1962, he thought it had been from an old shepherd, Archie Scott, when he was eighteen or nineteen, and by 1979, he had fixed the date as 1916 (when he was nineteen).[37]

Another distorting factor that we must be aware of is the tendency for notable singers – and compilers of large repertoires – to continue to be identified with their repertoires, even when the people naming them have learned the songs through intermediaries. There are some clear examples in G-D. For instance, Bell Robertson sources her version of Song 1092 to James Rankin (the assistant of song collector Peter Buchan). However, we know that Rankin died in 1831 (Walker, 1915: 78 n.), ten years before Bell Robertson was born.[38] Likewise, Bell Robertson describes Song 434 as a song of her grandmother's, but she also tells us that her grandmother died in 1837, again before she was born. Without this information, it would have been easy to assume that she learned the song directly from her grandmother. Another example is Song 309A from Mrs Lyall, which is described in two different MS sources (both cited in the song note) as being from her grandfather or alternatively 'from her mother, who received it from *her* father'. In the SSSA material, Willie Mathieson, for example, often names Sandy Ross as the source of a song, although he apparently inherited Ross's repertoire indirectly through his second wife, Ross's granddaughter.[39] Thus when grandparents are mentioned, there may be some doubt about whether the song was transmitted directly from the grandparent,

---

37 SA1956.172.A8, TaD 51212; SA1962.62.A4, TaD 12488; SA1979.160, TaD 83058.
38 Rankin is said to have sung the song to her grandfather. It is possible that her paternal grandfather could still have been alive when she was a child, so we take him to be her source, but this too is uncertain. Similarly, Annie Ritchie is said (in FoC, p. 474) to be nearly seventy c. 1925, and her d.o.b is confirmed as 1857 (p. 524, n. 6), but at Song 875C, noted in 1906, the note reads, 'Sung by Gamie [i.e. gamekeeper] Stewart at Brucklay sixty years ago', so it would appear that the note is not to be read as implying direct transmission of the song from Stewart to her.
39 E.g. SA1952.5.A5, TaD 15729.

which is entirely possible if the grandparent was still alive, or indirectly via a parent. Indeed, the answer may be 'both'.

1.6   The Benefits of a Quantitative Approach

The poor quality data are a challenge and an opportunity. We cannot go back and ask questions that were not asked or answered at the time, but we can put together what we have and interrogate it quantitatively. This study will weigh the catch in bulk, as it were, rather than counting each fish. Though the approach taken here is quantitative, it must be emphasised that the statistics arrived at are purely descriptive, since the original collections themselves are not any type of sample, and furthermore SSSA is not available in its entirety through the TaD database. We must be careful not to ask more of the data than they can deliver. Nevertheless, they are sufficiently voluminous that patterns in the findings may raise interesting questions. It is the patterns that are primarily of interest, rather than the raw figures.

This study is essentially a demographic one. It departs from the usual emphasis on the biographies of individual singers and their relationship with the folk tradition, usually interpreted in terms of their particular life experiences, sometimes as being characteristic of a group, such as farmservants or Travellers. The perspective of this work is necessarily broader: life experiences are seen mainly in terms of birth cohorts, and how the economic conditions and cultural milieu of a particular time might have affected the individuals growing up at that time. This is not to say that this milieu is assumed to be the same for all groups at the same time: rather it is treated as the result of a dynamic interplay of forces, those of modernity[40] on the one hand – literacy, mass education, commercial farming, rail communications, assembly line production, recording and broadcasting technology –, and those of tradition on the other – the extended family, high fertility, apprenticeship or informal education of children to follow in their parents' occupations, pre-capitalist production, and self-made entertainment. The balance of these forces is different for the Travellers in comparison with the general population, and, as Hughes (2008) also finds in relation to Japanese folk song, for rural in comparison with urban populations.

The present study relies heavily on work that has been done by the editors of *G-D* and by TaD to obtain basic biographical information (though it is now

---

[40]   In taking the opposite of *tradition* to be *modernity*, this work follows Hughes (2008: 4 ff.), himself following Rice (1994: 322, n. 1).

unfortunately often too late). Apart from this, however, there has been little study of the bulk of singers in the major collections of Scottish and English folk song. Attention has focussed, understandably, on the prominent figures, individuals who contributed large repertoires or were significant performers. An exception is a study by Bearman (2000)[41] of the social background of the singers from whom Cecil Sharp collected in Somerset in the first decade of the twentieth century. Bearman finds – perhaps surprisingly, since Sharp himself saw his collection as the remnants of the old 'peasant' culture (Sharp ed. Karpeles, 1965) – that these included clergymen and prosperous tradesmen, and their wives and daughters. At the same time, Bearman calculates (p. 760) that 40% of the 139 economically active males were indeed engaged in agriculture, considerably higher than the 25% figure in the 1901 Census results for Somerset.[42] The benefit of such an overview, then, is that it may serve to modify and refine impressions based on the notable singers or on the numerically dominant population sources.

Given a large enough database, such as the one compiled for this study, it is also possible to detect patterns that are not, as it were, visible to the naked eye. One such pattern in the present study is the dearth of singers born in the 1920s, which can be regarded as a trough between the main body of singers drawn from the general population, and a new cohort of Folk Revival singers born at later dates (Chapter 8). This study also reveals many detailed patterns of song transmission within and outside the family, between the sexes, and between Travellers and the general population (Chapter 4 and *passim*). There are also hints of an impact upon song transmission of the disruptive changes in rural life in the late nineteenth century, though the effect of formal education is seen more in the divergence of the general population from the more conservative Travellers than in any precisely dateable development (Chapter 7). A number of issues raised by previous scholarship are also addressed below, including:

– the reticence of female singers, something that is fleetingly mentioned by Porter and Gower (1995: xxv) (Chapter 5);
– the association, made by Child, amongst others, of women with the Child ballads (Brown, 1997; Bishop, 2004: 406) (Chapter 5);
– the greater success of collectors between the 1950s and 1970s in obtaining this sought-after type of material from Travellers than from the population at large (Chapter 6);

---

41 Drawing partly on unpublished research by David Bland, one-time librarian of the Vaughan Williams Memorial Library.
42 Bearman uses the narrow definition of that Census, which excludes, for instance, gamekeepers and jobbing gardeners.

– whether the wealth of material obtained from the Travellers in the mid twentieth century implies that they would also have been a richer source before the First World War – if only Greig and Duncan had sought them out, as lamented by Henderson, ([Henderson], 1975: 14) and others following him (Chapter 3).

The analysis touches many areas of enquiry, so I hope the reader will indulge occasional digressions into other topics, such as the prominence of the North-East as an area rich in folk song and ballads, and the tendency for the song culture to produce a few individuals who amass very large repertoires. As I am not a folk song expert, I do not go deeply into the matter of song repertoires. I rely on existing classifications, chiefly the Child ballads – the debateable validity of this category is discussed below (§6.1). I also make some limited use of the G-D corpus as a baseline against which to compare the SSSA Traveller corpus. (It is possible to search the TaD cataloguing database by Child, G-D, Roud and Laws numbers.[43])

What is described in this study is two very extensive song collections, not the song culture itself. Much of what singers are able to recall about their learning of songs is vague. It must be emphasised that the patterns we can see are only in terms of the data that we have: it is a matter of what people remember, what they convey to the collectors, and what is filtered through the TaD cataloguing. It is only a very imperfect window into the past. To return again to the fishing metaphor, we can only observe what came up in the nets: we have no way of knowing how representative it was of the life of the ocean at that time. Nevertheless, there is a tremendous volume of fragmentary information on record, assiduously collected, preserved, and catalogued, and the aim of this study is to find ways to utilise it.

---

43 Roud numbers refer to *The Roud Folk Song Index* (n.d.). Laws numbers refer to Laws' American ballad catalogue (1957). The *Tobar an Dualchais/Kist o Riches* website is also searchable by all four classifications.

CHAPTER 2

Weighing the Catch

This chapter is concerned with the criteria used to select data from the two collections. It details the varied approaches to the data in the analysis. It also gives an overview of the demographic make-up of the contributors to the collections, and addresses the reliability of the estimated d.o.bs. As the G-D material is published, it is open to other scholars to replicate the research reported here, and detailed comments have therefore been made in Appendix B below on the selection and interpretation of the data. The TaD database, on the other hand, is subject to ongoing modification, so it will not be possible exactly to reconstruct the data as they stood when the material was compiled, though it is unlikely that much new biographical information will be obtained at this stage. It would be redundant to comment on individual biographical details here, as the present author's additions – from documentary and online sources – have been entered into the TaD cataloguing database itself, with references.

2.1 The Data Sources

The School of Scottish Studies at the University of Edinburgh was a major inspiration for the Folk Song Revival of the 1950s and 1960s, and its Archives – containing recordings made by Hamish Henderson, Alan Bruford, Ailie Munro, Peter Cooke, and other staff, researchers and associates of the School – are a mainstay of research on traditional song in Scotland. It might seem that there is little left to learn from the collection: there have been many studies of individual contributors and their repertoires, and of songs and airs, and much has been written also about the ethnology of traditional singing. However, the digitisation of the sound archive and the re-cataloguing of the tracks by the TaD project make it possible to search the material in new ways.

Not all of the digitised tracks are available online, and some are permanently restricted, for various reasons, but the tracks in the TaD cataloguing database represent the greater part of the relevant material in SSSA for the 1950s–70s, plus some later material, though it is not possible to quantify exactly what proportion remains to be incorporated into TaD and catalogued within it. The biographical information in the cataloguing database is also more extensive and detailed than the often very brief notes on the website, and includes information on family relationships.

Some additional data on song transmission and biography have been added here from sources published by the SSSA and its staff, in particular the journal *Tocher*, the website 'Whalsay's Heritage of Song', Bruford (1976, 1986), Munro (1996), and sleeve notes to the LPs *The Muckle Sangs* (1975)[1] and *John MacDonald – The Singing Molecatcher of Morayshire* (1975); and also from MacColl and Seeger (1977), L. Williamson (1985), Douglas ed. (1992), Douglas and Miller eds. (1995), and E. Stewart ed. McMorland (2012), all of whose coverage overlaps with that of the SSSA. For simplicity, the material will be referred to in this work as if all of these data come from the SSSA via TaD.

With regard to G-D, there is sometimes a degree of uncertainty, as Lyle points out ('Editorial introduction', G-D vol. 1, p. xvi), as to whether a contact gave a song from his or her own repertoire, or collected it on behalf of Greig and Duncan. FoC helps to clarify the roles of intermediaries and contributors, but many individuals are both. The editorial treatment of material passed on by an intermediary is not entirely consistent across the eight volumes of the collection. For instance, songs from Mrs Lyall's husband are usually placed over her name in the main text, apart from Song 1170. In the 'Index of Singers/Sources' (in vol. 8), however, Mr Lyall is listed as the contributor of all of these items. When listing G-D contributors this study has been guided by the notes to individual songs (including Supplementary Notes in vol. 8) and by FoC, as well as the Index. William Walker and John Ord have been omitted, as they were major collectors in their own right, and therefore not representative of the patterns of song transmission within communities. Had Walker been included this would also have introduced a degree of circularity when the Child ballad material is examined, as he contributed to both Child (1882–98) and G-D. Further details of how the G-D data have been selected and interpreted are given in Appendix B below.

2.2 Selecting the Data

Some individuals are not counted here for one of the following reasons: they are of unknown sex; they act only as intermediaries in G-D; they contribute only children's songs, non-song material such as rhymes, or material from

---

1 The term 'muckle sang' for the big ballads is not one that was used by contributors themselves. Steve Byrne (personal communication, 14 April 2016) has found an earlier use in a sleeve note by Bruce Dunnet to a 1958 recording by Robin Hall. The note is reproduced at https://raretunes.org/robin-hall/ (accessed 9 October 2019).

printed sources;[2] or they contribute only material of their own composition. (See Appendix B for details of the G-D contributors in these categories.) Most of the contributors to both collections offer folk songs, but no attempt has been made to eliminate other material, except that individuals who contribute only children's songs are omitted. This is for purposes of the study of song transmission, as children's songs have their own typical pattern of transmission from peer to peer (Opie and Opie, 1959). A case could also be made for excluding bawdy songs, which are not acceptable in all company, but there are recordings of women singing the mildly bawdy and euphemistic ones, with only a 'thread of blue', leaving a negligible number of really filthy songs such as Roud 10122 or 10305, whose transmission, we can suppose, is indeed very selective. (The reference is to catalogue numbers in *The Roud Folk Song Index* (n.d.).)

Some SSSA Gaelic contributors were also recorded singing in Scots or English, and these are included. Their non-Gaelic songs are mainly art songs in English. Apart from Folk Revival singers, there are very few singers in the database whose repertoire encompasses traditional Scots or English and also Gaelic songs (leaving aside some macaronic songs with often garbled Gaelic choruses).[3] Both collections include some examples of non-traditional genres such as music-hall songs and art songs (and in SSSA even a few pop songs, especially when children were allowed to take the mike). As others, including Atkinson (2004: 145), Olson (2007a: 390) and Byrne (2010: 286), have pointed out, the distinction between folk or traditional and other types of material is not one that singers themselves made until influenced by the collecting process.

The singing culture represented in the collections was not, of course, a closed system. In particular, Olson (1995–96) suggests that there was a very substantial input into the already robust song culture of the North-East by the migrant workers from Ireland and elsewhere who arrived in large numbers to build the railways in the 1850s, and had already been present in smaller numbers to build the turnpike roads and other infrastructure from the beginning of the century. *Contributors* from outside Scotland are omitted here,[4] but in

---

2 However, individuals are included whose material came to G-D through their having published it themselves in periodicals.
3 Some instances are Maggie Wilson from Achnasheen (TaD ID 1705), and two Travellers, John MacPhee from Argyllshire (TaD ID 825), and Betsy Whyte (TaD ID 1955), whose family were from the Trossachs. This is not the Betsy Whyte who wrote *The Yellow on the Broom* (1979, 2001), and whose husband Bryce is mentioned above. All other references to Betsy Whyte in this work are to the latter, the Montrose Betsy Whyte (TaD ID 3523).
4 This includes unidentified singers at festivals, ceilidhs, etc. who could not immediately be confirmed as Scottish as their tracks were not online. However, Scottish emigrants recorded in Australia are included if it appears that they learned their songs before leaving the country.

order to obtain as full as possible a picture of song reception by the Scottish singers, the study does include non-Scottish *sources*. Likewise, while members of staff of SSSA are omitted as contributors, Hamish Henderson is included here as a source. He is more typical in this context, and was in fact an important source for numerous Traveller performers and other participants in the Folk Revival.

In relation to the family data, it is not possible to identify in-laws as a separate category, as common parlance does not distinguish between blood relatives and relatives by marriage where aunts and uncles are concerned. Step-parents are counted here simply as parents. The practice of children being brought up by relatives other than their parents is not taken into account: in these cases the actual relationship is counted.[5]

There is some limited data on childhood song acquisition. The analysis can only be very tentative, as this piece of information was not systematically sought by the collectors, and it may often be taken for granted or implied when recipients say that they learned their songs 'at home' or from parents or grandparents. Insofar as information on childhood song acquisition can be retrieved, it can be identified either by statements to that effect, by reference to biographical information, or by calculations based on when the song was learnt relative to the recipient's d.o.b. Also, some contributors were children when they were recorded. *Childhood* is taken here to mean under the age of fourteen (the school leaving age from 1883 to 1947), although at the time when many of G-D's contributors were children, it was normal to go out to work around the age of twelve. Someone still at school is assumed to be a child unless the age is given and is fourteen or over. In the G-D song notes, a frequent expression is 'in early life' (or a similar wording), and Bell Robertson says of several of her songs that she seems to have known them all her life. These expressions are taken as referring to childhood.

In the G-D data a problem is posed by the frequent mention of 'girl(hood)'. Whereas boys in the nineteenth century generally began their working lives in their early teens and entered the phase of 'youth', girls only entered into what would be the pattern of their adult lives when they married (or, if they did not marry, when they had reached some indeterminate age when they were

---

G-D's correspondents writing from furth of Scotland are assumed to be exiled North-Eastern readers of the *Buchan Observer* if there is no other information about their background.

5   Such arrangements are often permanent, but the anonymous author of a participant observation study in the 1970s also notes that at various times of the year Traveller children would go to stay with relatives, such as grandparents, aunts and sisters, possibly for reasons of meeting the education requirements (Anon., 1975: 94). (See below, §4.5, on the education requirements for Traveller children.)

no longer expected to). A period of employment between childhood and marriage was an interval during which the person was still referred to as a 'girl'. We can only take it that 'girl(hood)' refers to child(hood) if there is a qualifying term, such as 'little girl'. The picture is therefore incomplete. The G-D figures for females are calculated with and without the 'girl(hood)' data: the correct figure presumably lies somewhere between.

As the initial focus of the study was on song transmission, singers who contribute only their own compositions are omitted. Also omitted are individuals who contribute only tunes without lyrics. It is possible that where G-D is concerned this entails a false distinction between items that consist of music only, and items that have at least one verse of the lyrics, usually interlined with the music. For instance, the contribution from Miss Dunbar, Song 1239F, consists only of the tune, but Greig mentions that she gave a rendering of the song (FoC, p. 508). Both Greig and Duncan were, at least initially, more interested in the tunes than in the lyrics (Shuldham-Shaw, 1973, 1981: xiii; Campbell, 2002: 447): the latter had in most cases already appeared in print, often in fuller form than they were able to collect, while the former promised more in the way of new and unpublished material. Greig's *modus operandi* is described by McKean (2002: 590): Greig would write down a verse and use that as a skeleton around which to take down the tune in sol-fa. As Lyle points out, when there are both interlined lyrics and separately noted ones, they do not always correspond exactly ('Editorial introduction', G-D vol. 1, p. xv).[6] However, at the risk of leaving out the music-only material unnecessarily, the presence of at least one verse is taken here as an assurance that the contributor had an acquaintance with the lyrics.[7]

2.3   Approaches to the Data: Transmission

To compensate as far as possible for the limitations of the data, a variety of different ways of interrogating the data sets are employed in this study. The transmission data are ordered on the following bases:
- *instances* of transmission of particular song lyrics. If more than one means of acquiring the song is mentioned – e.g. it was first heard in performance,

---

6 Occasionally the words given with the music are actually from a different song, to which the tune commonly belongs, e.g. Songs 149C and 1785.
7 On this basis, John Fox and Mrs Stevenson are included, although FoC (p. 482) describes their contributions as 'tunes'.

then learned from another singer, then supplemented with further verses from a written source – all are counted as separate instances;
- individual song *recipients*. As explained above (§1.1), the recipients at first hand are that sub-set of contributors who provide transmission information; they are supplemented by additional information at second hand. Only 8% of the Traveller recipients are at second hand, in comparison with 12% of those in the general population. In G-D the figure is 24%. The recipients can be sub-divided according to the types of inter-personal transmission they participate in, namely *family* transmission – further sub-divided into *nuclear* and *extended* family transmission –, and *non-family* (i.e. other inter-personal) transmission;
- *pairs* of *recipients* and *sources* in inter-personal transmission, again further sub-divided into *family* and *non-family* pairs. The information about the sources is sometimes vague. Some occupations, e.g. whaler, can be assumed to be male, and farmservants are also assumed to be male unless stated otherwise. A source might be a family member of known sex but unknown relationship, or vice versa (as for instance with the sex-neutral term 'cousin'). The numbers used in the analyses therefore vary: they are stated in the captions to the relevant tables and figures;
- individual song *sources*.[8] Although most sources only figure once in the lists of pairs, there is in fact a many-to-one relationship in both directions between the recipients and the sources: e.g. an individual might transmit songs to more than one family member. Some influential singers, such as Jeannie Robertson, were sources for several others in the SSSA collection.

The various approaches listed above offer different perspectives on complex patterns of interaction. To use a metaphor, the song culture is like a market, in which the recipients are the customer base, the sources are the vendors, the pairs are the trading relationships, and the instances of song transmission are the transactions. Usually patterns derived from the different types of analysis agree; when they do not, this draws our attention to some distortion in the market, as it were.

2.4 Approaches to the Data: Chronology

The chronological dimension is an important one in many of the topics addressed, and there are various ways of capturing this in the data:

---

[8] Family trees have been taken into account where these are known, but it is possible that there could be some duplication of individuals: e.g. one contributor's grandmother might, unbeknownst, be the same person as another's aunt, and so on.

- The distribution of the SSSA contributors (and of the first-hand recipients, i.e. those who are a sub-set of the recorded contributors) can be tracked in terms of when they were first recorded.[9] This is tabulated in half-decades.
- The average (median) ages of the SSSA contributors when first recorded can be calculated, revealing differences between the sexes and amongst the demographic groups. However, as the range of ages is very wide, a clearer picture is obtained by calculating the percentages born before certain dates.
- Broad comparisons can be made between the 1950s collecting period, when contributors with a wide range of d.o.bs were recorded (going as far back even as the 1850s in one case),[10] and subsequently. This measure is informative about the decline in popularity of the Child ballads prior to the Folk Revival.
- The distribution of d.o.bs of the various categories of singers can be examined. This is tabulated in decades. This measure shows peaks and troughs in the numbers of contributors from successive birth cohorts recruited to the two collections. It reveals differences amongst the demographic groups, and is used to track changes over birth cohorts in various sub-sets of the song transmission data.
- Comparisons can be made between G-D's data (c. 1910) and the SSSA data (1951 to the late 1970s). For purposes of extending the distribution of d.o.bs, the G-D data can be combined with the SSSA general population or core population data. The validity of treating the two collections as broadly representing the same song culture at different time periods is discussed below (§6.2).
- Family pairs can be analysed in terms of generations. The same generation, including siblings, cousins[11] and spouses, is termed here *generation 0*; the parental generation, including aunts, uncles, etc. is *generation 1*; and the grandparental generation, including great aunts, great uncles, etc. is *generation 2*. Individuals in generation 3 are too few to analyse, and are included in generation 2. Younger generation sources are also too few to analyse and are omitted when the data are broken down in this way.

---

9   As the TaD cataloguing is incomplete, it is possible that earlier recordings of individual singers may exist.
10 Annie Grant from Glenlivet (born 1853).
11 Cousins are assumed to be in the same generation as the recipients unless there is information to the contrary.

2.5 Ballad Fragments: Definition

Although the picture of the SSSA collection obtained via TaD is incomplete, and would not be adequate to describe the repertoires of individual singers, in the aggregate there are enough data on the Child ballads to attempt a preliminary sketch at group level. That is, we can ask how many individuals in the group contribute only fragments, one ballad, two ballads, and so on. In practice, the numbers are clumped here to arrive at a more manageable number of categories (see below, Figure 5.9): these were chosen by eye according to what seemed natural break points along the number range (Figure 2.1).

It is necessary to have some measurable definition of a fragment, which must be to some extent arbitrary. The Child ballads vary considerably in length: many are very long, but singers often perform abbreviated versions. The TaD cataloguers sometimes describe renditions of six or more verses as 'fragmentary' if they consist of scattered verses that do not cohere into a narrative. However, in order to have an objective measure, the definition used here relies simply on the number of verses.[12] Four verses is perhaps the borderline: some ballads, and especially 'The Four Maries' (Child 173), can be abbreviated to four verses while remaining coherent. The ranking of the groups is the same

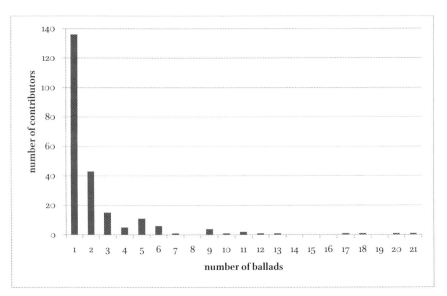

FIGURE 2.1 Numbers of SSSA contributors with Child ballad repertoires of different sizes

---

12   Most ballads have 4-line verses. In the case of exceptions, four lines are counted as a verse.

TABLE 2.1 SSSA Child ballad repertoire size – percentage of contributors with at least one whole Child ballad *versus* fragments only (Revival contributors omitted)

		Percentage of Child ballad contributors			
		All	Whole ballad	Fewer than 5	Fewer than 4
	n	%	%	%	%
Male core pop	79	100	70	30	25
Female core pop	53	100	62	38	36
Male Trav	45	100	76	24	13
Female Trav	44	100	82	18	11
All	221	100	71	29	29

Note: fragments can be defined as fewer than 5 verses, or alternatively as fewer than 4 verses: the former definition is used in subsequent analyses.

whether a fragment is taken to be fewer than five verses or fewer than four: in either case, the core population females have the highest percentage of repertoires that consist of fragments only, and the female Travellers the lowest (Table 2.1). For present purposes a ballad fragment is defined as fewer than five verses.

The TaD cataloguing does not always include the number of verses, and in these cases reference has been made to the audio recordings,[13] except for public performances, which we can assume are not fragmentary. Since public performance is part of the definition of Revival contributors, the Revival contributors are not included in this part of the analysis, in order to avoid circularity.[14] Where singers have contributed more than one recording of the same ballad, only the longest version is counted. Occasionally in SSSA, and more frequently in G-D, individual contributors give more than one version of a ballad, as remembered from different sources; these additional versions are only counted here if they are treated separately by the editors of G-D or the TaD cataloguers. In G-D, the editors divide some Child numbers into more

---

13 Including some not online, for which I am grateful to the School of Scottish Studies Archives for access.
14 It would also be pointless to quantify their repertoires in the data, as they have usually only recorded two or three ballads in SSSA (often in the context of festivals or competitions), which are not likely to be representative of their personal repertoires.

than one type, e.g. C7 'Earl Brand' appears in G-D as Song 220 'Lord Douglas' and also as 1026 'The Child of Elly' (see 'Index of Child and Laws songs in this edition', vol. 8, pp. 677 ff.). In SSSA, the TaD song cataloguers distinguish a parody version of Child 12 ('Lord Randal'); an American version, 'Matty Groves', of Child 81 ('Little Musgrave'); three versions ('Here's a Health to All True Lovers', 'I'm Often Drunk and I'm Seldom Sober' and 'Willy-o') of Child 248; a macaronic version with Gaelic chorus, 'Hame Drunk Cam I' of Child 274 ('Hame Cam Oor Guidman'); and a version, 'Davie Faa', with a Gypsy instead of a beggar, of Child 279 ('The Jolly Beggar') as well as Child's own separate 279 and 279A versions. Where contributors record at least one 'whole' ballad (defined as at least five verses), any additional fragments are ignored.

There can be a variety of reasons for only fragments of Child ballads being recorded in the data. Sometimes one verse is sung to illustrate the tune. It is possible that some individuals, if given the time to remind themselves of the words, and knowing that the big ballads were of particular interest to the collectors, could have sung more complete versions on a subsequent occasion. Some, especially if elderly, might have forgotten the words of songs that they could, at one time, have sung. Others might have picked up some of the words through hearing the ballads, without having set out to learn them. Unusually, Jane Turriff was recorded in the process of acquiring a ballad.[15] It is possible that different reasons might prevail in different groups. These questions can only be addressed in the context of a more detailed study of individual repertoires, which is not attempted here.

2.6 Outline of the Contributors, and a Note on the Reliability of Estimated Dates

This study has assembled data on 1,159 SSSA contributors, of whom 535 have known d.o.bs, with another 242 able to be estimated, leaving a third unknown.[16] Figure 2.2 shows the numbers of SSSA contributors first recorded in each half-decade in the data. The fluctuations may to some extent be an effect of the incomplete TaD coverage, and this is certainly the case after the late 1970s, but for the most part they probably do reflect different amounts of fieldwork done at different times. For all groups there is a dip in the numbers of those first recorded in the second half of the 1960s, then more new contributors in the 1970s, although for Traveller contributors this second peak, which

---

15 'Lang Johnny More' (Child 251) on SA1972.220.A7.
16 For a breakdown by sex and social background, see Table A1a.

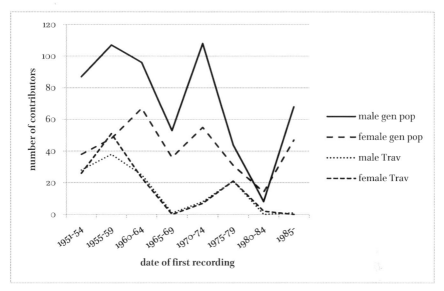

FIGURE 2.2 Numbers of SSSA contributors by half decade of first recording

is attributable in large part to recordings of Duncan Williamson's circle, does not come until the second half of the 1970s.

Figures 2.3 and 2.4 show the median ages of SSSA contributors in each half decade of recording, with and without the estimated d.o.bs. When we take only known d.o.bs in Figure 2.3, it would seem that the median ages of females in the general population are under-estimated in the recording periods 1951–54 and 1955–59, where a relatively large number of children skews the medians downwards: six out of fifteen general population females with known d.o.bs recorded in 1951–54 are under fourteen, and five out of 21 recorded in 1955–59. The skewing is corrected to some extent when the estimated d.o.bs are added in Figure 2.4, and in general the patterns are smoothed.

Nevertheless, the wide range of ages – from four to 105[17] – means that the median ages do not give a very clear picture. Instead Tables A5a and A5b show the percentages born before certain dates (1900 and 1920).[18] The percentages are very similar with and without the estimated d.o.bs: in either case, the female Travellers stand out as having a smaller proportion born at the earlier periods, i.e. the fieldwork was not reaching so far back in time to find contributors from this group. When the figures are broken down further by recording

---

17   Maggie Clouston, born in 1880, recorded in 1985.
18   The choice of break points is necessarily arbitrary: 1920 is chosen as the start of a decade of particular interest (see Chapter 8), 1900 simply as the start of the century.

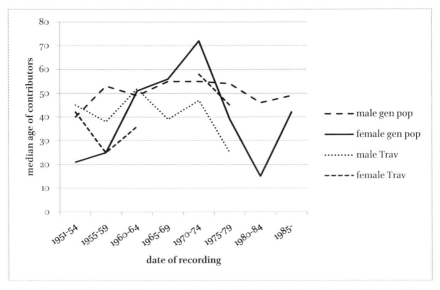

FIGURE 2.3 Median ages of SSSA contributors by half decade of first recording (known dates of birth only)

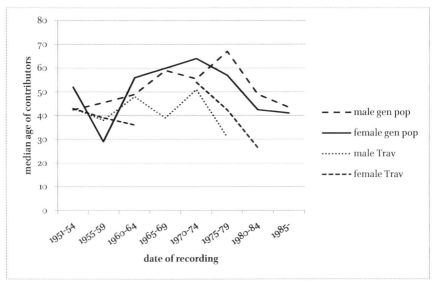

FIGURE 2.4 Median ages of SSSA contributors by half decade of first recording (known and estimated dates of birth)

date, the patterns with and without the estimated d.o.bs are again broadly similar (cf. Tables A6a and A6c with A6b and A6d).

There are data for 308 SSSA contributors of Child ballads.[19] In this data set it is possible to quantify the Folk Revival contributors separately (Figures 2.5, 2.6 and 2.7). The Revival contributors become more numerous as we approach more recent decades of birth, producing a pronounced double peak, or bimodal distribution, of decades of birth (Figure 2.8). This is discussed below (§8.1). The Revival contributors are not separated out in the overall SSSA data set, but the bimodal distribution, with its trough in the 1920s, reveals their presence. This pattern is evident when we take only known d.o.bs (Figure 2.9), but becomes particularly clear when we add the estimated d.o.bs (Figure 2.10).

The unknown d.o.bs in SSSA can be incorporated into a timeline on the basis of the *terminus ante quem*, assuming that an adult first recorded in the 1950s has a d.o.b before 1930, and so on. Figure 2.11 shows the cumulated percentage of each group that has been reached by each date. The graph for the female Travellers, who tend to have more recent d.o.bs, climbs more slowly at first, but the graph for general population females crosses below it prior to 1930, again pointing to the 1920s as the transition from the older core population to the younger Folk Revival singers.

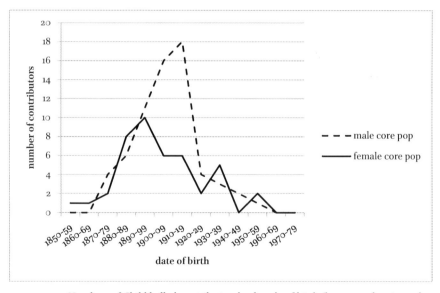

FIGURE 2.5 Numbers of Child ballad contributors by decade of birth (known and estimated dates of birth): SSSA core population

---

19   See Table A1d.

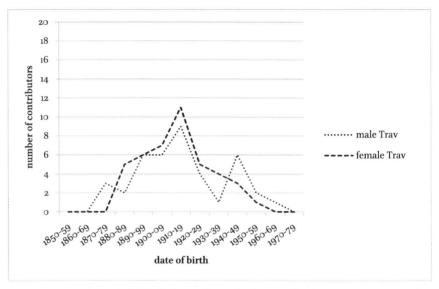

FIGURE 2.6   Numbers of Child ballad contributors by decade of birth (known and estimated dates of birth): SSSA Travellers

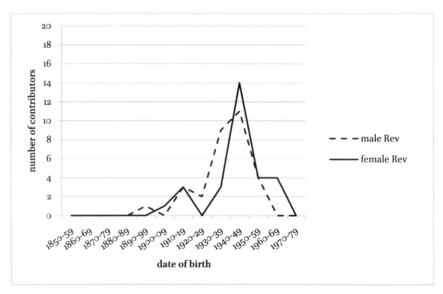

FIGURE 2.7   Numbers of Child ballad contributors by decade of birth (known and estimated dates of birth): SSSA Revival contributors

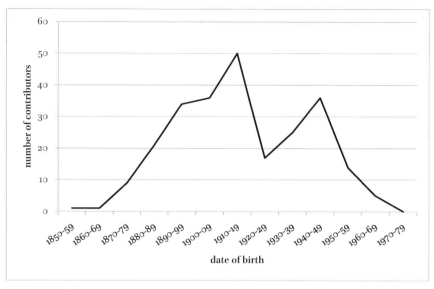

FIGURE 2.8 Numbers of Child ballad contributors by decade of birth (known and estimated dates of birth): all SSSA

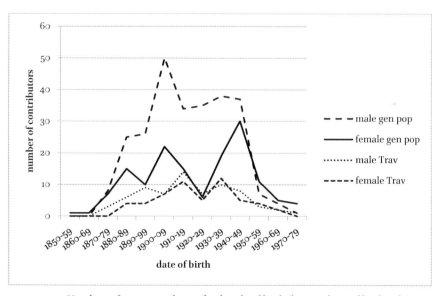

FIGURE 2.9 Numbers of SSSA contributors by decade of birth (known dates of birth only)

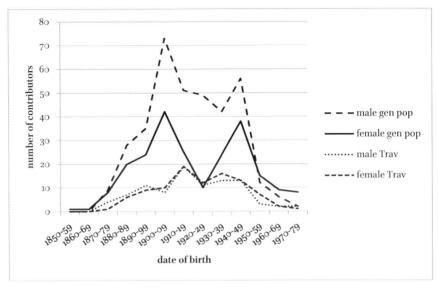

FIGURE 2.10   Numbers of SSSA contributors by decade of birth (known and estimated dates of birth)

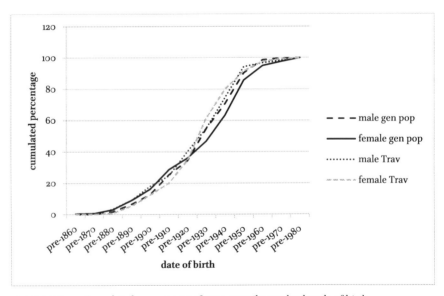

FIGURE 2.11   Cumulated percentages of SSSA contributors by decade of birth

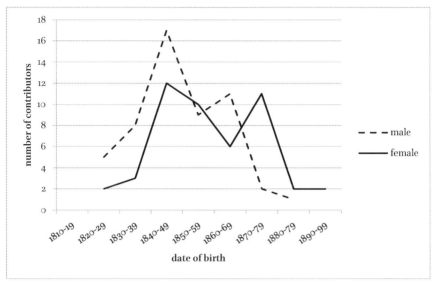

FIGURE 2.12   Numbers of G-D contributors by decade of birth (known dates of birth only)

From G-D there are data for 478 contributors, of whom 56% have unknown d.o.bs.[20] The patterns by decade of birth are very similar with and without the estimated d.o.bs (Figures 2.12 and 2.13), though the 1840s peak is perhaps exaggerated in Figure 2.13, as the estimated d.o.bs for individuals described as 'old' when collected (over a relatively short period) are compressed into this decade.

Overall, the estimated d.o.bs appear to be distributed across the SSSA recording period, and across decades of birth in both SSSA and G-D, in a fairly reliable fashion, judging by the broad agreement, when the estimated d.o.bs are added, with the patterns established by the known d.o.bs, but with the smoothing of some anomalies. The estimated dates also compensate to some extent for an apparent under-representation of female contributors in SSSA if only known dates are used. This suggests that without the estimated d.o.bs, the number of female contributors is under-represented, probably because of social constraints on asking the age of women. Males outnumber females 63% to 37% if we rely only on known d.o.bs.[21] Taking known and estimated d.o.bs together, the difference is reduced to 59% males and 41% females.

In what follows, the estimated d.o.bs will, in most cases, be included without also showing the results for known d.o.bs only, in order to avoid a proliferation

---

20   See Table A1a.
21   For numbers, see Table A1a.

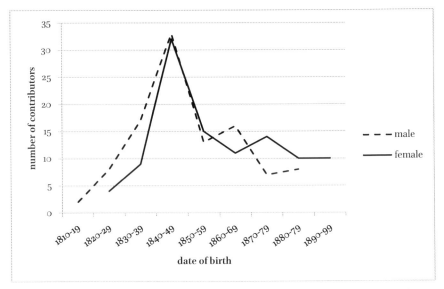

FIGURE 2.13   Numbers of G-D contributors by decade of birth (known and estimated dates of birth)

of figures and tables. However, when considering the sources (i.e. individuals identified by contributors as the sources of particular songs), both will be shown, as the percentages of known d.o.bs of sources are very small,[22] and the addition of the estimated d.o.bs suggests patterns, especially for the earlier decades of birth, that are not apparent when only known d.o.bs are taken into account (see below, §5.3.2).

---

22   See Table A1c.

CHAPTER 3

Did Greig and Duncan Neglect the Travellers?

Disclaimer: in order to discuss historical material, this work refers to a number of terms that are now considered offensive, in particular *tinker* or *tinkler*. No offence or criticism is intended towards present-day Gypsies or Travellers. Nor does the author wish to assert that any of the historical groups or individuals discussed here are ancestral to any present-day Gypsies or Travellers, apart from the undisputed continuity of certain Gypsy surnames associated with Kirk Yetholm.

3.1 The Fog of Euphemism

It can be difficult to discern Travellers in the historical record, even as recently as G-D, because of the various terms and euphemisms used to refer to them.[1] For the current usage, SND (s.v. *travel* v. 4) quotes Gentleman and Swift (1971: 7) to the effect that *traveller* (*sic*, without capitalisation) 'has been adopted by the majority of the community' as a specific self-designation. It difficult to pin down the first reference to Travellers in this sense in the dictionary record: in Older Scots (i.e. before 1700) *traveller* has the general sense of a wayfarer, and the specific sense of someone travelling with merchandise (DOST s.v. *travalour*). A 1699 reference to '[t]he travelling people' (SND s.v. *travel* v. 4) does seem to refer to itinerants as a distinct group, but thereafter it is the mid-nineteenth century before we have references to the group's own use of the term (NSA for Yetholm, 1845: III, 166; J. Simson, 1866: 427, 432).

Until quite recently, when it was rejected as derogatory, the usual term was *tinker*, in Scots also *tinkler*. Hamish Henderson (e.g. 1981a: 229) sometimes uses Robert Burns' term *tinkler-gypsy*,[2] which is also used in the title of McCormick (1907). *Tinker* converged with, and from the eighteenth century largely replaced, the term *Gypsy*, except with reference to some communities, particularly in Kirk Yetholm, who continued to identify themselves as Gypsies. In 2008 an industrial tribunal hinged on the ethnic identity or otherwise of the Scottish Travellers (Anon. 2008). The ruling was in favour of regarding them as

---

1 This section is based on Macafee (2019), q.v. for a much more detailed discussion and further references.
2 In 'The Twa Dogs', l. 18.

a distinct ethnic group. They are now commonly referred to in official sources as *Gypsy/Travellers*, and Roma descent is perhaps more likely than in the recent past to be self-asserted (cf. Turbett, 2009; Anon., 2011).

The *Roma* (also known as *Romany*, but this term is sometimes reserved for the language) generally presented themselves in fifteenth century Europe as *Egyptians*, specifically Christian Egyptians, i.e. Copts, wandering as pilgrims (Grellman trans. Raper, 1787: 99; Pitcairn, 1833: 591). (The word *Gypsy* is a shortened form of *Egyptian*.) Their presence in Scotland is reliably documented from 1505 on (Pitcairn, 1833: 592; MacRitchie, 1894: 29), when a group entertained at court. (A breakaway group from this band were also the first documented in England.) They subsequently travelled the country under royal protection. This was temporarily withdrawn in 1541, in view of numerous complaints against them (W. Simson ed. J. Simson, 1866: 106; MacRitchie, 1894: 41). By the end of the century, they were the object of several ineffectual statutes aimed at either expelling them or forcing them (along with other vagabonds) into employment or servitude, but references to them still pursuing their own lifestyle continue to appear in the next century, from Shetland to the Borders. Under a statute of 1609,[3] however, they did so under pain of death, and some were indeed hanged, especially in the first half of the seventeenth century. W. Simson (ed. J. Simson 1866: 344–5) was informed that the press-gangs took large numbers of Gypsies during the American War of Independence (1775–83) and again in the Napoleonic Wars (1803–15).

The historical persecution of the Gypsies naturally made them reluctant to identify themselves as such. J. Simson (in W. Simson ed. J. Simson, 1866: 7 n. 4) states that *tinkler* was the itinerants' own preferred term, rather than *Gypsy*. Tinkering – working in metal, and mending pots and pans – was an occupation that they followed. The earliest occurrence of *Tinkler* is as a surname in the late twelfth or early thirteenth century (*DOST* s.v. *tynklar*). The source is *Liber Ecclesie de Scon*, the register of Scone Abbey, where a portion of land is specified 'que iacet inter terram serlon incisoris et terram Jacobi tinkler' (1843: 30).[4] This passing mention of a medieval land-holder has been made to bear a great deal of weight. It is quoted by Crofton (1880, 2001: 1), who writes: 'Between the years 1165 and 1214 *James "Tinkler"* held land in the town of Perth.' This should be read as 'At some time between the years …': the dates quoted are those of the reign of William I, the original text being arranged by reigns, not dates. Crofton's words are quoted by MacRitchie (1894: 4–5); both are careful to point

---

3 'Act regarding the Egyptians' (12 April 1609), in 'Records of the Parliaments of Scotland to 1707' (in Modern English translation).

4 'Which lies between the land of Serlon the cutter and the land of James Tinkler.'

out that someone who is a 'tink(l)er' need not therefore be an itinerant, but MacRitchie would clearly like to entertain the possibility, and subsequent writers have often taken it as fact. Thus we read about 'the ancient Celtic tinsmith caste (mentioned in the twelfth century in Perth)' (Gentleman and Swift, 1971: 9); and we are told that 'Gypsy/Travellers have been part of Scotland's economic and cultural life since at least the 12th century' (C. McDiarmid and Watson, 2015).

It is clear from the quotations in *DOST* s.v. *tynklar* that, besides the twelfth century James Tinkler, there were 'tink(l)ers' who held land (sixteenth century quotations) and 'tink(l)ers' who were admitted to Hammermen's guilds and to burgess status (seventeenth century quotations). Such individuals were presumably sedentary. The chief indication that some 'tink(l)ers' were set apart from the general population is the process of pejoration that the term undergoes. However, this is evidenced only from 1560 onwards: 'To tryit tinklaris tell thy taill ... For honest folk few will set by thé' (*DOST* s.v. *tynklar*). Indications of 'tink(l)ers' who were itinerant date only from 1567 in England (*OED* s.v. *tinker*) and from the seventeenth century in Scotland.

Prior to the arrival of the Roma in 1505, there is no evidence of itinerants in Scotland except for *sorners* and Highland bards, and (mentioned alongside bards) pretend ('feigned') fools (*DOST* s.v. *bard*). Sorners went about in armed bands in the Highlands and adjoining areas 'extorting free quarters and provisions' (*DOST sorning* vbl. n.). Bards demanded hospitality with the promise of entertainment, on the one hand, and the threat of blazoning the victim's meanness in scurrilous verse, on the other (cf. Watson, 1937: 272–3). There is no evidential basis for the idea that there was an existing ancient Celtic caste of itinerant metalworkers, or that the Roma merged with such an entity. This notion, promoted by the poet Lewis Spence (1920: 367, s.v. *Shelta Thari*; 1955), and encouraged by Henderson (1974, 1992: 174; 1981a, 1992: 229), is now widely accepted.[5] It is built on fanciful Victorian theories about the Bronze Age and the supposed antiquity of the Irish Travellers' secret language, known as Shelta.[6] It does appear, however, that the small band of Roma who originally brought the gypsy way of life augmented their numbers over time from the indigenous population, including 'the descendants of itinerant craftsmen, broken clansmen, outlaws, mendicant soldiers, deserters, Irish exiles, fugitives and refugees from dynastic and religious hostilities' (Leitch, 1988: xxii).

Travellers were also referred to in terms of other occupations, as well as tinkering, in which they engaged, in particular hawking. Hawkers mentioned in

---

5   It is repeated, for instance, by Cooke (2007: 213) and by L. Williamson (1985: 1).
6   For a detailed discussion, see Macafee (2019).

G-D might well be Travellers, as might some street singers. In principle tramps are completely distinct, being lone individuals, but descriptions are sometimes ambiguous. Irishmen mentioned as sources in G-D might be Irish Travellers, or part of the broader influx of Irish poor into Scotland in the early nineteenth century (even before the Potato Famine of 1845–49). W. Simson ed. J. Simson (1866: 356) writes of bands of extremely impoverished itinerants arriving from Ireland from c. 1820 onwards and to some extent forcing Scottish Gypsies off the roads and into settled occupations.

3.2 The Supposed Neglect

When scholars began to take an interest in the Travellers and Gypsies in the nineteenth century, they found them very wary of outsiders. Only a handful of individuals, for whom it became a life's work, were able to gain the itinerants' trust, notably Walter Simson, David MacRitchie, and Andrew McCormick in Scotland; and in England George Borrow, John Sampson, Francis Groome, and Charles Leland. This wariness arose both from the consciousness that they did not live entirely within the law, and from the harshness with which they were generally treated by the authorities. For instance, under the Reformatory Schools (Scotland) Act 1854 vagrant children could be compelled by local magistrates to attend a residential 'industrial school'. Subsequent legislation consolidated these powers, and from the 1880s on the Royal Scottish Society for the Prevention of Cruelty to Children was active in bringing cases of perceived neglect before the courts (Kelly, 2016: 72). The Children Act 1908 (§58(6)) stipulated that non-attendance at school was grounds for sending a child to an industrial school. By the 1950s, with the advent of the Welfare State, the face that the authorities turned towards the itinerants was a more benign one; but magistrates, the police, local government officials – and later also social workers – still had extensive powers to disrupt and interfere with their lives, and other professionals such as doctors and the clergy were still conduits by which information about them might reach the ears of those with power to interfere.

When Hamish Henderson began to record the Travellers, he had the advantage of being young and unthreatening. He also had a legendary ability to put people at their ease, and was happy to drink with the men and go on escapades such as what he euphemistically terms 'scrounging' peats ([Henderson], 1975: 14). So he was entitled to congratulate himself on breaking through the barrier of distrust. Unfortunately, he chose to counterpoint that success by suggesting that Greig and Duncan had neglected the Travellers, and that the reason was fear of social disapproval (Henderson and Collinson, 1965: 2; [Henderson], 1975: 14). The idea that Greig and Duncan, men of mature years who were pillars of the community, would have suffered a loss of social status from consorting with Travellers appears to be a projection of experiences like that described later by Rehfisch (1975: 274), of being shunned by the general population of Blairgowrie after an initial warm reception, when the fieldworkers threw in their lot with the Travellers.[7] Henderson's complaint about Greig's and Duncan's supposed neglect of the Travellers has been echoed by later writers (MacColl and Seeger, 1977: 2; Shoolbraid, 2010: 20), and even by G-D's own editors (Lyle, 'Introduction', vol. 8, 2002: xxiii). They lament the lost riches that might have been collected if only Greig and Duncan had deigned to 'learn from the Travellers' (Campbell, 2009: 54). Munro (1991: 149) quotes from a 1990 letter of James Porter's to the effect that Greig and Duncan 'ignored the travellers because of class and other biases common among professional people of the period', and she reiterates that they 'would appear to have avoided the travelling people, or at best been unaware of the treasures hidden amongst them' (p. 158). However, she adds in an endnote that the evidence for or against this 'hitherto accepted view' must await a study of Greig and Duncan's contributors. With the publication of G-D, this is now possible.

3.3 Travellers in *Greig-Duncan*

Since both collections relied heavily on family and social networks to discover and recruit singers, it was probably inevitable that particular demographics would be either over-represented or under-represented. Nevertheless, far from shunning the Travellers, Greig had a Traveller contact, Geordie Robertson, whom he engaged as a musician, as Henderson and Collinson acknowledge. It appears that Duncan did attempt to cultivate Travellers, visiting the markets and fairs where they gathered (P. S. Duncan, 1966: 66–7). However, it would have been surprising if a man occupying his position in the community could have mingled with them freely; and although he carried a flask of whisky to lubricate social interaction (Olson, 2002a: 544, citing a letter of Alexander Keith), he himself was a teetotaller.

---

7 There was more going on: in 1956 Hamish Henderson and Farnham Rehfisch took the part of the Stewart Traveller family when they were unfairly targeted by sanitary inspectors and were subject to other legal action, apparently because of local antagonism after they made the move from fruit picking to fruit growing in their own right. Henderson recruited a prominent lawyer, Lionel Daiches, who successfully defended the Travellers (S. Stewart, 2006: 126; Neat, 2009: 79).

There are three contributors in G-D who were most likely Travellers:
- Miss Henderson, 'a wandering damsel who sang for coppers' (note to Song 783A), who contributed seven songs;
- a 'wandering wife' (note to Song 1528B);
- Lizzie Stewart, 'a hawker girl ... travelling with her father, who was a hawker' (note to Song 1038G).

It is noticeable that two – and possibly all three – of the Traveller contributors in G-D had put themselves forward to sing in exchange for money, as opposed to being solicited to sing by the collectors: the girl called Henderson sang for coppers, and Lizzie Stewart sang at Duncan's door. Some other buskers who are mentioned in G-D are 'an old woman on the streets of Peterhead' (note to Song 112H), a 'blind old minstrel who stands and sings near the entrance to the Joint Station' (note to Song 113B), and 'a wandering tramp' (note to Song 951D, via Mrs Lyall).[8] Street singers might be Travellers: Maggie Stewart (an aunt of the famous Traveller singer Jeannie Robertson), for instance, made her living in this way as well as by hawking.[9] The fact that singing was used by Traveller women and children – as well as by tramps and the blind and infirm – as a cover for begging might also have made it awkward to ask for songs from Travellers, especially men.

It is possible that Greig and Duncan did make successful contact with Travellers, but did not obtain anything of interest from them beyond the few items that are in G-D. For instance, Greig mentions, in relation to 'The Tinkers' Weddin'', that he had 'heard it sung by a genuine tinker – a high compliment surely to the author' (quoted in the head note to Song 609), but he gives no additional text from that source. Such a selective approach to what was taken down is not unusual in G-D, presumably because the same lyrics were already in their collection, or in published collections (see above §2.2).

There is a curious comment by Bell Robertson about the singing of a 'tinker boy' from whom she picked up a verse of 'The Bonnie Banks o' Airdrie':

> They [the 'tinkers'] used to camp beside our house and the children came in to beg. My brothers ... used to ask them to sing. Of course they did not realy [sic] sing – it was a kind of chant ...
>
> G-D, note to Song 199B

---

8 Apparently recently, as she originally gave only a fragment recalled from her mother's singing. She is therefore treated here as an intermediary for this item.

9 SA1954.96.A2, TaD 1059; [Henderson] (1975: 26–7).

This is reminiscent of the 'declamatory style with variable intonation' of Martha Johnstone[10] (born 1901), described by Linda Williamson, and recognised by Duncan Williamson as a style characteristic of older women Travellers (L. Williamson, 1985: 230 ff.). McCormick (1907: 12 ff.) recounts an anecdote dating to 1789 of men overhearing Gypsies singing in a wood at night, and mistaking the singing at first for psalms. The lead singer was joined in the chorus by others, so this may have sounded like precenting. Bell Robertson's 'of course' suggests that she regarded chanting as the usual Traveller style. Since Greig and Duncan were primarily interested in tunes, this might have made Traveller performances of less interest to them, if this was indeed usual amongst Travellers at the time, or if it was believed to be.

As a side note, the continuation of Bell Robertson's comment is even more curious: '... but at the end of every verse they spat and said Paat and Sandy laughd [sic].' This sounds like a child's carry-on: perhaps it happened once by chance, and seeing that it raised a laugh, the children repeated it. However, it can also be compared with McCormick's (1907: 163–4) description of Mary Kennedy, a 'Tinkler' woman, giving a ludicrous performance of 'The Boatman's Dance'[11] with a dance between verses. McCormick also describes a 'Tinkler' boy singing and acting 'The Strodgribber', a song, partly in cant, about a shoemaker (p. 301). Buffoonery had, after all, long been part of popular entertainment.

3.4   A Very Small Fraction of the Population

Reliable figures for the number of Travellers in Scotland in the past are not to be had. W. Simson (ed. J. Simson, 1866: 367) estimates the numbers with some knowledge of Romany words at c. 5000. Since his work remained unpublished for twenty years, this is perhaps c. 1846. From the late nineteenth century on there are estimates based on reports by Chief Constables, but these include vagrants of all kinds. These numbers vary from 6,654 to 10,049 between 1889 and 1906 (Departmental Committee on Vagrancy in Scotland, 1936: 22). In 1917 there were reckoned to be 2,248 'tinkers', many living in houses, not including 309 men in the Army and 171 children in industrial schools (Departmental Committee on Tinkers (Scotland), 1918: 9). The Departmental Committee on Vagrancy in Scotland gives a figure, on the basis of the Chief Constables' reports, of 4,864 to 7,317 vagrants in the two years prior to 1936, but comments:

---

10   Also known, by her surname from her first marriage, as Martha Reid.
11   This can be found in G-D as Song 484.

> The evidence furnished to us, as regards the proportion of all vagrants who could be classed as 'habitual' has proved so conflicting that it is hardly possible for us to give the approximate number of this class.
> DEPARTMENTAL COMMITTEE ON VAGRANCY IN SCOTLAND, 1936: 22

Nevertheless, they venture the figure, on the basis of their own enquiries, of 1,266 'tinkers' and Gypsies not in houses. Additionally, there were 1,530 individuals holding pedlars' certificates or hawkers' licences,[12] some of whom would also have been Travellers (1936: 40–1). An attempt at enumeration in 1969 located 1,452 individuals in March and 1,598 in August, with only about 50% overlap between the two sets (Gentleman and Swift, 1971: 19). The population of Scotland at the 1901 Census was 4,472,103 ('1901 Census', n.d.) so the Traveller population would have had to be approaching 22,500 to represent even half of 1% of that. The Travellers were presumably a higher proportion of the rural population, but even so, with three Traveller contributors out of c. 500,[13] G-D does not appear to under-represent this population group at 0.6% (or 1.2% if we include the additional three itinerants and street singers).

In the G-D transmission data the contributors identify 515 source singers, and a few of these are described as itinerants or as singers in streets or markets, but it is not always possible to distinguish Travellers as such amongst the 'travelling' or 'wandering' characters, hawkers, pedlars, tramps and beggars. There are about sixteen of these, or 3% of the sources. Robert Alexander describes his source for 1219B as 'pedlar people'. These were probably Travellers, if they were going about as a group. It is unclear how many different individuals he is referring to as his sources of Songs 282, 429A, 1372B, and 1531B. Charles Farquharson, a 'travelling character, partly deranged, who had been in better circumstances' (note to Song 429A) was evidently a tramp. Farquharson also provided 1372B, but may or may not have been the same person as a 'travelling character' (Song 282) and a 'travelling man' (Song 1531B). Likewise Bell Robertson's three mentions of a 'tinker boy' (Songs 199B, 693B and 1018R) may or may not refer to the same person. Others are: two Gypsy girls living in a cave near Portgordon, who were George Innes' father's source for Song 42;[14] a travelling fiddler's wife who was Mrs Gillespie's source for 233E; Johnny Rainy

---

12   Under the Pedlars Act 1871 (§3), pedlars, i.e. hawkers doing business on foot, were exempted from the licence fee for hawkers with transport, and had instead to obtain a less expensive certificate from the local police. In colloquial usage, women Travellers on foot were often referred to by the more general term, as hawkers.

13   The figure used here for analysis is only 478 because of the exclusions mentioned above (§2.2).

14   George Innes was born c. 1823.

or Rennie, 'a half-witted character ... whose sister carried besoms for sale' who was Mrs Gillespie's source for 471C, 802A and 1367; 'a man who came through Rosehearty begging when Bell [Robertson]'s grandmother was a lassie circa 1775', who was the source for 643; Blind Bob, singing in Porter Fair, who was J. Sim's source for 649D; 'a beggar man who came from Skye', who was William Farquhar's source for 733; a man and a woman singing in Strichen market, who were Bell Robertson's sources for 1210; and Mr Rettie, 'a wandering servant' (presumably a farmservant), who was Annie Shirer's source for 164G; an Irishman singing on the streets of Peterhead, who was William Spence's source for 262B; and an Irish hawker, who was one of Bell Robertson's sources for 1098I (supplementary song note in vol. 8).

There are also sources not counted here, for reasons explained above (§2.2): William Walker's source for 233I, described as 'a broken down precentor' (so presumably a tramp); Mrs Aiken, a blind woman, who was Walker's source for 981F; and four tunes collected from Mrs Forbes that might have been learnt from 'a tinker who visited Skellybogs' (Lyle, 2002a: 525, n. 27). In a discussion of 1142 'Mormond Braes' (quoted in the head note to the song), Greig also mentions a neighbour's recollection of 'a wandering minstrel from the south' who made the mistake of singing, in a Strichen market, the rival version of the song, set in Blairgowrie.

3.5   Traveller Songs

What might the supposed lost riches consist of? The only specific suggestion is Campbell's mention of the more elaborate singing style of the Travellers (2002: 453). Munro (1970: 177) suggests that this stylistic tradition might have been shared with street singers (some of whom, as we have seen, would themselves have been Travellers), and singers in pubs and music-halls. This is the style now associated with the Travellers, in contrast to the chanting mentioned above.

Olson (2003–4: 163) and Cooke (2007: 214) have both pointed out that the Traveller song repertoire was substantially the same as that collected from earlier generations of country people, amongst whom they moved. The song collector Pete Shepheard, recorded by SSSA in 1986, likewise regards the Traveller repertoire as little different from that of the general population.[15] There are no previously unknown narrative ballads collected for the first time from Travellers. Instead, the most that has been said is that some Child ballads have variants specific to them, and Hall (1975) identifies two that were rarely

---

15   SA1986.172, TaD 84118.

preserved except by Travellers: 'Son David' (Child 13), recorded by Jeannie Robertson,[16] and 'The Cruel Brother' (Child 11), recorded by Martha Stewart, both in the 1950s; while members of the Johnston family sang the rare 'Young Johnston' (Child 88) (Cooke, 2007: 214).

Had the Travellers possessed a traditional repertoire beyond that of the Lowland population in general, there are certain items that we might have hoped to find, including perhaps some of the lost songs known only from their titles in *The Complaynt of Scotland* of c. 1550 (Wedderburn ed. Stewart, 1979: 51),[17] the traditional version of Child 293 (now widely known in Sir Walter Scott's rewritten version, 'Jock o' Hazeldean'), and likewise the traditional song re-written by Burns as 'The Birks of Aberfeldy' (see below, §3.6). If Macafee (2012, 2014) is correct in authenticating Allan Ramsay's ballad of Harlaw as a copy of a 16th century text, and therefore a candidate to be the ballad ('the battel of the hayrlau') mentioned in *The Complaynt of Scotland*, we might likewise have hoped to find this preserved orally.[18]

Ian Olson (personal communication, 26 June 2014) takes issue with the claim of Bruford (1975: 265) that the Travellers preserved a hypothetical older traditional song about a whisky still that was supposedly the inspiration for Rev. John Skinner's composition, 'The Ewie wi' the Crookit Horn',[19] and which he must then have bowdlerised to make it literally about a favourite ewe. Olson points out that none of the supposed precursors – even to the title of the tune – can be shown to have existed prior to the time of Skinner's composition,[20] while the conceit that the ewe is really a whisky still is traceable to William Stenhouse in his notes ('Illustrations') to the second edition of *The Scots*

---

16   Hamish Henderson describes the recording of Jeannie Robertson singing Child 13 as 'a spectacular disproof' of the belief that it had died out in Scotland (1986, 1992: 83).
17   In particular, Child (vol. v, 1898: 235) quotes the fragment 'god sen the duc hed byddin in France and delaubaute hed neuyr cum hame' as a possible lost ballad.
18   Greig is prepared to accept that the Ramsay ballad is not Ramsay's own work but is older. However, he objects that its stanza form is not conformable to the usual structure of ballad tunes. See the note to Song 112 in G-D.
19   Bertie (2005: 341) tentatively identifies the place of publication of the first extant text, a broadside, as Newcastle. If so, this might explain the written form *ewie* rather than the more usual Scots *yowie*.
20   See Bertie (2005: 341) on the date of composition; and, on supposed precursors, Walker (1883: 105–6), Bertie (2005: 6), Glen (1900: 156, no. 293), and Laing's notes on the song in the third edition of *The Scots Musical Museum* (1853: vol. IV, 412*–3*; and see p. 402* for details of his MS source). Personally, I find Walker convincing when he claims that a contemporary gave Rev. Skinner three lines to start off the song, as he appears to be relying on Skinner family sources, but Bertie disagrees on circumstantial grounds.

Musical Museum.[21] The problem with hypothesising a purely oral descent for something that exists in print is that once it is in print it is in the public domain for the whole of society (even if not accessible at will: see below, §4.1).

'The Strodgribber' (see above, §3.3) is one of four songs of which McCormick (1907) gives fragments. Cooke calls them 'travellers' songs' (2007: 215), but the others are more general in character. Mary Kennedy's song, 'The Boatman's Dance', was mentioned above. The information about Mary Kennedy dates from around the 1850s. She had a brother, Sandy (McCormick, 1907: 149), who would sing for the young people of a farm as he sat in the cart shed making spoons and baskets (p. 153). McCormick quotes from a song he sang called 'McGuire's Grey Mare', about a horse race (p. 155). The fourth song, sung by a 'Tinkler' child, was a sentimental song about how nice it is to have a little house of your own (p. 361). Titles of other songs mentioned by McCormick as sung by 'Tinklers' are:

- 'The Plains of Waterloo' (p. 153). G-D has this as Song 152;
- 'The Merry Masons' (p. 164). This is possibly the West of Scotland children's rhyme quoted by Dick (1903: 441, note to Song 236): 'Hey the merry Masons, and ho the merry Masons, / Hey the merry Masons goes marching along,'
- 'The Tinkler's Waddin'' (p. 183), Song 609 in G-D, written by William Watt (1792–1859),[22] and sold as a broadside ('Broadside ballad entitled "The Tinker's Wedding"', 2004);
- 'Willie, We have Missed You' (p. 501), written by Stephen Collins Foster (1826–64) and sold as a broadside ('Willie, We have Missed You', n.d.).

There is a small hint in G-D that there was a concept of 'tinker song' in Duncan's circle: his brother George so describes Song 1785 'Tilly Illy Rey Dum Dee' (see the note to the song). Duncan might therefore have been hoping to collect 'tinker song' when he sought out Travellers. The songs composed by Travellers and peculiar to them appear to be mostly:

- short lyrics showcasing cant vocabulary, e.g. – besides 'The Strodgribber' – 'Jimmy Drummond',[23] 'O What did he Feck ye?'[24] and 'Bing Avree, Barry Gadgie';[25]

---

21 See the second edition (1839, vol. III, p. 287) or the third edition (1853, vol. IV, p. 287). In the third edition the 'Illustrations' (which run through the second edition with their own page numbering) are gathered in one volume, vol. IV, with the addition of further notes by Laing. See further below, Chapter 4, n. 63.
22 See note to G-D Song 280, also by Watt.
23 See e.g. SA1967.141.A3, TaD 99116.
24 See SA1962.74.A1–4, TaD 18105.
25 See SA1962.75.B7, TaD 36755.

- occasional verses, often about people known to the authors (L. Williamson, 1985: 59), e.g. Belle Stewart's 'Frank and Ruby', about her friends the Kelbies,[26] or the adaptations of popular songs sung by sisters Katie Johnston and Betsy Whyte, which change the lyrics or add to them to refer to Traveller families;[27]
- jibes and bawdry, often extempore (Cooke, 2007: 220–1).

3.6 The Traveller and G-D Repertoires: Two Exercises in Comparison

The question of what, if anything, Greig and Duncan missed by not collecting more intensively from Travellers cannot now be addressed. The proposition that the 1950s Traveller repertoire is substantially that of the general population at a somewhat earlier point in time, on the other hand, is testable, but it must be left to others to compare the entire G-D and SSSA Traveller repertoires. Two small exercises in comparison are undertaken below. Although there is only partial access to the SSSA catalogue via TaD's database, this is the greater part of the relevant material, and it has the benefit that the Scots songs have been classified by Child and G-D numbers. The Child ballad repertoires in TaD and G-D are compared below, and the more marginal, fragmentary material of G-D is searched for in TaD.

None of the Child ballad contributions in G-D come from Travellers (unless the 'old woman on the streets of Peterhead', who sang Child 163 'Harlaw', was a Traveller). We can therefore regard G-D as a baseline for the general population, roughly speaking (see §6.2 below). There are 121 different Child ballads in the G-D data.[28] The Folk Revival singers arguably belong to a different cultural context, and they introduce some ballads not recorded otherwise in the data. Leaving them aside, in the remainder of the SSSA data there are 94 different Child ballads, 26 of which are not found in G-D. Only eight of these are recorded exclusively from the Travellers in SSSA: Child 13, 183, 3, 35, 37, 77, 78, and 255 'Willie's Fatal Visit' (which Lizzie Higgins tells us Hamish Henderson gave to Jeannie Robertson to expand her repertoire).[29] Since the G-D material comes almost entirely from the North-East,[30] and the SSSA material from

---

26   See e.g. SA1955.54.A2, TaD 28989.
27   SA1976.148.A4, SA1975.99.B15.
28   Not counting sub-divisions where the G-D editors have given different numbers to different variants.
29   SA1987.14.3, TaD 80508.
30   The only exception so far as Child ballads are concerned is Jeannie Brown, Margaret Gillespie's servant in Glasgow, who is one of several contributors of Child 12; but her father was from the North-East.

all around the Lowlands and Northern Isles, it is not surprising that there are some additional items in the latter, but the SSSA Traveller contribution is not especially remarkable in this context.

It is also worth asking whether the Travellers provided any fuller versions of songs that G-D collected only as fragments. (The term 'fragment' is used loosely in this section for any very small piece of a song. The strict definition set out in §2.5 above is used in the analysis of Child ballad repertoires in Chapter 6.) There are about 320 songs of this kind in the collection. It is difficult to be sure whether some very short songs, e.g. love songs and nonsense songs, are incomplete as they stand – even if longer versions exist in other collections, they might have circulated in G-D's catchment in shorter forms. There could be various accidental reasons for G-D lacking complete texts of particular songs; for instance it might happen that all of the specimens concentrate on the music rather than the lyrics – and a few of these items are indeed well known and well represented in the SSSA collection, e.g. 1528 'The Bonnie Banks o' Loch Lomond';[31] or the song might refer to places elsewhere; or conversely it might be about minor local happenings or characters and thus by its nature ephemeral. Nevertheless, taken in the aggregate, the fragmentary songs form an outer margin to the collection, and we might expect, if the Travellers did indeed have a richer store than the rest of the population, that some of these might have turned up when the SSSA collected from them.

Of the 320 fragments-only items identified in G-D, only 58 appear in TaD. Travellers provide instances of 17 of these 58,[32] but only three are uniquely recorded from Traveller individuals: Songs 751, 132, and 801. However, the last is not G-D's 'Birks o' Abergeldie' but the Burns version 'The Birks of Aberfeldy', based on it. Travellers outnumber others for another three songs: 199 'The Bonnie Banks o' Airdrie', 1166, and the nonsense or nursery song 1703. Interestingly, 'The Bonnie Banks o' Airdrie' is a song that Bell Robertson heard from a 'tinker boy' (see above §3.3).

This is a limited exercise, but it tends to confirm the impression of Olson (2003–4: 163) that the Traveller repertoire of the 1950s was more or less the G-D repertoire of the 1900s. The comparisons made above do not encourage the idea that Greig and Duncan had somehow missed the opportunity to tap into a source of songs separate from, and richer than, the (extremely rich) general song culture. Olson very much doubts that the Travellers in Greig and Duncan's time

---

31   Likewise 609 'The Tinker's Weddin'', 776 Burns' 'Rattlin Roarin Willie', 1201 'She Put her Hand into her Bosom', 1277 'The Jolly Minister', 1303 'The Muckin' o' Geordie's Byre', 1329 'The Russian Girl', and 199 'The Bonnie Banks o' Airdrie'.

32   Of which six are well represented in the SSSA collection (see previous note).

had a unique body of Lowland song, unshared by the rest of the community, handed down secretly and orally over the years or even centuries. This is not only hard to prove, but judging from Greig and Duncan's huge haul from the region, highly unlikely.

OLSON, 2003–4: 165

3.7 The Traveller Mystique

As Lyle says in her 'General Introduction' to G-D (vol. 1, p. vii), '[T]he collection is, in a way, the outcome of a corporate effort by the community of Aberdeenshire ... as well as of the individual efforts of the two collectors.' The Victorian period, which coincided in large measure with the lives of G-D's contributors, was the great age of taxonomy. The *pax Britannica* allowed the scientific exploration of most of the globe, and the painstaking assemblage of specimens, in fields such as palaeontology, mineralogy and anthropology, as well as in biology, where there was still much to add to the classification established in the previous century by Linnaeus. The collection of antiquities and folk song fitted naturally within this intellectual project to document and classify the whole world of knowledge. It was a period of democratic participation in scholarship not repeated until the participative effort of our own times to populate the internet with content.

The aims of the collectors were not nearly so clear to the contributors when the SSSA began recording in the early 1950s. The age of taxonomy was past, and the intellectual labour was now to interpret, compare, and theorise. For the public, however, collecting still made sense primarily as a taxonomic activity. For instance, Betsy Whyte describes how she began trying to find songs for Peter Cooke, Linda Williamson, and Hamish Henderson, not realising that they knew far more than she did.[33] The other way in which the SSSA collecting made sense to the public, now that recording equipment was involved, was as a search for talent, which of course tends to exclude most people from consideration.

The SSSA concentrated a large part of their collecting effort on the Travellers. What the Travellers made of it at the time is anybody's guess, but it is highly unlikely that they saw themselves as partners in the way that many of Greig and Duncan's contributors evidently did. Betsy Whyte was quite intimidated once she learned that Peter Cooke was a highly-respected scholar, not the student or dilettante she had originally taken him for. Whereas some of G-D's

---

33 SA1978.122, TaD 64239.

contributors seem to have been aware of the importance of detailed and accurate documentation of their contributions, implying a relationship between themselves and posterity, for the Travellers the relationship was with the collectors, whom they were prepared to humour and oblige.

Some of the finest of the Traveller singers became performers and recording artists, and prominent source singers for the Folk Revival. It would not have been surprising had they made sense of their role by assuming that there must be something about themselves, as Travellers, that added an extra dimension to the song repertoire. In this they were encouraged by Ewan MacColl (Douglas, 2002: 127). Since song transmission within Traveller families had attracted scholarly interest, the singer's own pedigree would be offered to audiences to valorise the performance. Scholars, folksingers and audiences have all deferred to this Traveller mystique, and so we arrive at the present situation where the song tradition of the Lowlands is regularly presented as 'Travellers' songs' (as in the title of MacColl and Seeger, 1977) or 'Traveller ballads' (e.g. McCleery *et al.*, 2008: 13), and G-D, which could hardly have been more voluminous in its collection of a regional repertoire, is found wanting because it does not have enough Travellers.

CHAPTER 4

Song Transmission

4.1 Historical Stages of Song Transmission

The relationship between oral culture and a literate society is complicated. It is the result of a sequence of historical developments that do not replace each other, but accumulate and interact; and the impact of mass literacy on the dissemination of songs is not felt only by those who are themselves literate. Five cumulative stages of song transmission can be identified: oral tradition, publication in print, dependence on literacy, audio recording, and (which does not concern us here) digitisation.[1]

Although the term 'oral tradition' is used in the folk song literature, this is within the context of a society that possessed literacy as far back as folk song can be traced (Atkinson, 2010: 145). However, so long as the majority of people were illiterate, we can assume that for the most part songs were learned by ear and memorised. Though this process is criterial for an oral culture, it remains, of course, a possibility in later periods also. There are reports of individuals learning songs at a single hearing: for instance Peter Pratt from Orkney (born 1880) remembered a song of seven stanzas apparently heard once seventy years previously (Bruford, 1986: 112). It is hard to know how typical this talent was, but it would seem that in the normal situation where songs were learned aurally, they were sung repeatedly. For instance Willie MacPhee, a Traveller (born 1910), discussing storytelling by the campfire, recalls, 'That's the way ye learned sangs tae, just gettin tae ken them by hearin them owre and owre an owre again' ([Douglas], 1992: 83). Jock Ainslie from Fife (born 1900) describes learning songs while living in bothy accommodation as a farm worker: 'Ye learnt off o one another … Yir mate mebbe sut an sung a song quite unconsciously an you were pickin up the words' ([Ainslie and Henderson], 1991: 53). Even when a song was heard on a single occasion, for instance the man overheard by an unidentified SSSA contributor singing 'The Greenock Railway' while repairing a bridge,[2] it is possible that the singer might have sung it over several times. The song recipient could also be pro-active in the process: Jeannie Robertson describes learning songs as a child by getting her mother to sing them over

---

[1] This section is based on Burnett, Macafee and D. Williamson (2017), where the analysis is structured in terms of knowledge management theory.
[2] SA1978.154, TaD 89037.

and over to her,[3] and similarly Belle Stewart and her daughter Sheila describe learning 'False, False hae ye been' from a relative who sang it repeatedly for them until they had learned it.[4]

The next stage is the collection and dissemination of song lyrics in print. In the eighteenth century there was an interest in recovering old traditions that were perceived to be disappearing. However, the medium of print entailed a major loss of information, as the song lyrics were detached from their tunes. The songs that were most sought after by early collectors such as Bishop Percy and Sir Walter Scott were the long narrative ballads. Their publication recast them for those outside the folk tradition as poems. In the twentieth century many Scottish schoolchildren encountered their song heritage only in this way. For instance Oliver and Boyd's *A Scots Reader Book II – Senior* of c. 1937 includes 'Get Up and Bar the Door', 'Sir Patrick Spens', 'Thomas the Rhymer',[5] 'The Twa Corbies' and a number of others. In 1963 Hamish Henderson was still trying to persuade the BBC to present ballads in sung rather than recited form (Henderson, 1963a, 1992: 44).

Bell Robertson and Mrs Gillespie (the sister of Rev. Duncan), who were very prolific contributors to G-D, both used printed sources as an *aide memoire* (Petrie, 2002a: 564; Petrie, 2002b: 584). However, naïve traditional singers could, as individuals, be quite isolated from the knowledge held in printed collections. For instance, Charlotte Higgins (born 1895) patiently learned 'The Road and the Miles to Dundee' and 'Lord Gregory' from an old lady whose memory was failing.[6] Charles Fiddes Reid from Aberdeenshire (born 1907) advertised in a newspaper for the words of 'The Laird o Esslemont',[7] which his mother had sung. Duncan Williamson took five years to get the whole of 'Green the Ganger'.[8] In some sense everybody was now within a national culture that included this knowledge, but they could not necessarily access it at will. Nevertheless it could find its way to them. Songs passed through print and re-entered oral tradition, e.g. Scott's version of Child 293, 'Jock o' Hazeldean', replaced the traditional one in popular currency. Fragments of Scott's version were recorded from Traveller singers Betsy Whyte and Stanley Robertson.[9] Olson (2003–4: 165) makes the point, with reference to Greig and Duncan's time, that 'the powerful "print to oral" transfer process' implies that there must

---

3   SA1977.221.B4.
4   SA1974.41.3, TaD 67921.
5   Cf. §1.5 above.
6   SA1962.68.A1; SA1962.68.A4, TaD 38725; SA1962.68.A3, TaD 38727.
7   SA1980.104, TaD 49286.
8   SA1978.138.
9   SA1975.150, TaD 77221, and SA1983.45.2, TaD 69995. See also Chapter 1, n. 10.

have been a considerable transfer of song from print via the literate settled community to the Travellers. Two of the songs mentioned by McCormick (1907) as sung by 'Tinklers' are by known authors and were sold as broadsides (see above, §3.5). Some more recent examples are discussed by Byrne (2010: 293–7).

The third stage is dependence on literacy. It is at this stage that there is the greatest divergence between the Travellers and the general population. Bruford (1986: 114) notes that in the early part of the twentieth century, songs often changed hands on scraps of paper, and these might be copied into a personal song-book. Grace Anderson (from Shetland, born 1924) mentions that her father (unlike herself) knew all the words of 'The Sheffield Apprentice' 'without the book'.[10] Likewise Robbie Murray (born before c. 1920?) mentions that his father did not write any songs down, as he had a very good memory, but Mr Murray wishes he had copied down the songs before his father passed away.[11] Many individuals did copy songs down: Campbell (2007: 431) observes that what she calls 'self-collection' has been relatively common in Scotland. G-D was able to draw upon notes made in 1875 and 1885 by George Duncan, the brother of Rev. Duncan, from the singing of their parents (Lyle, 2002a: 514). Two major SSSA contributors, Willie Mathieson (born 1879) and Willie Mitchell (born 1904), collected songs in Aberdeenshire and in Kintyre respectively, in Willie Mathieson's case from boyhood on (Henderson, 1963b, 1992: 32).

Writing things down to preserve them for future reference is of course a natural thing for a literate person to do, given access to affordable writing materials. This is simply a manifestation at a popular level of the same impulse that prompted George Bannatyne to compile the Bannatyne Manuscript, our main source for Older Scots poetry, in 1568, or prompted the anonymous seventeenth century compiler of the manuscript song collection that forms the core of Percy's *Reliques of Ancient English Poetry* (Groom, 1996). With reliance on writing, oral skills degenerate (Ong, 2002). The significance of this was grasped by prescient contemporaries: the Lady of Lawers prophesied in the seventeenth century that 'the feather of the goose would drive the memory from man' (quoted in translation from the Gaelic by Cowan, 1980: 1). That is, the capacity to commit material to memory goes unexercised and is consequently under-developed. Bruford (1986: 114) remarks that some singers, like Ethel Findlater (from Orkney, born 1899), clearly liked to have the 'psychological prop' of the written word, even if it was not really necessary. Byrne (2010: 315, n. 37) observes that on the digitised versions of the SSSA tapes it is sometimes possible to hear pages being turned as contributors sing from books or

---

10 SA1974.7.5, TaD 37930.
11 SA1986.5.B2.

manuscripts. Greig makes a similar point in relation to the long bothy ballad, 'The Boghead Crew', which runs to 26 verses in G-D:

> It takes a bit of memory to carry compositions of this length in one's head; and in this respect the exponents of our older minstrelsy put to the blush most of those who go in for modern compositions; for, while the former will sing songs and especially ballads of almost interminable length, which, as likely as not, they may never even have *seen* in print or writing, the latter will hardly embark on a song of three or four verses without the printed sheet to refresh their memories.
>
> G-D, note to Song 409A

There are many comments in the SSSA archive that point to a dependence, amongst individuals in the general population, on literacy to acquire the text of a song heard aurally. Unfortunately, it is not possible to extract data from the collections on the means of transmission between individuals: this is not mentioned in most cases. There are, however, enough examples to show that it was not uncommon for sources either to write lyrics down for the recipient, or to dictate them. For instance, Gordon Adam (born c. 1920?) learned 'If you Ever Go across the Seas to Scotland'

> from a conductor on an Aberdeen Corporation bus. He learned the words by writing them down while the conductor slowly recited them. He was only planning to travel half-way, but in the end went one and a half times round the route, and it did not cost him a penny.[12]

Ethel Findlater learned 'Half-Past Ten' from a neighbour; she heard him sing it while he was cutting peats, and later got him to repeat the song while she copied it down.[13] Annie Grant from Glenlivet (born 1853), describes learning 'The Bonnie Lass o Bennachie' at the age of seven from a transcription made by her brother of the singing of an old travelling man.[14]

In the fourth stage, audio recording and broadcast transmission were, of course, a great improvement over print in their ability to capture songs. Gramophones were commercially available before 1900 and became increasingly popular and affordable as time went on. BBC radio broadcasts began in 1922. Television broadcasting began in Scotland in 1952. When people

---

12   SA1956.44.A3, TaD 48749 (quoted from the Summary).
13   SA1969.52, TaD 64122.
14   SA1956.41.A2, TaD 12179.

reminisce about life before these new media, a frequent theme is that they made their own entertainment, in fact *had* to make their own entertainment. The availability of professional entertainment on demand, within the home, removed the incentive for everybody to contribute:

> Before 1914 in Orkney ... singing was the regular entertainment at weddings and harvest homes ... and could often be part of an ordinary evening visit. As in the Victorian drawing-room, everyone had a 'party piece' ... and many had sizable repertoires, though with the coming of the wireless and the gramophone few people continued to remember the songs they once knew....
> BRUFORD, 1986: 97

4.2 Outline of the Data and a Note on Selection

Information about song transmission in G-D comes mainly from the notes to the songs, with some additional details from the biographical essays and Lyle's (2002a) chapter on 'The formation of the collection', all in vol. 8, and from Campbell (2009). The SSSA data come primarily from the tracks indexed in the TaD database with the label 'song transmission'.[15] The cataloguers' summaries of these tracks were examined.[16] Some reference was made to audio to clarify particular points, but it was not possible, within the scope of this study, to listen to all of the relevant tracks, which number c. 2000, many not online. The number of song transmission instances is larger than the number of tracks, as recipients quite often identify multiple sources for a particular song (see above, §1.5).

The transmission data can be analysed in a number of different ways, as described above (§2.3). In the SSSA data there are 2,279 *instances* of song

---

15 These are mainly song tracks, though there are also some other tracks where the transmission of particular songs is mentioned. Only a limited amount of indexing was possible towards the end of the main phase of TaD funding, but attention was focussed on the Scots song material. Some additional data come from published sources listed above (§2.1); for simplicity, this information will be referred to as if it also comes from the SSSA via TaD.

16 The extent of detail in the track summaries, and even whether relevant information has been included at all, is dependent on the individual cataloguer (subject to pressures of time at different stages of the project). The instructions given to cataloguers encouraged them to include in the summaries of song tracks any information mentioned on the track, but there may of course have been omissions.

learning,[17] by 560 *recipients*, of whom 467 have known or estimated d.o.bs.[18] For the most part the recipients are a subset of the contributors, except for 64 who are not themselves recorded, but for whom information is available at second hand, usually when individuals provide information about their sources' own sources.[19] The recipients participate in 649 non-family *pairs* and 513 family pairs.[20] In the G-D data, there are 1,906 instances of song learning by 228 individuals, of whom 154 have known or estimated d.o.bs. Transmission information is at second hand for 54 recipients. There are 415 non-family pairs and 176 family pairs.

The recipients are broadly similar to the contributors in the breakdown into demographic groups (but with a higher proportion of Travellers, as discussed above §1.5),[21] and the 496 actually recorded by SSSA are likewise broadly similar in their distribution over the recording period. The distributions by decade of birth are also similar (cf. Figures 4.1 and 4.2 to Figures 2.10 and 2.13), but the dip in the 1920s in the SSSA data is only seen for females. The additional recipients for whom the data come at second hand naturally increase the proportions at earlier dates.

In order to maintain a consistent approach and a clear delimitation of the data, transmission information is only used where a specific song is identified. Thus if a contributor says, for instance, that he or she learned all of his or her songs from a grandmother, this information is not used unless a specific song learned from the grandmother is identified. This inevitably produces some distortion, and an under-estimation of family sources in particular.[22] However, there is no reason to believe that any one group would be more affected by this source of error than another, or that the reliability of comparisons amongst groups would, therefore, be compromised. The approach taken here seeks to complement the usual one that relies on contributor biographies, which are

---

17   See Table A2a.
18   See Table A1b.
19   As with first-hand data, non-Scottish individuals are omitted, including, in G-D, Jeannie Brown's Irish grandmother.
20   See Table A8a. When these data are analysed in more detail, some pairs are omitted, either because the data are vague with regard to some details, or because the source is of a younger generation than the recipient, a category of transmission too small to quantify. The same applies to the G-D data.
21   See Table A3a.
22   Also, sources who are specified by family relationship may not be uniquely identified. It is not clear, without further detail, whether a grandmother or brother, for instance, mentioned more than once, is the same grandmother or the same brother. In such cases, only one grandmother or brother is counted: the range of family members involved in song transmission pairs will therefore again be somewhat under-estimated.

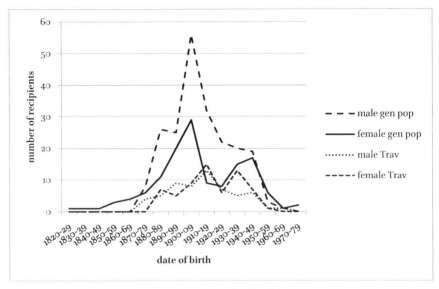

FIGURE 4.1 Numbers of SSSA recipients by decade of birth (known and estimated dates of birth)

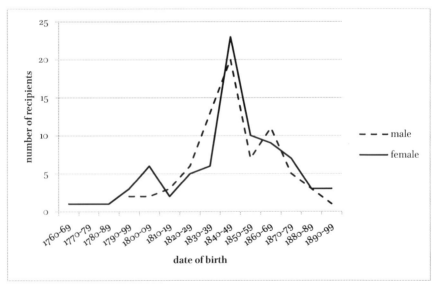

FIGURE 4.2 Numbers of G-D recipients by decade of birth (known and estimated dates of birth)

only available for the better-documented contributors. The two perspectives are two different lenses through which we can view the same subject, but we cannot look through both at the same time, since we cannot combine both types of information into one data set.

The under-estimation of family sources is balanced by the vagueness that often surrounds song transmission outside the family, leading to an under-estimation of non-family source individuals. Vague information that cannot be specified in terms of inter-personal transmission is counted here under the heading 'time or place'. However, it can be assumed that songs learned by farm-servants 'in the bothy' (i.e. in their accommodation on the farm) were learned from males.[23]

4.3   Categories of Song Transmission Information

Unsurprisingly, since traditional singing was the focus of the collections, the main type of information in the data concerns inter-personal transmission, with 1,870 out of the 2,279 instances (i.e. 82%) falling under the headings of *family* or *non-family* (i.e. other inter-personal) transmission,[24] and indeed the form of the question often prompts contributors to answer in this way. It is not always clear whether an individual who moved in folk circles learned directly from a performing or recording artist whom they might have known personally; direct contact is assumed in these cases.

When we come to the Folk Revival, audio and written sources become more important: 18 out of 44 Child ballad transmission instances (i.e. 41%) detailed by Revival singers in the data are from these sources.[25] Nevertheless, family transmission did continue to be one source for individuals born in the 1930s and later, including such prominent singers as the Fisher family,[26] Phyllis Martin,[27] Jean Redpath,[28] Isla St Clair,[29] Dick Gaughan[30] and Joe Rae.[31]

---

23   There are seventeen 'bothy' instances of this kind in the SSSA data, where no specific individual is identified. Some contributors source multiple songs in this way, but without further details to distinguish the sources, such as different times or places, all that can be done with this information, so far as inter-personal transmission is concerned, is to count 'the bothy' as one individual, so again there is under-estimation.
24   See Tables A2a and A2b.
25   See Table A2c.
26   SA1987.25, TaD 88294, 88295.
27   Douglas and Miller (1995: 138, note to song 58).
28   Various tracks on SA1960.205, TaD 76764, 76766, 76781, 76784.
29   SA1966.113.A10, TaD 57242; SA1971.195.3, TaD 43654.
30   SA1966.114.A9.
31   Douglas and Miller eds. (1995: 124, note to song 2).

Recipients are sometimes vague about family sources; they are very often vague about other sources. If they do not identify a specific source, contributors often relate their learning of a song only to a place or a period in their lives (listed as 'time or place' in the tables). There is not much that can be done with this information, apart from using it in some cases to identify songs learned in childhood. The expression 'learned/heard at home', which occurs several times in the G-D data without further details,[32] may well indicate family transmission, but given the importance of servants as song sources, this cannot be taken for granted, and these instances are counted as 'time or place'. 'The old folk' is another expression, used quite often by Travellers, that may well refer to family sources, but again this cannot be taken for granted. Males in the G-D data are particularly apt to give only contextual information about how they learned songs. They often mention farms where they were working at the time.[33] Even individuals who were in different occupations later in life would often have spent their youth as farmservants, if they came from the large rural population of small farmers and crofters that was a characteristic feature of the North-East in the nineteenth century (Carter, 1979: 109–10).

Unsurprisingly, very few songs are sourced by Traveller contributors to 'school or church' (which includes youth groups, Temperance meetings, evangelical meetings, etc.). The females in the general population form a disproportionate number of this (small) category.[34] By 'written sources' here is meant published materials and archives: when song lyrics are passed from hand to hand in writing, this is taken as inter-personal transmission. It is not possible to separate the categories of live performance and recordings in the SSSA data, as the ambiguous wording 'from the singing of' is often used. In the G-D data, broadside sellers singing their wares are counted in the performance category.[35] Male and female Travellers each have 2% from audio sources or performances. The Travellers, like the general population, listened to gramophone records (an electrically-powered gramophone could be run off a car battery) and sang the popular songs of the time (Olson, 2007b: 3), but on the whole this material was not of interest to SSSA and was not sought out. There is

---

32   Chiefly from Mrs Walker, but also once from Mrs Gillespie.
33   FoC includes an index of place-names (vol. 8, pp. 526–9).
34   This is a residual category – in a few cases where specific individuals, e.g. teachers, are named this is counted as inter-personal transmission.
35   Songs 205, 314A and 394 are described as sung and sold at markets or fairs. Others described as sung at markets or fairs – 447A, 1508 and 393 – are also counted in this category, though it is possible that they may have been sung by street singers rather than broadside sellers.

a surprisingly small proportion of cases (0.9%) in the SSSA data where contributors say that they cannot remember anything about how they learned a song. This type of comment could easily have been omitted by the TaD cataloguers, and therefore under-estimated, so it is reassuring to find that the proportion is also very small in G-D (again 0.9%).[36]

Contributors sometimes mention the social context in which songs were learned, including social events ranging from house parties to weddings. Willie Mathieson learned a number of songs at social evenings following communal farm work, either harvesting[37] or threshing;[38] and some other men also mention the former.[39] Jeannie Williams from Shetland (born 1897), mentions a carding, a party of women and girls assembled to socialise and card wool together.[40] It is sometimes difficult to distinguish the social element of such contexts from singing at work: there are also numerous unambiguous mentions of the latter, including work on farms, in woollen mills, and at tasks ancillary to fishing. Unfortunately, this type of information is not systematic enough to quantify.

4.4 Inter-Personal Transmission

The various population groups differ in their relative proportions of family and non-family song transmission, and within each of these categories a number of differences amongst the population groups emerge from the analyses.

4.4.1 *The Predominance of General Population Males as Non-family Sources*

Males are the most numerous non-family source for both sexes in G-D (Figure 4.3). In SSSA, general population males are likewise the most numerous non-family source for all groups except the female Travellers, whose non-family sources are mostly other Travellers (Figures 4.3 and 4.4).[41]

---

36 Figures in Table A2b are rounded.
37 See e.g. SA1952.01.B1 (B12), TaD 4447.
38 See e.g. SA1952.1.B9 (B20–B21), TaD 4463.
39 E.g. Jimmy Taylor (born 1886) on SA1952.32.A7, TaD 46758, John Strachan (born 1875) on SA1952.27.B5 (B14), TaD 10167. See also Chapter 5, n. 50.
40 SA1974.13.3.
41 Core population males are less prominent as a source for male Travellers in the Child ballad sub-set of the data: cf. Figure 4.5.

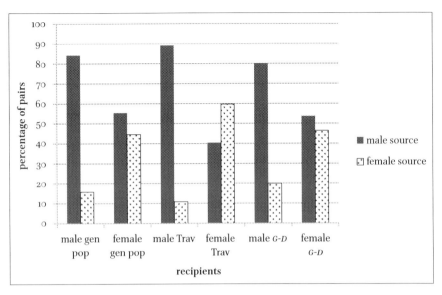

FIGURE 4.3 Percentages of male- and female-sourced SSSA and *G-D* non-family transmission pairs. Figures based on 380 SSSA pairs with male general population recipients, 101 with female general population, 46 with male Travellers, 67 with female Traveller; and 170 *G-D* pairs with male recipients, and 222 with females.

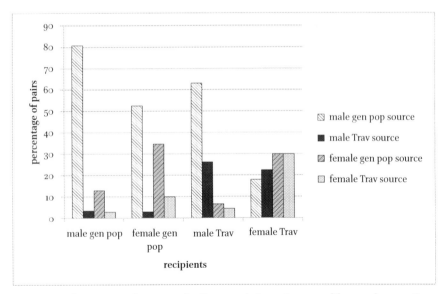

FIGURE 4.4 Percentages of SSSA non-family transmission pairs sourced from each group. See note to Figure 4.3.

4.4.2 The Relative Lack of Non-family Transmission from the Travellers to the General Population

Correspondingly, the Travellers form only a small proportion of sources for the general population in the data, which is not surprising as they are and were a tiny proportion of the Scottish population. Certain female Traveller singers became influential in the Folk Revival (cf. Figure 4.5), but traditionally female Travellers whose singing was heard by the general population tended to be hawkers and street singers, while the few male Travellers who were sources for either sex of the general population tended to be hawkers and casual farm labourers.

Before the improved communications of the nineteenth century, itinerants such as chapmen, travelling tailors and 'tinkers' brought news and entertainment to isolated country districts. McCormick describes the performance of Mary Kennedy (see above §§3.3, 3.5), who 'would enter a house and ask for a penny, some tobacco, etc, then make a feint to leave, and would be reminded "that she had forgotten to favour the company with a song"' (1907: 163). Olson (1992: 46–7) quotes (from a letter of 1989) Flora Garry's description of a Traveller woman, Mrs McGuire, singing in the farm kitchen after selling from her pack. Flora Garry was born in 1900; this was when she was a little girl on a farm near New Deer. Even as late as 1916–17, the Chief Constable of Forfarshire told the

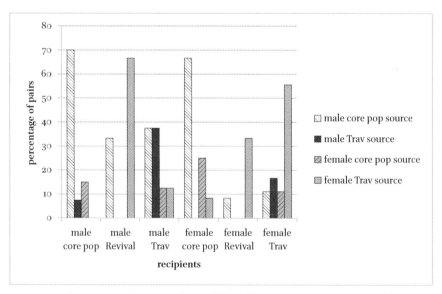

FIGURE 4.5 Percentages of SSSA non-family Child ballad transmission pairs sourced from each group

Departmental Committee on Tinkers (Scotland) that 'in Forfarshire, the tinkers are well known and "they are made, as a rule, pretty welcome. The tinkers are almost the only strangers that the country people have among them, and the people get news from the tinkers"' (1918: 13).

4.4.3   The Female Preference for Family and Female Sources

The G-D females agree with other female groups in the data in having a higher proportion of family than non-family transmission, in terms of song *instances*, and also in terms of *recipients*.[42] They differ from the other female groups in having a high proportion (68%) of their *pairs* in the non-family category,[43] but the figures here are distorted by the large range of identified contacts of a few individuals, namely Bell Robertson, Mrs Gillespie and Annie Shirer. Without these three, the percentage would be 44%,[44] similar to the figure for the SSSA general population females. Nevertheless, non-family sources are not unimportant, and this may be relevant to the unexpectedly small overlap between the repertoires of two female cousins in the G-D corpus in Campbell's (2003) study.

The sources that females draw upon in non-family pairs include a large proportion of other females (Figure 4.3). For female Travellers, female-sourced non-family pairs are the majority at 60%. General population and G-D females have much higher percentages than the corresponding male groups: 46% for G-D females in comparison with 20% for G-D males; the proportions for general population females are similar. Several of the G-D females' sources are servants, so the context, though not familial, is still in many cases domestic.[45] As Laslett (1983: 91–2) points out, we tend not to appreciate what a large proportion of the population was in service in the past, including servants in quite modest households. At the 1891 Census, 190,067 females aged ten and upwards, or 11.88% of the female population in that age group, were engaged in 'domestic' occupations. In 1901 the corresponding figures were 174,475, or 9.75% ('Census of Scotland, 1901 – Appendix Tables', p. xxx).[46]

---

42   See Table A2b for instances and A9a for recipients.
43   See Table A8a.
44   Without these prolific contributors, the G-D females have 68 non-family transmission pairs, and 85 family pairs. In Child ballad transmission pairs (Table A8b) the percentage of non-family pairs for G-D females falls to 29% with this adjustment, based on 12 non-family pairs, and 29 family pairs.
45   For instance, Mrs Gillespie, Annie Shirer, Bell Robertson, and Mrs Lyall all acquired songs from female servants, when they were growing up or in adult life, or both.
46   The apparent drop in numbers may owe something to the very early cut-off at age ten.

4.4.4 *The Male General Population and Male G-D Preference for Non-family Sources*

Male recipients in G-D and the SSSA general population participate much more in non-family than in family transmission. This is seen in all three analyses:

- In terms of song *instances*, SSSA general population males identify 27% of their song learning as coming from family members, 51% from non-family; the corresponding figures for G-D males are 31% family, 37% non-family.[47]
- In terms of individual *recipients* who participate in either type of transmission, 41% of SSSA general population males participate in the family transmission category, 59% in the non-family; the corresponding figures for G-D males are 39% family, 56% non-family.[48]
- In terms of recipient-source *pairs*, SSSA general population males identify 27% in the family transmission category, 73% in the non-family; the corresponding figures for G-D males are the same.[49]

The evident wealth of opportunities for males to learn songs outside the home probably reflects their greater participation in the workplace. However, the fact that the G-D figures for *instances* are closer together suggests a high volume of songs being passed on in the family transmission that did take place for these male recipients.

4.4.5 *The Traveller Preference (Both Sexes) for Family Sources*

Although Traveller men were involved in casual farm work by the late nineteenth century (see below, §6.9), they preferred self-employment if possible. This is perhaps why male Travellers differ from the other male groups in their balance of family and non-family transmission. Travellers of both sexes strongly favour family sources. The figures for male Travellers are:

- 66% of song instances from family members, 23% from non-family;[50]
- 71% of male Travellers participating in family transmission as against 43% in non-family transmission;[51]
- 63% of transmission pairs in the family category.[52]

The corresponding figures for female Travellers are for the most part even higher:

- 71% of song instances from family members;
- 81% of recipients participating in family transmission;
- 62% of transmission pairs in the family category.

---

47 See Table A2b.
48 See Table A9a.
49 See Table A8a.
50 See table A2b.
51 See table A9a.
52 See table A8a.

The high level of family transmission amongst the Travellers may be a trait of great time depth, as Douglas (2004: 431, quoted below, §4.5) suggests, but there is no objective way to confirm this, since the d.o.bs of sources only go back to the beginning of the nineteenth century.[53] It is certainly compatible with the importance of the extended family in the Traveller way of life. The Travellers' high level of extended family transmission is discussed below (§7.5).

4.4.6 *Same-Sex and Opposite-Sex Transmission Pairs within the Family*

Almost all groups in the data have more female- than male-sourced family *pairs* (including both nuclear and extended family pairs), overwhelming so in the case of the G-D females (Figures 4.6, 4.7 and 4.8). The exception is the SSSA general population males. The SSSA general population to a large extent corresponds to G-D, with a slight overlap in d.o.bs, so we can combine the two sets of data into a single graph to examine whether there is a change over time (Figure 4.9). The numbers are small and the graph consequently erratic, but it can be seen that the apparent increase in male-male family transmission between G-D and SSSA rests on the particularly high percentages in the 1880s

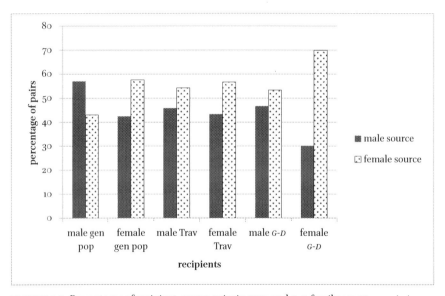

FIGURE 4.6   Percentages of recipient-source pairs in SSSA and G-D family song transmission, by sex of source
Note: based on 144 SSSA pairs with general population male recipients, 132 with general population females, 83 with male Travellers, and 127 with female Travellers; and 60 G-D pairs with male recipients and 104 with females.

---

53   See Figure 5.13 below.

SONG TRANSMISSION 69

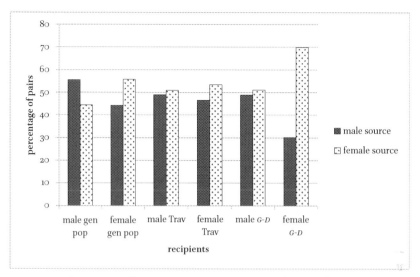

FIGURE 4.7 Percentages of recipient-source pairs in SSSA and G-D nuclear family song transmission, by sex of source
Note: based on 108 SSSA pairs with general population male recipients, 104 with general population females, 51 with male Travellers, and 73 with female Travellers; and 45 G-D pairs with male recipients and 63 with females.

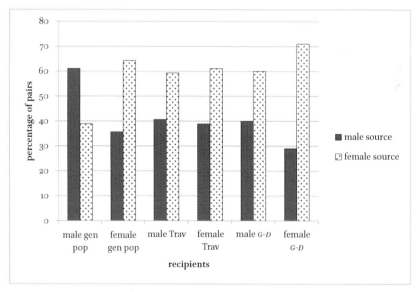

FIGURE 4.8 Percentages of recipient-source pairs in SSSA and G-D extended family transmission, by sex of source
Note: based on 36 SSSA pairs with general population male recipients, 28 with general population females, 32 with male Travellers, and 54 with female Travellers; and 15 G-D pairs with male recipients and 41 with females.

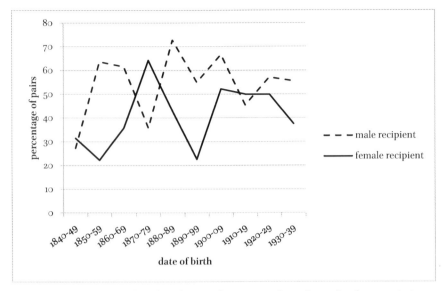

FIGURE 4.9 Percentages of combined G-D and SSSA general population family transmission pairs that have male sources, by date of birth of recipient (known and estimated dates of birth, 1840–1939 decades of birth of recipients, outliers omitted)
Note: based on 71 SSSA pairs with general population male recipients, 41 with general population females; and 18 G-D pairs with male recipients and 24 with females.

and 1900s birth cohorts (all from SSSA data, as it happens). However, the figure is also over 50% for male sources at several earlier points, so there is no consistent trend over time.

An odd thing about the graph is that the male and female recipient lines mirror each other at several points (though they agree in showing a dip in male-sourced pairs for the 1890s birth cohort, to which we shall return below, §7.6). What this implies is that the male and female patterns of same-sex versus opposite-sex pairs tend to coincide to some extent over time (the data are rearranged to show this more clearly in Figure 4.10). In particular, the 1850s birth cohort seems to have experienced a high level of same-sex family song transmission; the 1870s a low level; then both lines rise to overlapping peaks and fall again to around the 50:50 mark.[54]

If this is not simply coincidence, there could be several different factors at work that it may not now be possible to disentangle. Different birth cohorts

---

54 Family transmission is dominated by Generation 1 (mainly parents, with some uncles and aunts, and a few more distant relatives), and indeed the graphs are very much the same if we take only the Generation 1 pairs, but the numbers are very small at this degree of sub-division of the data, so this figure is not used here.

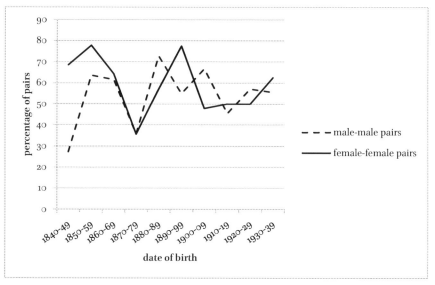

FIGURE 4.10   Percentages of combined G-D and SSSA general population family transmission pairs that are same-sex, by date of birth of recipient (known and estimated dates of birth, 1840–1939 decades of birth of recipients, outliers omitted)
Note: for numbers, see note to Figure 4.9.

may have experienced different patterns of work and leisure interaction between the sexes within the family, or different degrees of rigidity in gender roles. Changing tastes may have affected the transmission of the older generations' repertoires: detailed study of repertoires and their transmission to different birth cohorts might throw some light on the question. It is possibly relevant that there is a relationship between Child ballad transmission and family transmission from female sources. The percentage of recipients who participate in family transmission from female sources correlates strongly with the percentage of recipients who participate in Child ballad transmission (correlation coefficient = 0.88). The equivalent correlation for male sources is much weaker (correlation coefficient = 0.43). The declining popularity of the big ballads is discussed below (Chapter 6).

4.5   The Travellers Embedded in a Literate Society

Family sources have been seen as implying a continuity of oral transmission, possibly of great time depth. For instance, Douglas (2004: 431) writes, 'The oral tradition was presumed to have died out in the eighteenth century … … The secret of its preservation can be found in family tradition.' Douglas is writing about Belle Stewart, a Traveller (born 1906) who was an important source singer for the Folk Revival.[55] Her daughter Sheila Stewart (born 1935) said that before they were discovered as singers, they sang only within the family, not for audiences (McColl and Seeger, 1986: 33). As we saw above (§4.4.5), the female Travellers source a very high proportion of their song transmission in the data to family members. Also, the male Travellers – unlike males in the general population or in G-D – are not very much below the females in this respect.

Social network theory informs us that the crucial elements in the spread of ideas, information, and so on, are the weak ties between networks, not the strong ties within them (Granovetter, 1973). The Travellers may have had only weak ties with the general population, in contrast to their strong family ties, but the former provided bridges across which songs could be exchanged, with the result that the repertoire that circulated within Traveller families was largely the same as that of the general population, and accordingly just as likely to have printed texts not far back in the line of transmission.

A documented case of the recent introduction of a song into Traveller family transmission is Child 255 'Willie's Ghost' or 'Willie's Fatal Visit'. Lizzie Higgins had recently started to sing it in 1987. She recalls that it was given to her mother Jeannie Robertson by Hamish Henderson, so that she could expand her repertoire.[56] Stanley Robertson, Jeannie Robertson's nephew, also acquired it, and having only ever heard it from Jeannie Robertson, he regarded it as a Traveller song and presented it as such.[57] Another example is 'The Queen amang the Heather', a song made popular by Belle Stewart. By her own account, when recorded in 1953, although she had heard parts of it sung by her mother, the version that she sang was acquired from her brother, who had overheard it sung by a ploughman.[58]

When the Travellers were discovered as singers in the 1950s, a great deal of importance was attached to the oral nature of their culture, of which their low level of literacy was the guarantee. At that time, many Travellers were still non-literate. In the 1969 survey reported by Gentleman and Swift (1971: 58) (see

---

55   Ironically, Douglas is referring here specifically to Belle Stewart's signature song, 'The Queen amang the Heather', which she believes was one of Belle Stewart's father's songs, received via her brother (their father having died when Belle was a baby). See below, however, on her brother's acquisition of his version of the song. MacColl and Seeger (1986: 31) give two separate pieces of information from Belle Stewart: the statement that she learned most of her songs from her brother, who had learned songs from their father; and an account of how their father acquired 'The Queen amang the Heather'. It would be easy to conflate these.
56   SA1987.14.3, TaD 80508.
57   SA1979.133.A4, TaD 67495.
58   SA1953.238.B6, TaD 26110.

above, §3.4), about two thirds of the Travellers over the age of five said they could read and write, with the numbers declining with age for those of 35 and over. A higher proportion of females were literate, except amongst those of 65 and over (i.e. those born before c. 1900), where the positions of the sexes were sharply reversed. However, as Gentleman and Swift point out, this self-reported literacy might mean no more than an ability to fill out simple official forms. The Travellers had largely evaded the compulsory schooling that was imposed by the *Education Act* of 1872, and in 1908 the Children Act came part-way to meet their itinerant lifestyle by requiring school attendance for only 200 half days a year.

Travellers sometimes remark that people picked up songs by ear *because* they were non-literate: for instance, Jane Turriff talking about how her mother and grandmother learned 'Andrew Lammie';[59] or Belle Stewart talking about how she learned 'The Twa Brithers' from her brother, Donald, who could not write.[60] Nevertheless, the Travellers were embedded in a literate society, and thus even individuals who were not themselves literate were open to a flow of information from printed sources. They also had literate individuals amongst them. Jeannie Robertson recounts that when she was about twelve she had books of old songs acquired as scrap from big houses, and she used to learn the words and fit a tune to them. The only song that she specifically identifies from this source is 'Cruel Fate', i.e. Robert Burns' 'The Northern Lass'.[61] The book is not identified, but the song, which is not one of his best known works, appears as no. 118 in vol. II of *The Scots Musical Museum*.[62] Hamish Henderson is reported to have found copies of *The Scots Musical Museum* in Traveller camps (Olson, 2007a: 401, n. 5).[63]

---

59 SA1974.150.2.
60 SA1972.234.A1–A2, TaD 100310.
61 SA1973.153, TaD 82390.
62 Vol. I in the third (1853) edition where the volumes are doubled up.
63 The relevant volume of either the second or third editions would have given access to Stenhouse's 'whisky still' reading of 'The Ewie wi' the Crookit Horn' (see above, §3.5). It is not impossible, of course, that this interpretation was inadvertently suggested to Traveller singers by the fieldworkers themselves. Ian Olson (personal communication, 26 June 2014) observes that Jeannie Robertson added a verse pertaining to the 'whisky still' interpretation. This is not sung on her recordings for the SSSA on SA1955.176.B2 (TaD 18726), SA1955.177.B1 (TaD 30057) or SA1959.106.A2 (TaD 39053), but it can be heard, for instance, on her EP *Jeannie Robertson and 'The Gallowa' Hills'* (1958). The extra verse hints at the 'whisky still' reading, but in a sleeve note to the EP, Hamish Henderson spells the idea out distinctly: 'This ... song ... is about the misfortunes of a moonshiner, or distiller, of illicit whisky. The "yowie" ... was the pet-name for the still in which Highland potcheen was produced.'

The Travellers, then, did not stand completely apart from the written word. Three per cent of the female Travellers' instances of song transmission in the data, involving eight individuals, are from written sources, and 1% of male Travellers', involving two individuals.[64] Where the Travellers differed most profoundly from the general population is that they did not exhibit the dependence on literacy to acquire and remember lyrics that has been noted anecdotally amongst the latter.

---

64 See Table A2b. These instances include Child ballads (see Table A2c), but the written sources in these cases are mainly in a secondary role, providing additional verses: for instance Betsy Whyte augmented her family version of Child 203 'The Baron o Brackley' by reference to Child (L. Williamson, 1985: 96), a copy of which Linda Williamson had given her (p. 287, n. 2).

CHAPTER 5

The Reticence of Female Singers

5.1   Older and Younger Women

Women are greatly outnumbered by men as contributors in the SSSA general population group, where 63% are male.[1] Amongst the general population individuals identified by contributors as their sources for songs, 69% are male.[2] The differences are not so large in G-D – 59% of contributors are male, and 57% of sources. For the Travellers the sexes appear in roughly equal numbers in both capacities (48% of contributors and 51% of sources are male). Since the sources are likely to be a more random selection than the contributors, these figures suggest that the under-representation of general population females in the SSSA data, and females in the G-D data, is not simply an artefact of the collection process. A small indication that general population females were more difficult to recruit as contributors in SSSA is that, in contrast to the other groups, higher numbers of new contributors were recorded in the early 1960s than in the 1950s (see Figure 2.2 above, and cf. Figure 5.1 for core population Child ballad contributors), so far as can be told from the TaD-derived data. By the 1960s the recordings include Revival singers such as Jean Redpath, Gordeanna McCulloch and Isla St Clair.

Two explanations have been offered in the literature for the lower public profile of women singers in the past: the more limited activity of women outside of the domestic sphere, and traditional ideas of propriety that might have made younger women, in particular, more reticent to perform in mixed company. Porter and Gower observe that amongst Travellers it was only post-menopausal women who were encouraged to perform. Indeed they comment that in any society, 'Women are discouraged from public performance … young women's public musical behavior [sic] often is limited because of their sexual attractiveness, to which performance draws attention' (1995: xxv). Linda Williamson (1985: 54 ff.) makes a similar point about jealous husbands amongst the Travellers preventing their wives from socialising.

There are several findings in this study that tend to confirm that there was a dampening effect of social constraints upon public performance by younger

---

1   See Table A10a. It is extremely unlikely that the data are unrepresentative of the SSSA collection in this respect.
2   See Table A10b.

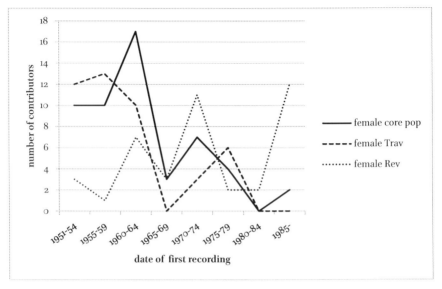

FIGURE 5.1   Numbers of female SSSA Child ballad contributors by half decade of first recording

women. The general population females tend to be older than other groups when first recorded (see above, Figures 2.3 and 2.4),[3] at least up until the mid-1970s, when the large number of young Folk Revival singers reverses the trend. As we saw above (§2.6), the median age of this group is skewed downwards in the early years of recording by the large number of children in the data: in fact, the number of young women is relatively small until the Revival singers begin to appear. Of 53 female general population contributors who were aged 16–39 when first recorded,[4] forty (i.e. 74%) were recorded in or after 1960, and 24 (i.e. 44%) in or after 1970. There are several well-known Revival singers amongst them, but this study does not attempt to differentiate between the core population and the Revival singers in the full data set. By contrast, of 31 female Travellers in the same age range, only thirteen (i.e. 42%) were recorded as late as the 1960s, and seven (i.e. 23%) as late as the 1970s.

A slight majority – 54% – of both sexes in the general population were born before 1920.[5] It is when we look at the percentages born before 1900 that a marked difference between the sexes emerges. Nearly half – 48% – of the

---

3 As noted in Chapter 2 n. 9, it is possible that earlier recordings of some individuals might exist, since the TaD cataloguing is incomplete.
4 On the basis of known or estimated d.o.bs.
5 On the basis of known and estimated d.o.bs. See Table A6b.

general population females recorded in the first few years of fieldwork were born before 1900; and even as late as the early 1970s, the proportion is 34%.[6] By contrast, the percentage of general population males born before 1900 is only 35% in the first years of fieldwork, and drops to 20% by the early 1960s. The sexes are more similar in G-D in their distribution by d.o.bs (cf. Figure 2.13 above), but the collection method was very different from SSSA, and there was an intention to collect from older singers.

5.2 (Older) Women and the Child Ballads

5.2.1 *The Established Association between Women and the Big Ballads*
A complicating question is whether an association between older women and the Child ballads might have led to a bias towards older women in the SSSA fieldwork. We shall digress slightly at this point to consider women and the Child ballads. (The validity of using Child's ballad catalogue as a category is discussed below, §6.1.)

The first mention of ballad singing in Scotland is in Barbour's *Brus*, where Barbour writes briefly of a feat of arms of fifty men against three hundred horsemen, then adds:

> I will no*cht* rehers ye maner
> For quha-sa lik*is* yai may her
> 3oung wemen quhen yai will play
> Syng it amang yaim ilk day.[7]
>
> M. MCDIARMID and STEVENSON eds., 1981, vol. III, Book XVI, ll. 527–30

A number of nineteenth century collectors identified ballad singing as a largely female practice (Brown, 1997), including Child, who regarded women as the principal preservers of ballads, singing as they worked around the home (Bishop, 2004: 406). Hamish Henderson has a term 'kitchen singer' that he applies to Jean Elvin, from whom he recorded 'Andrew Lammie': 'Jean was strictly a kitchen singer ... I just happened to go into the house, and to hear her singing all by herself' ([Henderson and McNaughton], 1991: 41). Likewise, Duncan was not directed to Bell Duncan, later a major contributor of ballads to James Madison Carpenter, although she lived quite near to one

---
6 On the basis of known and estimated d.o.bs. See Table A6d.
7 'I will not rehearse the manner / For who-so likes, they may hear / Young women when they want to play / Sing it among them each day.'

of his contributors (Bishop, 2004: 396). For women singing around the home, 'Their audience ... was often provided by children, their own or others', and this may account for the frequent citing of women as first sources of songs' (Petrie, 1997: 266).

5.2.2 The Contribution of Females in the Child Ballad Data

Given the emphasis in the literature on female ballad singers, a preponderance of females would have been expected in the Child ballad data. Some results do point in that direction:

- As *contributors*, general population and G-D females are not quite so much out-numbered by males in the Child ballad data as in the overall data. Females comprise 43% of the SSSA general population (40% of the core population, i.e. with Revival singers omitted), compared with 37% for songs overall.[8] In G-D likewise, the female Child ballad contributors comprise 46%, compared with 41% overall. (The split is already fairly even for the Travellers in the overall data, and is 50:50 in the Child ballad data.)
- As *sources*, general population females are likewise not quite so much out-numbered in the Child ballad data: they comprise 40% (core population 41%), in comparison with 31% overall.[9]
- As *sources*, G-D and Traveller females actually out-number the males, very considerably in the case of the G-D females, with 64% of Child ballad sources, compared with 43% overall.
- In *family* pairs there are larger percentages of female- than male-sourced pairs for all groups of recipients in the Child ballad data, even the male core population[10] (Figure 5.2; contrast Figure 4.6, above, for family pairs overall, where the general population males stand out for their preponderance of male-sourced pairs).
- In *non-family* pairs, female-sourced pairs predominate for G-D females in the Child ballad data, in contrast to songs overall (Figure 5.3; cf. Figure 4.3 above). (The female Travellers already stand out in the overall data as having more female-sourced non-family pairs.)
- The numbers of ballad types and tokens recorded from female Travellers outnumber those recorded from male Travellers in the first great decade of

---

8 See Table A10a.
9 See Table A10b. It is not surprising that the male majority in the set of contributors is reflected in the sources. Core population males – like general population males in the overall data – have a higher proportion of non-family than family pairs (see Table A8b for the Child data; cf. Table A8a for pairs overall), and they very much favour male sources in these pairs (see Figure 5.3 for the Child data; cf. Figure 4.3 for the overall data).
10 Pairs with Revival recipients are too few to analyse and are omitted.

THE RETICENCE OF FEMALE SINGERS

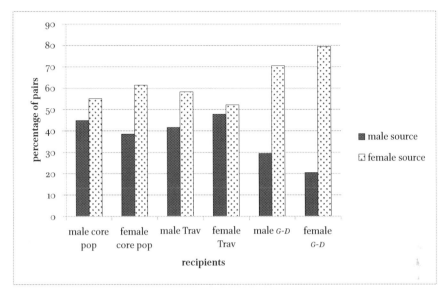

FIGURE 5.2 Percentages of male- and female-sourced SSSA and G-D family Child ballad transmission pairs (Revival recipients omitted). Figures based on 29 SSSA pairs with male core population recipients, 26 with female core population, 36 with male Travellers, and 67 with female Travellers; and 17 G-D pairs with male and 39 with female recipients.

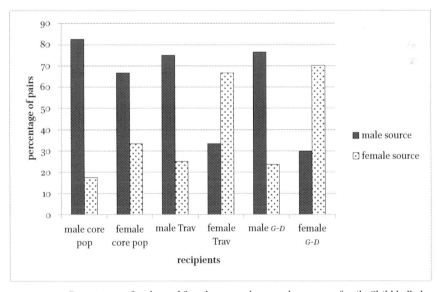

FIGURE 5.3 Percentages of male- and female-sourced G-D and SSSA non-family Child ballad transmission pairs (Revival recipients omitted). Figures based on 40 SoSS pairs with male core population recipients, 12 with female core population, 8 with male Travellers, and 18 with female Travellers; and 17 G-D pairs with male recipients and 47 with females.

recording, in the 1950s.[11] The numbers of male and female contributors are about equal, but the females outnumber the males in types by 1.5 to 1, and in tokens by 2.4 to 1. G-D females likewise, although somewhat outnumbered by male contributors, exceed them by about half as much again in both types and tokens.[12]

- A much higher percentage of Traveller females contribute two or more ballads – 43% compared with 24% of males.[13] The same sex difference is found in G-D – 32% of females compared with 23% of males. (The lower figures for G-D than for the Travellers are probably misleading: see below, §6.6.)

Conversely, there are patterns that might have been expected, but are not found:

- General population females do not outnumber the corresponding males as Child ballad contributors, comprising only 43% (core population 40%);[14]
- nor do they outnumber the males as Child ballad sources, comprising only 40% (core population 41%).[15]
- In non-family pairs, core population female recipients have more male than female Child ballad sources (Figure 5.3).
- In the 1950s recording period, core population females contribute many fewer Child ballad types and tokens than males, relative to their numbers as contributors. The males outnumber the females 1.7 to 1, but in ballad types 2.5 to 1, and in ballad tokens, 3.8 to 1.[16]
- Only 21% of the female core population females in the Child ballad data contribute two or more ballads, in comparison with 27% of the corresponding males.[17]

5.2.3 Decline in the Female Contribution over Time

The contrast between the G-D and the SSSA general (and core) population findings suggests change over time. This is confirmed by Figure 5.4, which combines the Child ballad contributors from the SSSA core population and G-D, and shows the percentage who are female in each decade of birth. Disregarding the rather erratic figures at either end of the graph, it is in the 1900s birth cohort that the percentage of female *contributors* falls considerably below 50%. A similar graph for Child ballad *sources* declines more steadily

---

11 See Table A11d
12 For numbers, see Table A11a.
13 Cf. Figure 5.9 below.
14 See Table A10a.
15 See Table A10b.
16 For numbers, see Table A11d.
17 Cf. Figure 5.9 below.

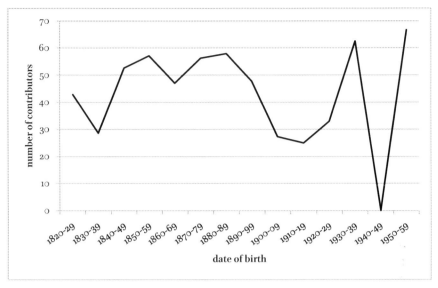

FIGURE 5.4 Percentages of combined G-D and SSSA core population Child ballad contributors who are female, by decade of birth (known and estimated dates). For numbers, see Figures 2.5 and 5.7.

from very high values between the 1780s and 1810s to well below 50% in the 1900s (Figure 5.5).[18]

Turning now to the age patterns of Child ballad contributors, a comparison with contributors overall is complicated by the generally younger Revival singers, who form a considerable proportion – 28% – of the Child ballad data.[19] The Child ballad core population (i.e. with the Revival singers omitted) and the overall general population are not directly comparable, but it can be said that:
- although the SSSA recruited larger numbers of core population females after the 1950s,[20] they tended, up to the early 1970s, to be drawn from the same birth cohorts as those recorded in the 1950s;[21]
- the median ages of SSSA core population and Traveller Child ballad contributors, of both sexes, are particularly high, especially the figure for the core population females, at 62;[22]

---

18 See below (§6.2) for discussion of the validity of combining G-D and SSSA data.
19 For numbers, see Table A1d.
20 See Table A11d.
21 See Tables A6e and A6f.
22 See Table A12.

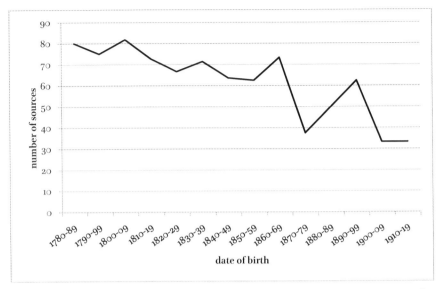

FIGURE 5.5 Percentages of combined G-D and SSSA core population Child ballad sources who are female, by decade of birth (known and estimated dates, outliers omitted). For numbers, see Figures 5.6 and 5.8.

– likewise, the percentages born before 1900 are relatively high for the Child ballad data. The core population females have a very high percentage born before 1900: 51% in total (in the first years of fieldwork 88%), in comparison with 24% in total for the general population females in the overall data;[23]
– for female Travellers the percentage born before 1900 is 26% for the Child ballad data in comparison with 17% for songs overall;
– the distribution of the core population females by d.o.b peaks in the 1890s, with twelve (out of 43) of the core population women born before that decade (one in the 1850s). This peak is two decades earlier than that of the core population males. By contrast, in the overall data both sexes of the general population peak in the same decade, the 1900s;[24]
– the d.o.b distribution of the Child ballad *source* singers tracks that of contributors thirty years earlier. The tracking is not surprising, given the high proportion of family transmission of Child ballads, which tends to produce regular generational intervals. The core population females thus have the

---

23 See Table A6f for the Child ballad contributors and cf. Table A6d for the overall contributors.
24 Shown as graphs in Figures 2.5 and 2.10; and see Table A13 for an overview of modal decades of birth in various sub-sets of the data.

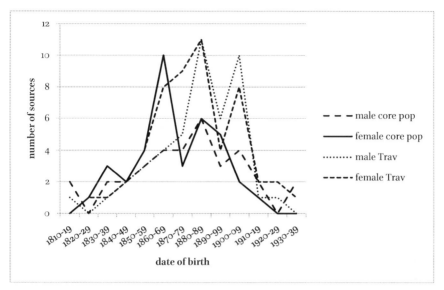

FIGURE 5.6   Numbers of SSSA Child ballad sources by decade of birth (known and estimated dates of birth, Revival sources omitted)

peak, or modal value, in the 1860s, two decades earlier than the core population males or the Travellers (Figure 5.6).

The pattern in G-D is very different:

− The numbers and distribution of male and female Child contributors are broadly similar across decades of birth, and their modal decades of birth are the same (Figure 5.7).
− Moreover, the distribution closely follows that of contributors overall (cf. Figure 2.13 above): that is, the Child ballads are not associated with older contributors in general, or with older women in particular in G-D, though it should be remembered that a large proportion of G-D's contributors were drawn from an older generation in any case.
− More tentatively, since we rely heavily on estimated d.o.bs for the sources, the modal decade of birth of sources is the same as that of contributors, i.e. the 1840s (Figure 5.8).[25]

This suggests a robust culture of ballad singing in the North-East in the first half of the nineteenth century, with peer-to-peer transmission as well as ballads being passed down the generations.

---

25   The method of estimation of d.o.bs tends to cluster dates at this point, as stated above (§2.6): some of these individuals, both contributors and sources, were doubtless born earlier.

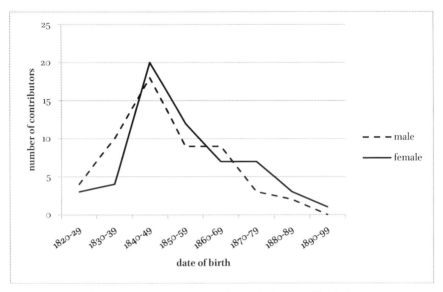

FIGURE 5.7 Numbers of G-D Child ballad contributors by decade of birth (known and estimated dates of birth)

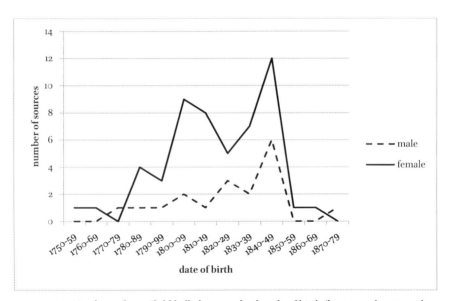

FIGURE 5.8 Numbers of G-D Child ballad sources by decade of birth (known and estimated dates of birth)

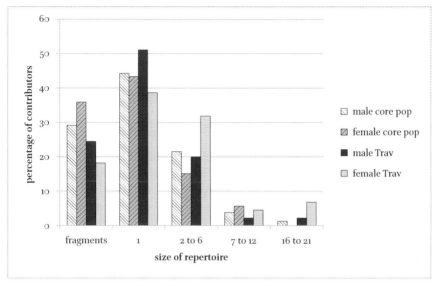

FIGURE 5.9 Percentages of SSSA Child ballad contributors with repertoires of different sizes (Revival contributors omitted). Figures based on 79 male core population contributors, 53 female core population, 45 male Travellers, and 44 female Travellers.

It would seem, by contrast, that in the SSSA core population many of the females who might at one time have been singers of ballads were to be found amongst elderly, sometimes very elderly, women. Fading memories may also explain why core population females have a particularly high percentage of Child repertoires in the data that consist of fragments only (Figure 5.9).[26] This is not to say that young female singers are entirely lacking in any group of the Child ballad singers: there are six under the age of thirty, at the time of recording, in the core population (out of 43 with known or estimated d.o.bs); and seven under the age of thirty amongst the Travellers (out of 42). Nevertheless, we have found reason to believe that there is some degree of association between the Child ballads and older women amongst the core population and the Travellers, and to the extent that this might have directed the fieldwork towards older women, it detracts from the argument that the greater age of the women recorded indicates some reticence amongst younger women. However, as we shall see, the patterns of song transmission do provide support for the argument.

---

26   For the definition of 'fragment' used in this analysis, see above, §2.5.

5.3 Sex and Age Patterns in Non-family Song Transmission

5.3.1 *Sources and Recipients in Non-family Transmission*

We turn now to the overall set of SSSA data (i.e. not only the Child ballad data). We have already seen that general population males are by far the highest percentage source in non-family pairs for each SSSA group except the female Travellers.[27] The latter is the only group with mainly female-sourced pairs.[28] Where female Travellers do have non-family male sources, these come largely from within the Traveller population. For G-D females, the balance between male- and female-sourced pairs is more nearly equal.[29]

From the other side of the non-family pairs, who are the recipients that the sources transmit their songs to? For female sources, same-sex transmission pairs dominate outside the family (Figure 5.10). This is very marked for the female sources in G-D and for the female Travellers. The more balanced distribution between the sexes for general population female sources may be explained by the high proportion of the female-to-male pairs in this group that

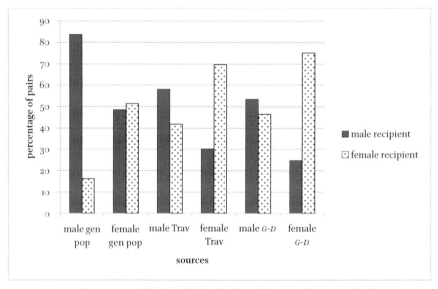

FIGURE 5.10 Percentages of male- and female-directed SSSA and G-D non-family transmission pairs
Note: this corresponds to Figure 4.3 with the axes transposed.

---

27 See Figure 4.4.
28 See Figure 4.3.
29 See Figure 4.3.

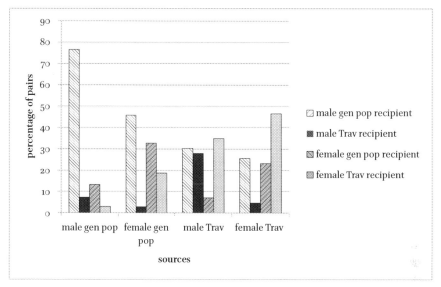

FIGURE 5.11　Percentages of SSSA non-family transmission pairs directed towards each group
Note: this corresponds to Figure 4.4 with the axes transposed.

have a farming context (at least twenty out of 49); we shall return to this point below (§5.4). There is also some distortion created by the multiple female sources of Willie Mathieson and Willie Mitchell, both amateur collectors of songs (see §4.1), who are the recipients in seven and five female-sourced non-family pairs, respectively.

At the same time, the SSSA general population males form a not insubstantial proportion of the non-family recipients for all source groups (Figure 5.11), which is unsurprising, given their numerical dominance as recipients. Even the female Travellers have some transmission to general population males, though this is mainly in the context of the Folk Revival, with Jeannie Robertson, in particular, being a source for many younger singers including Andy Hunter, Arthur Johnstone, Jimmie MacGregor and Norman Kennedy; and her daughter Lizzie Higgins being a source, for instance, for Cy Laurie.

5.3.2　*The Ages of Source Individuals*

We have already seen that the SSSA general population female contributors tend to be older than the males. This tends to make for older sources also, especially given this group's preference for family transmission,[30] which

---

30　See Table A8a.

favours sources one or two generations older than the recipient. The number of known d.o.bs of the 988 source individuals in the SSSA data is very limited, with only 9% being known,[31] and consequently the distribution by d.o.b is not very informative for known d.o.bs only (Figure 5.12). If we can rely on the estimated d.o.bs, which give us another useable 50% of the total, the SSSA pattern does suggest a somewhat older population of female sources (Figure 5.13). Additionally:

- Male sources in the general population have a modal value in the 1870s, a generation (three decades) older than those from the same demographic group who figure as recipients. The corresponding females have their modal value four decades earlier, in the 1860s.
- Likewise, a higher percentage of general population female sources have d.o.bs before 1900: 81% compared with 70% of the corresponding males.[32]
- 54% of general population female sources have d.o.bs before 1880,[33] compared with 46% of the corresponding males.
- The Traveller figures are somewhat lower, but there is the same sex difference.
- There is a large difference between the general population sexes in *non-family* transmission specifically, with 75% of female sources but only 59% of males born before 1900, and 43% of females but only 30% of males born before 1880.[34] This does suggest a greater prominence of older rather than younger women singers outside the family sphere.
- The *non-family* figures for the Traveller sources, whose numbers are small, are not so clear-cut, with a lower percentage of females born before 1900, but, going back further in the age groups, a higher percentage born before 1880.

In the G-D data for sources, however, the sexes are broadly similar:

- In the distribution of d.o.bs (Figures 5.14 and 5.15), the female modal value is in the 1840s, the same as the modal value for recipients, and the male modal value only slightly earlier, in the 1830s, suggesting – as already observed in relation to the Child ballad data (§5.2.3 above) – a robust song culture amongst peers.
- There are similar percentages of female and male sources born before 1840, and a slightly lower percentage of females born before 1800 (14% of females and 19% of males).[35]

---

31   See Table A1c.
32   See Table A14a.
33   This date is chosen as being a point of interest in Chapter 7.
34   See Table A14b.
35   See Table A15a. The date 1840 is chosen as being the start of the modal decade of birth, 1800 simply as the start of the century.

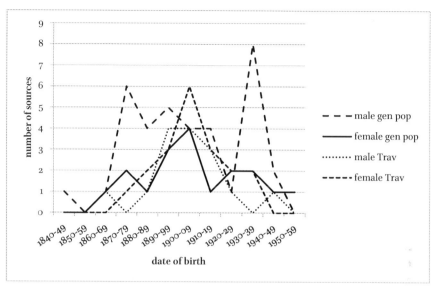

FIGURE 5.12   Numbers of SSSA sources by decade of birth (known dates of birth only)

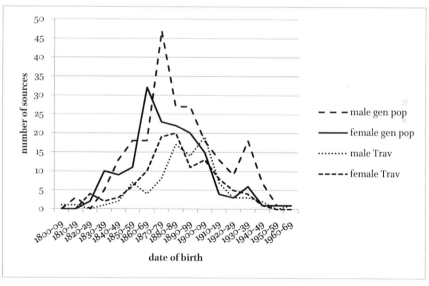

FIGURE 5.13   Numbers of SSSA sources by decade of birth (known and estimated dates of birth)

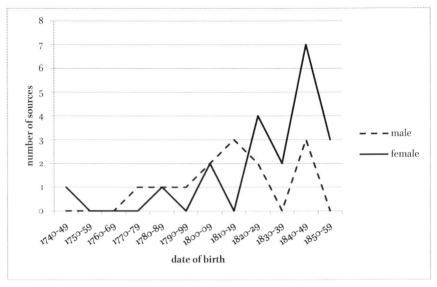

FIGURE 5.14   Numbers of G-D sources by decade of birth (known dates of birth only)

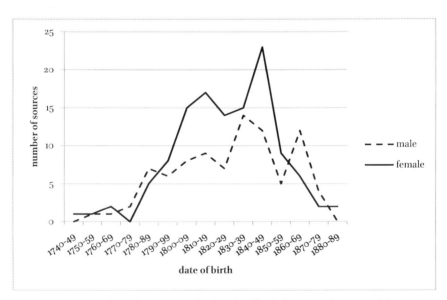

FIGURE 5.15   Numbers of G-D sources by decade of birth (known and estimated dates of birth)

- This is even more marked in *non-family* transmission, with 50% of female sources compared with 61% of males born before 1840; and 5% of females, 18% of males before 1800.[36]

This tendency towards younger female sources in G-D appears to be at least in part because of several young female servants who are song sources for both male and female recipients in G-D. Songs learned by men from servant girls include 96G, 1044C, 212A, and 404A. Sources described as Highland girls (Songs 1844, 735) were quite possibly also servants, as were, in all likelihood, some other girls whose roles cannot now be identified.

5.4 Domestic and Non-domestic Spheres

We are not looking at an absence of female-to-male song transmission outside of the family, but rather an under-representation. Porter and Gower may be correct about the reticence of younger women in contexts of performance, and this seems to be a factor in the SSSA collection, where contributors were indeed asked to perform for the tape-recorder. However, this seems to have affected the recruitment of general population women, and not the Travellers to whom Porter and Gower's observation refers. Possibly the contexts of recording tended to be more convivial for the latter, with larger groups assembled, making the fieldworker and the tape-recorder less central to the occasion.

The impression given by the person-to-person pairs is that general population men were the group whose singing was most widely heard outside of the family. To some extent this reflects the male-dominated environment of farmservants, especially after 1870 when innovations in agricultural equipment meant that fewer women were employed in field work (Carter, 1979: 102), though there would still generally be what was called in the North-East a kitchie deem[37] assisting the farmer's wife with indoor work. Many of the older men recorded by SSSA came from this background, and describe learning songs from each other 'in the bothy'. Many of the male contributors to G-D likewise came from this milieu. Traveller men also interacted with it, either as casual farm workers, or as visitors in the evenings (Cooke, 2007: 214). Traveller women apparently did not interact with general population men to any great extent.[38]

---

36   See Table A15b.
37   Literally a kitchen dame.
38   Ian Olson (verbal communication, 11 May 2016) recalls that when he was working for an Aberdeenshire tree grower in 1955, in his school holidays, everyone sang as they worked,

Traveller women seem to be the most restricted to their own family circle. They are a very minor source even for male Travellers outside the family.[39] The female Travellers who are sources for the general population are almost entirely singers who became well known through the Folk Revival (chiefly Jeannie Robertson, Lizzie Higgins and the Stewarts of Blair),[40] apart from Margaret MacDonald (a street singer who is counted here as a likely Traveller), who was the source of a song for 'Blin Jimmy' Bowie (born in Elgin some time after 1916);[41] and an unnamed Traveller girl who came round hawking and was a source for Willie Mathieson in 1896.[42]

The women in G-D also pass on songs mainly in single-sex contexts outside the family (Figure 5.10). As noted above, a number of the female sources identified by female recipients in G-D are servants: many girls in nineteenth century society spent some years in domestic service before they married. In relation to the G-D collection, the family/non-family distinction may not be the correct one to make. The real difference may be between domestic and non-domestic contexts. The domestic category would include domestic servants, including most female farmservants.

Domesticity would perhaps also be a better perspective from which to view farm contexts in SSSA. The unmarried men and the women servants living on a farm were to some extent in a domestic relationship with each other. Depending on the size of a farm and the social relations existing within it, the domestic sphere of the farmhouse itself might also extend to the male as well as to the female farmservants, though by the nineteenth century the old kindly relations no longer obtained on the large commercial farms, except perhaps for the farmer's children. Rural businesses like the millwright's belonging to the father of Rev. Duncan were also physically and to some extent socially an extension of the owner's domestic sphere: Duncan's sister Margaret, later Mrs Gillespie, learned numerous songs as a child from the carpenters employed by their father (Petrie, 2002a: 560).

In workplaces where people sang habitually to pass the time as they worked, those who overheard should probably not be regarded as the audience of a

---

except Traveller women, who did not join in.
39 See Figure 4.4.
40 In the transmission data used here, Belle Stewart and her daughter Sheila Stewart.
41 SA1952.30.B6 (B16). After his mother's death, Bowie was brought up in various institutions, including Craigmoray in Elgin, which dates from 1930. He may have been a street singer or tramp.
42 SA1952.17.B10 (B18), TaD 20828.

performance as such.[43] For instance, the ploughman from whose overheard singing Donald MacGregor learned 'The Queen amang the Heather'[44] may have been completely unaware that he had passed on the song. Farm work is one of the contexts of female-to-male song transmission that is mentioned in SSSA. For instance, Willie Mathieson heard 'Ta Clerk in ta Ofish' from Annie Massie when she was milking the cows.[45] George Hay from Aberdeenshire (born 1878) learned 'The Convict Maid' from Jean Lobban while harvesting.[46] Herring gutting is also mentioned. For instance, George Hay heard 'The Ball of Kirriemuir' (!) from herring gutters when he was a boy.[47] Bert Coull from Angus (born c. 1912) heard 'Don't Let us be Strangers' from fisherwomen, again when he was a boy.[48] Like much farm work, gutting was done in the open air, where a singer could easily be overheard.

Petrie (1997: 266) suggests that 'For many women, marriage and its attendant domestic ties, must have marked a withdrawal or at least restricted access to communal singing,' and in support of this there is a remark by Willie Scott to the effect that his wife used to sing a lot before they were married.[49] There is no obvious reason, however, why married women would be excluded from social occasions where there was singing. Rural gatherings, such as a meal-and-ale,[50] would include women singers. For instance, Willie Mathieson heard 'Barbara Allen' from a woman at a threshing – i.e. communal work on a farm when the travelling threshing machine visited, followed by a social evening.[51] Similarly, Donald MacMartin from Berwickshire (born 1904) learned 'A Pretty Fair Maid' from a woman who sang it at barn dances.[52] There is little indication of the typical age of such performers, but notice that the singers above are described as 'women' rather than 'girls' (on the terminology of 'girlhood' see above, §2.2).

However, women did expect to withdraw from work outside the home when they married, and it is thus in the workplace that younger women were

---

43 McKean (2018), discussing Willie Mathieson, makes a similar point, that the primary audience for traditional singing is the individual himself or herself.
44 SA1953.238.B6, TaD 26110.
45 SA1952.9.A2, TaD 17152.
46 SA1952.9.A7, TaD 17162.
47 SA1952.16.B10 (B22).
48 SA1952.53.A6, TaD 4339.
49 SA1962.27.A8, TaD 57710. There are several contributors of this name in the SSSA collection. This is the well-known singer Willie Scott (TaD ID 2894).
50 *Meal-and-ale* was the North-Eastern term for a harvest feast; it was named after the dish of oatmeal and ale, plus whisky, that was traditionally served on the occasion (*Scottish National Dictionary* s.v. *meal* n.¹, v.¹). Further south the harvest home was called a *kirn*.
51 SA1952.15.B4, TaD 2742.
52 SA1965.159.B19, TaD 28061.

much more likely than older ones to find themselves in contact with men who were not members of their families. This would imply that women were more active as singers outside the home when they were younger and unmarried. Conversely, Porter and Gower suggest that younger women were more reticent in mixed company. Indeed, both tendencies may have been at work in opposite directions, and there were probably subtleties with respect to the occasion and the company, so that young unmarried women, like Mary Bennett in *Pride and Prejudice*, might be allowed to 'exhibit' amongst friends.

There appears to be a different balance between the two opposing tendencies in G-D. Non-family transmission from females is very much tilted towards other females, but age does not seem to be a factor. Female servants are frequently mentioned as sources of songs for both sexes, and these are sometimes specifically identified as girls or young women. The boundary between the domestic and the outside world would have been more important for a woman than a man, entailing different codes of conduct, in the same way that a woman would have been at liberty in a domestic context to go about 'in her figure', as people used to say, but outside of that context would have worn a jacket or shawl to obscure her form. As suggested above, women in farm service might have been able to go about the farm singing without feeling inhibited.

The idea of young women's reticence does find some support, as we have seen, in the age distribution of the SSSA *contributors*, with women tending to have earlier d.o.bs.[53] We must be cautious in interpreting this finding, however, as there is an association between older women and the Child ballads, which might conceivably have steered the fieldwork towards older women. However, general population female *sources* also have earlier d.o.bs than male ones in SSSA (as do female Traveller sources, depending on the cut-off point). An examination of the contributors in relation to their sources confirms that men were much more prominent as singers outside of the family context. In SSSA there appear to be different dynamics at work in the recruitment and recording of women Travellers and those from the general population. While the women Travellers were recorded (often by male fieldworkers) in roughly equal numbers with men, their pattern of song transmission nevertheless suggests that they normally had limited interaction with men outside the family, until a few individuals were introduced to audiences through the Folk Revival.

---

53   The sexes are more similar in G-D in their distribution by d.o.bs, but the collection method was very different from SSSA.

CHAPTER 6

The Devolution of the Child Ballads to the Travellers

6.1 The 'Child Ballad' – a Valid Concept?

The 'Child ballad' is used as a category in this analysis, but it must be borne in mind that the Child ballads cannot be characterised by objective criteria. Indeed, Olson (1996–97: 163) describes the Child corpus of 305 types as 'a rag-bag' and warns, 'No statistical analyses … could be accepted from such an ill-assorted array of samples from such a non-uniform population.' Some well-known ballads in G-D that are not in Child include Song 1396 'Bogie's Bonny Bell', Song 1403 'Allan MacLean', both in the first person; and Song 1462 'Rosie Anderson'. Nevertheless, the Child catalogue does have an internal coherence, as a body of narrative songs – mostly lengthy, mostly third person, often dealing with historical subject matter, some very old.

The main reason for using the concept of the 'Child ballad' is that it was adopted by the SSSA collectors themselves and influenced the direction of the fieldwork:

> After the foundation of the School of Scottish Studies, systematic collecting with tape-recorders began in the North-East; the School's research-workers were looking for everything that came under the general heading of oral tradition, but priority was naturally given to [the] classic or 'Child' ballads. This led in 1953 to the discovery in Aberdeen of the great Jeannie Robertson …
>
> HENDERSON, 1981b, 1992: 24

Also, pragmatically, the fact that Child's ballad classification has been applied to the relevant songs in the TaD database makes it possible to search for and extract a manageable, pre-determined set of data from each demographic group. The G-D editors have also provided an Index of the Child ballads in G-D.[1] The Child ballad collection is not used here as a data set in itself, but as a probe for making comparisons within the data of this study. Ultimately

---

1 'Index of Child and Laws songs in this edition', vol. 8, pp. 677–81.

the justification for using this category is that it does reveal salient differences amongst the groups.

6.2   Combining the G-D and SSSA Data – a Valid Approach?

The G-D and SSSA collections are taken here as views at different times of the same song culture, roughly speaking, G-D having the modal value of its contributors' d.o.bs in the 1840s, and SSSA in the 1900s for the general population and the 1910s for the Travellers. It is necessary to be aware, however, that the North-East, where Greig and Duncan collected their material, had a reputation throughout the nineteenth century as a region rich in traditional song, especially ballads (Goldstein and Argo eds. in Greig, 1963: i; Buchan, 1972, 1997: 5; Henderson, 1981b, 1992: 23). Olson (1995–6: 115) judges that this was a real phenomenon, and not merely the result of collecting efforts being concentrated in this region.

The Scots song material in SSSA, by contrast, comes from all over the Lowlands and Northern Isles, with a few items from the Highlands and Western Isles. However, in this collection too the North-East is prominent both overall and for Child ballads in particular. The North-East provides at least 16% of overall general population contributors, and at least 33% of core population Child ballad contributors, so far as the geographical origins of the SSSA contributors in the data can be ascertained (for numbers, see Table 6.1).[2] To put these figures in perspective, the North-East (understood as Aberdeen, Aberdeenshire and Moray) presently has 10.7% of the Scottish 'usual resident population' as of the 2011 Census (percentage based on figures from 'Scotland's Census', n.d.).

The famous Traveller singer Jeannie Robertson was from the North-East, and Hunter pays tribute to her as a North-Easterner, and an exponent of the local singing tradition of the North-East ('Editor's Introduction' to G-D: IV, xvii). However, many of the Travellers in SSSA have complex geographical backgrounds, so Table 6.1 does not attempt to categorise them geographically. The Revival singers are also omitted, as they are not so well documented. Besides

---

2   Recall that for contributors as a whole the *general population* includes the Revival contributors, so the general and core population figures are not directly comparable. In some cases the geographical origin of the individual is assumed on the basis of family connections. The division of the country into culture areas in Table 6.1 is loosely based on the map of the traditional Scots dialect areas in *SND* (vol. I, p. xv). At the time of writing, there is a link to this map (Map 2) in the online version of *SND* at 'About Scots' > 'The Scots Language' (§6). A revised version is included in *The Concise Scots Dictionary* (Map 1 in the 1st edition, p. xxxvii in the 2nd edition).

TABLE 6.1 Geographical distribution of SSSA general population contributors and core population Child ballad contributors

	All gen pop	Child core pop
North-East	147	44
Unknown	91	1
South-East	91	5
Shetland	74	13
West Highlands, Western Isles	68	5
Borders	65	6
Glasgow	57	1
Orkney	54	15
West (excluding Glasgow)	51	10
Angus	46	9
Dumfries and Galloway	45	5
Lowland Perthshire	24	2
Fife	28	0
East Highlands	21	8
East Sutherland and Cromarty	19	2
Kintyre	17	5
Caithness	9	1
TOTAL	907	132

the North-East, Shetland also ranks high as an area in which SSSA found Child ballad contributors amongst the core population, and Orkney and the West (in practice Ayrshire and Lanarkshire) are also more productive of Child ballad contributors than their overall rank would predict; Edinburgh and the South-East, Glasgow, and the Borders less so.

As we saw above (§3.6), the wider geographical catchment of SSSA produces 26 Child ballads not in G-D (i.e. 8.5% of the catalogue), but G-D has 40% of the catalogue and SSSA only 31%, if we omit the Revival contributors. Taking G-D to stand for the nineteenth century thus perhaps over-estimates the country-wide popularity of the Child ballads by that time, but it no doubt under-estimates the number of ballad types that could have been collected in a country-wide search. Famously, King Orfeo (Child 19), which is not in G-D, has been collected only from Shetland, with a refrain in corrupted Norn. With these reservations, G-D data and SSSA core population data are tentatively combined at some points in this work to extend the timescale of the d.o.bs and to provide a large enough body of data for analysis when sub-divided. It would, of course, be more valid to compare the G-D data with those from North-Eastern contributors in SSSA specifically. However, this must be left to some other hand. For this first attempt at a quantitative analysis of the two collections, the emphasis is on assembling as much data as possible, in order for any patterns to emerge more clearly.

6.3 Decline in Child Ballad Contributors and Contributions

Taste in songs, as in other things, changes over time. The long, narrative ballads were, by all accounts, declining in popularity over a long period before they found a new niche in the Folk Revival. Rev. Duncan observed in 1908 that:

> there are only a few that now sing the old traditional songs, and in many cases those that have them can hardly be said to sing them, though they can recall them when required. Indeed this has changed very much within my own memory: thirty or forty years ago these songs were often sung, though the young people were already beginning to take up with more modern productions; but now they are mostly known only to old people, or to a few in middle life who have been [able] to learn them in favourable circumstances from the former generation … … Now, however, the actual singing of the ballads has pretty well disappeared. They are too long for the patience of either singers or hearers.
>
> SHULDHAM-SHAW and LYLE, eds., 1974: 7–8

There is no inconsistency in the fact that the perceived decline of the ballad tradition can be dated to any point between the mid-eighteenth century, when Bishop Percy expected to find 'curious old Songs' only in 'remote and obscure parts' (Letter, 1761, quoted by Rieuwerts, 2002: 151), and 1925, when Keith described ballad singing as 'only now dying out' in Aberdeenshire (Greig ed. Keith, 1925: xv). Each observer is presumably comparing the situation as he finds it with the more robust level of activity that he remembers in the past, with the baseline shifting over time.[3]

---

3 In explicit contradiction of these pessimistic judgements, Henderson (1981b, 1992: 24) emphasises that the SSSA found many ballad singers, while Olson (2003–4: 163) describes Keith's choice of 'last leaves' for his title as 'perverse'. Henderson and Collinson (1965: 1) write: 'This elegiac note, as Keith himself has readily and generously admitted, was premature,' but they add, 'It is true, to be sure, that since Greig's day there has been a certain falling away …'

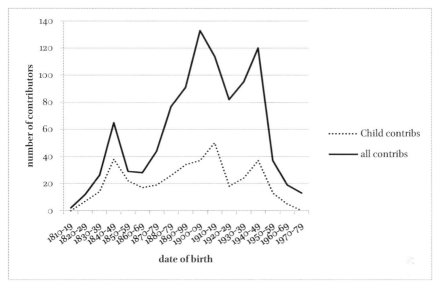

FIGURE 6.1 Numbers of combined G-D and SSSA contributors compared with Child ballad contributors by decade of birth (known and estimated dates of birth, outliers omitted)
Note: the G-D numbers are under-represented because of the large proportion of unknown dates.

Combining the data for all G-D and SSSA groups, the Child ballad contributors track the overall contributors in terms of peaks and troughs across decades of birth (Figure 6.1). However, as a *percentage* of all contributors, Child ballad contributors shows a mainly downward trend from the 1850s birth cohort on (Figure 6.2). This is largely attributable to G-D and to the Travellers in SSSA, both groups who peak at relatively high percentages then fall away (Figure 6.3). From the 1870s on, the general population maintains a relatively low level, wavering either side of 30% (leaving aside extreme values in Figure 6.3 for the 1850s and 1860s, which represent single individuals).

6.4   G-D as a Baseline

Taking G-D as a baseline from which to compare the ballad singing culture of the nineteenth century with that of the twentieth, the following trends emerge (in addition to the progressive decline, just mentioned, in the proportion of contributors who provide ballads or ballad fragments):

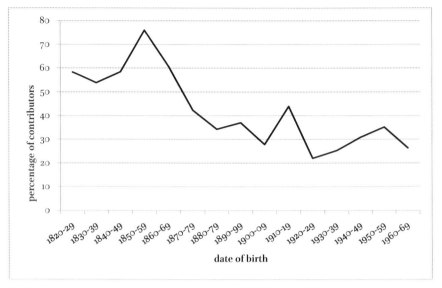

FIGURE 6.2 Combined G-D and SSSA Child ballad contributors as a percentage of all contributors, 1820–1969 (known and estimated dates of birth, outliers omitted)
Note: for numbers, see Figure 6.1.

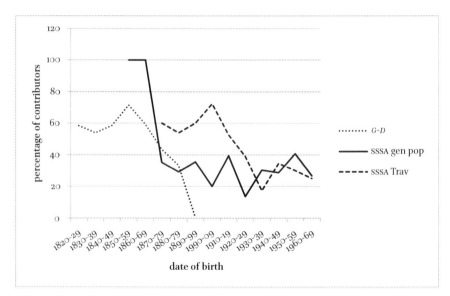

FIGURE 6.3 SSSA and G-D Child ballad contributors as a percentage of all contributors, 1820–1969 (known and estimated dates of birth, outliers omitted)
Note: extreme values are based on very small numbers. In order to relate the Child ballad contributors to the contributors overall, figures are given for the SSSA general population (i.e. the core population and the Revival contributors combined). For numbers, see Figures 2.10 and 2.13 for all contributors, and 2.5, 2.6, 2.7 and 5.7 for Child ballad contributors.

- The Child ballad contributors and sources cease to be female-dominated. The association made by a number of observers between women singers and the Child ballads is largely borne out in the G-D data, as we saw above: despite forming slightly less than half of the contributors, the females contribute considerably more ballad types and tokens, and a higher percentage of them contribute two or more ballads. They also form a clear majority of the sources. The female Travellers follow the same pattern in relation to male Travellers. With regard to the core population females, however, the association between women singers and the Child ballads is a thing of the past by the 1950s (see §5.2.3).
- An age gap opens up between sources and contributors.
- The overall ballad repertoire narrows, until the Folk Revival.
- Transmission is increasingly family-dominated.
- The more marked decline in contributors, sources and repertoire amongst the core population leaves the Travellers as the group most productive of ballads by the 1950s.

The last four points are discussed below.

6.5 Age Gap between Contributors and Sources

It appears that there was a robust culture of ballad singing in the North-East in the nineteenth century, as reflected through G-D. The Child ballads are not particularly associated with older contributors. Also, so far as we can estimate, the modal decade of birth of the Child ballad sources is the 1840s, the same as that of the contributors, implying a degree of peer-to-peer transmission. By contrast, all SSSA groups have a higher median age for Child ballad contributors than for contributors overall, and there is a generational gap between contributors and sources (see §5.2.3).

The Child ballads in G-D are *less* strongly associated with transmission from Generation 2 (the grandparental generation) than are songs overall (cf. Figures 6.4 and 6.5). Instead, the Child ballads in G-D are strongly associated with transmission from Generation 1 (the parental generation). This is largely attributable to mothers as sources: there are twenty pairs sourced to mothers and ten to fathers in the G-D data.[4] The SSSA core population, by contrast, have a higher level of family transmission pairs sourced to the grandparental generation for Child ballads than the general population do for songs overall.

---

4 See Table A16b.

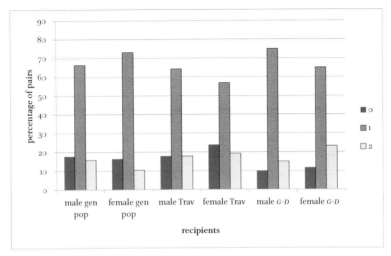

FIGURE 6.4 Percentages of SSSA and G-D recipient-source pairs in family transmission sourced to each generation
Note: generation 0 is the same generation as the recipient, 1 is the parental and 2 the grandparental generation. Figures based on 146 SSSA pairs with general population male recipients, 134 with general population females, 84 with male Travellers, and 130 with female Travellers; and 60 G-D pairs with male recipients, and 104 with females.

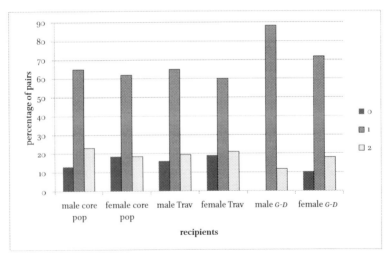

FIGURE 6.5 Percentages of SSSA and G-D Child ballad recipient-source pairs in family transmission sourced to each generation (Revival recipients omitted)
Note: generation 0 is the same generation as the recipient, 1 is the parental and 2 the grandparental generation. Figures based on 31 SSSA pairs with core population male recipients, 26 with core population females, 37 with male Travellers, and 67 with female Travellers; and 17 G-D pairs with male recipients, and 39 with females.

6.6 Narrowing Ballad Repertoire

G-D has a larger number of Child ballad types than any of the SSSA groups in the data, even if the very prolific Bell Robertson is excluded.[5] Between G-D and the SSSA *male* core population there is a roughly proportionate change in the numbers of Child ballad contributors and the numbers of Child ballad types and tokens recorded from them.[6] The picture is very different for core population *females*, with a negative percentage change in numbers of types (−113%) much larger than the change in numbers of contributors (−47%). The Revival singers have a substantial repertoire: between G-D and the Revival, the drop in the number of types is much smaller, proportionately, than the difference in the numbers of contributors involved.[7] Between G-D and the Travellers, however, the drop in the numbers of Child ballad types and tokens collected is smaller than the difference in contributor numbers, if the distorting effect of Bell Robertson's contribution in G-D is taken into account (Table A11c).

With regard to group repertoires, the SSSA and G-D data can only tentatively be compared, as the collection methods were very different, with the SSSA seeking out singers, and making extensive and repeated recordings of selected individuals, whereas G-D collected through intermediaries as well as directly, and also solicited particular songs through Greig's articles in a local newspaper. Also, G-D's emphasis on tunes, which were often taken down with a single interlined verse, means that figures for fragments[8] are unreliable, and the numbers of whole ballads will be correspondingly under-estimated. So while the G-D group figures for those who contribute two or more whole ballads – at 23% of males and 32% of females – are lower than those of the Travellers at 24% of males and 43% of females, this is probably misleading.

Within the SSSA data, the numbers with two or more whole ballads decline after the initial phase of fieldwork in the 1950s, which scooped up in one decade contributors born between the 1870s and the 1930s, and a few even earlier. This is seen for all groups, apart from females in the core population, whose high point of collection is in the early 1960s.[9] The tailing away after the 1950s is particularly noticeable for male Travellers (Figure 6.6).

---

5 Out of 40 types that occur only once in the G-D data, she accounts for 31, of which only nine subsequently appear in the SSSA data as we have it via TaD. Twenty of these one-offs of Bell Robertson's are sourced to her mother.
6 See Table A11a.
7 See Table A11b.
8 The definition of 'fragment' used in this part of the study is discussed above (§2.5). A rendering of at least five verses is counted as a whole ballad.
9 This is likewise the high point for general population females in the overall data (Figure 2.2).

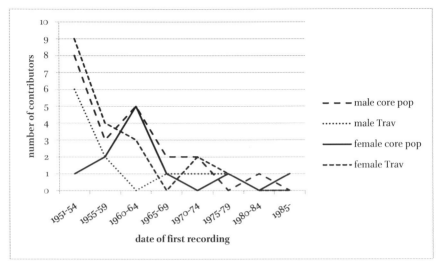

FIGURE 6.6 Numbers of SSSA contributors with two or more whole Child ballads in the data, by half decade of first recording (Revival contributors omitted)

Before we leave the topic of repertoires, it is worth digressing to consider the phenomenon of individuals with very large Child ballad repertoires. Although TaD's coverage of the SSSA collection is not adequate, as mentioned above, to describe the repertoires of individuals, some do stand out, even if the list of their relevant recordings may not be quite complete in the data. These are the Travellers Jeannie Robertson (born 1908), her daughter Lizzie Higgins (born 1929), and her nephew Stanley Robertson (born 1940); and also Martha Johnstone (born 1901). The younger relatives of Jeannie Robertson might, however, more properly be seen as Folk Revival singers. Hamish Henderson himself described Lizzie Higgins as 'a child of the Revival' (quoted by Olson, 2007b: 2).

These Travellers are matched for size of Child ballad repertoire only by a single individual in the SSSA core population, Willie Mathieson. He was as much a collector as a singer (Henderson, 1981b, 1992: 25). He was perhaps never what MacColl and Seeger (1977: 19) call a 'Singer' with a capital S, although in some respects he was what Niles (1995) calls a 'strong tradition bearer': that is, he was deeply engaged with the tradition, acquisitive of songs, and critically aware of them (McKean, 2018: 48). As it happens, Duncan Williamson (born 1928), Niles' type of the 'strong tradition bearer', is under-represented in the data, and this is a useful reminder that these data provide only a partial window into the SSSA collection, itself an imperfect window into the musical lives of the people recorded. Linda Williamson (1985, 290 ff.) gives slightly longer lists of

Child ballads (and other traditional narrative songs) for some of the Traveller contributors in the Williamson circle.[10]

In G-D, a few individuals likewise contribute very large Child ballad repertoires. These are:

- Mrs Gillespie (born 1841), who contributes 47 types (of which 35 have at least five verses);
- Annie Shirer (born 1873), who contributes 25 types (of which 21 have at least five verses);[11]
- Bell Robertson (born 1841), who makes an extremely large contribution,[12] although she apparently did not sing, with 92 types (of which 66 have at least five verses).

Buchan (1972, 1997: 5) writes, 'The Northeast is fortunate in having a singer with a sizeable recorded corpus for each of the significant stages of the tradition's evolution.' He focuses specifically on:

- Mrs Brown of Falkland (born 1747), whose MS was drawn upon by Sir Walter Scott (pp. 62 ff.);
- James Nicol, a source for the collector Peter Buchan in the 1820s (pp. 223 ff.);
- Bell Robertson (pp. 247 ff.).

We have no way of knowing whether these contributors were unusual in their own day, but it is a characteristic of both the G-D and SSSA data that there are a few individuals who took a particular interest in the long narrative ballads and acquired large repertoires of them. Likewise in the James Madison Carpenter collection, collected between 1929 and 1935 in England and Scotland, there is one particularly prolific contributor, Bell Duncan from Aberdeenshire (born 1849), who contributed c. 66 Child ballads (Bishop, 2004: 404).[13]

The limited information we have confirms the importance of family sources for some of the individuals with the largest Child ballad repertoires. An aunt

---

10   Excluding fragments, she lists 23 Child ballads for Martha Johnstone (there are 21 in the data used here, including Williamson's own transcribed items), seven for Betsy Whyte (here six), five for Johnnie Whyte (here four), four for Mary Williamson (all in the data here), and thirteen for Duncan Williamson (here eleven). As explained above (§2.1), the TaD data have been supplemented from Williamson (1985) and other sources; but in order to maintain a consistent definition of a fragment, her data are used only for songs for which she gives a transcription.

11   These appear to be from her own repertoire, not collected in her capacity as an intermediary. There is information about her sources for thirteen of them; they are mostly from her father or uncle.

12   As noted above (§4.1), both Bell Robertson and Mrs Gillespie used printed sources as an *aide memoire*.

13   Depending on what is included and how different versions are counted.

of Mrs Brown of Falkland was the source of much of her repertoire (Buchan, 1972, 1997: 63–4); Bell Duncan's mother was the source of many of her songs (Bishop, 2004: 396). However, individuals who assembled large collections of ballads (and songs generally) drew also on whatever sources were available to them, including singers outside the family, and also printed sources such as broadsides. Bishop (2004: 402) shows that two of the ballads provided by Bell Duncan (and omitted by Carpenter in his fair copy) clearly derive from print. It is not clear whether Bell Duncan herself obtained them from printed sources, or whether these sources were further back up the line of transmission.

It is worth asking whether there are also such individuals, with large Child ballad repertoires, amongst those named as sources in the data. Bearing in mind that generalised information about sources (e.g. 'I learned most of my songs from my grandmother') is not in a form that can be quantified, the sources who stand out in the SSSA data for the transmission of specific Child ballads are:

- David Whyte (a Traveller born ?c. 1840), who was the source of eight Child ballads for his great-granddaughter Martha Johnstone;
- Elizabeth MacDonald (a Traveller born in 1901), who was the source of seven Child ballads for her son Stanley Robertson;
- Maria Stewart (a Traveller born ?c. 1880), who was the source of ten Child ballads for her daughter Jeannie Robertson and granddaughter Lizzie Higgins.

To give a perspective on how much – or how little – of the relevant information is being captured in this way, Jeannie Robertson is herself named as a source (especially by younger relatives and by Revival singers) of only thirteen Child ballads, whereas her own Child repertoire in the data comprises eighteen ballads of at least five verses[14] and four fragments.

There are some particularly well-documented sources in the G-D data, probably because the recipients were able to recall and assemble the information at their own leisure:

- William Duncan (born in 1814) is the source of eight Child ballads for his son James Duncan (the collector), and for James' siblings Mrs Gillespie and George Duncan.
- Their mother is the source of fifteen for the same three recipients and also another one for their sister Elizabeth (Mrs Milne).[15]
- Annie Shirer (born 1873) names her father (born 1827) as the source of seven.

---

14   Including two different versions of Child 279 as well as Child's 279 Appendix, and the American version of Child 81.
15   The information about Mrs Milne's song acquisition comes at second hand from her daughter Jemima Milne.

- Mrs Lyall (born 1869), who mostly gives tunes with interlined text rather than full texts of her sixteen Child ballad contributions, names her mother (born 1847) as the source of eleven.
- Bell Robertson identifies sources for 86 of her 92 Child ballads (including fragments): 58 come from her mother (born in 1804). Of these, eighteen are identified as coming to Mrs Robertson from her own mother.

As well as songs, Willie Mathieson also collected sayings and lore of various kinds (McKean, 2018: 46); and Bell Robertson was described by someone who knew her as 'a perfect mine of local traditions'.[16] Something else that these two individuals had in common was their limited schooling. The rural North-East was notable for the high standard of its schools in the nineteenth century (see below, §7.3), but attendance was not compulsory until the Education Act of 1872, and another characteristic of the North-East was the large proportion of small farms and crofts that relied on family labour, including that of children (Carter, 1979: 28–9, 58 and *passim*). In some areas where there was not enough fieldstone for dyking, children were employed in herding cattle. Hawthorn hedges did not flourish in the North-East, so in these areas enclosure had to wait until the introduction of wire fencing after the middle of the century (Carter, 1979: 42–3). Mrs Lyall (born 1869) left school at the age of ten to herd cattle (Neilson, 2002: 566). In principle the school-leaving age was thirteen, but an exemption could be made if the child had reached a certain standard (Knox, n.d.). Willie Mathieson (born in 1879) left school at eleven to work as a ditcher.[17] In Bell Robertson's case, distance from the parish school meant that she could not attend, and she received her few years of schooling from a neighbour who kept a dame school. As Petrie (2002b: 582) puts it, 'In the absence of ready access to books or conversation, songs, particularly their narrative content, were always important to Bell.' For individuals like these, whose intellectual capacity was not matched by their formal education, their mental and imaginative sustenance had to come largely from the Bible, inexpensive chapbooks, and the great store of oral literature.

6.7 Transmission is Increasingly Family-Dominated

As the Child ballad transmission data become more concentrated in the Traveller group, transmission also becomes even more family-dominated. There is a very strong correlation between the percentage participation in

---

16   Mrs Frank Russell, who helped to publish Bell Robertson's poems (quoted by Buchan, 1972, 1997: 249).
17   SA1952.5.A10, TaD 15745.

TABLE 6.2   Correlation coefficients between percentage participation in Child ballad transmission, and in family and non-family transmission (across both sexes in G-D, SSSA male and female general population, and male and female Travellers)

	Correlation coefficients			
	Family	Nuclear family	Extended family	Non-family
Instances	0.92	0.70	0.97	−0.79
Pairs	0.80	0.50	0.96	−0.80
Recipients	0.86	0.81	0.96	−0.50

Child ballad transmission and in family transmission, whichever measure is used – song transmission instances, recipient-source pairs, or recipients who participate in various categories of song transmission. The correlation coefficients (see Table 6.2) are 0.80 or above for family transmission in general, lower for nuclear family transmission, and higher (0.96 or above) for extended family transmission. Conversely, there is a negative correlation between the percentage participation in Child ballad transmission and in non-family transmission (−0.50 or below).

By all the measures used in this study, the Child ballads are particularly associated with family transmission, more so than songs overall.[18] However, there is still room for a small increase between G-D and SSSA in the percentage of Child ballad transmission that is in the family category:[19] from 58% to 61% of instances, from 46% to 60% of pairs,[20] and from 58% to 62% of recipients. This is attributable to the very high family transmission figures reported by the Travellers, of both sexes. Indeed, as we saw above (§4.4.5), the male Travellers differ from the other male groups in having more family than non-family transmission on all measures. Even in non-family pairs in the Child ballad data, the core population males as sources for male Travellers are only at an equal level

---

18   Cf. Tables A2b and A2d in terms of instances, Tables A8a and A8b in terms of recipient-source pairs, and Tables A9a and A9b in terms of recipients. Apart from the female general population figures in Table A9b, family transmission is higher for the Child ballad data even with the Revival contributors included (i.e. the general population as opposed to core population figures).

19   See Tables A2d, A8b and A9b.

20   As explained above (§4.4.3), the low percentage of family pairs in G-D is attributable to the large range of identified non-family contacts of a few individual women contributors.

with other male Travellers, in contrast to the predominance of general population males as sources for this group in the data overall (cf. Figures 4.5 and 4.4 above).

The Travellers comprise 25% of the overall SSSA *recipients* and 39% of the Child ballad recipients, with even higher percentages of family recipients: 35% overall, 53% for Child ballads, and for extended family recipients rising to 47% overall and 62% for Child ballads.[21] The large amount of information that we have about Traveller song transmission, especially within the family, means that they form an even higher proportion of identified *sources*: 24% overall, 46% for the Child ballads, with even higher figures for family sources: 39% overall, 59% for the Child ballads. For extended family sources the percentages go up to 50% overall, 65% for the Child ballads.[22]

As discussed above (§1.5), a remarkably high proportion of female Travellers in the data have transmission information associated with them, and this is particularly so in relation to the sought-after Child ballads. This peculiarity may be the result of a selective focus in the fieldwork, and perhaps also an appreciation on the part of these contributors of the interests of the collectors. Considering that a very high proportion – 77% – of this group's Child ballad transmission instances fall under the head of family transmission,[23] it is possible, too, that female Travellers, more than other groups, had the sort of sentimental associations to particular songs, especially the long narrative ballads, that Linda Williamson's (1985: 61 ff.) sources describe, as reminders of family members who had sung them.

6.8 Greater Retention amongst the Travellers

The Traveller Child ballad contributors in SSSA tend to be younger than the core population and to contribute more Child ballad material:
– The median age of the Travellers (at the time of first recording) is lower than that of the core population: 52 for females (compared with 62 for core population females), and 50 for males (compared with 57).[24] See Figures 6.7 and 6.8 for a breakdown by recording period.[25]

---

21 See Tables A3a and A3b. It should be borne in mind, however, that the identification of contributors' backgrounds is in some cases tentative (see above, §1.4).
22 See Tables A4a and A4b.
23 See Table A2d.
24 See Table A12.
25 It might be objected that the younger average age of the male Travellers is an artefact. Indeed, if the core and Revival populations are recombined, the median ages are much

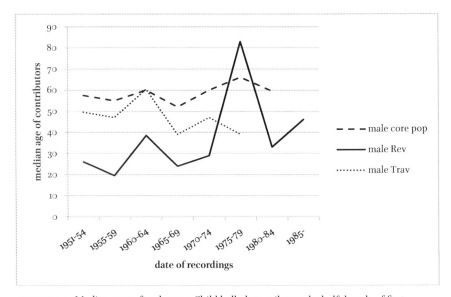

FIGURE 6.7 Median ages of male SSSA Child ballad contributors by half decade of first recording (known and estimated dates of birth)
Note: figures based on 65 core population males, 30 Revival males, and 40 male Travellers. The patterns over time are somewhat erratic because of the low numbers: note that there is a median age of 83 for male Revival contributors in 1975–79 that actually represents a single individual. This atypical individual is Douglas Neil Kennedy, director of the English Folk Dance & Song Society, who lived in Scotland up to the age of about fourteen (see *Oxford Dictionary of National Biography* s.v.). He belongs rather to the first than to the second Folk Revival (see above, §1.1).

- A smaller proportion were born before 1920: 69% of female Travellers (compared with 79% of core population females), and 65% of male Travellers (compared with 85% of core population males).[26]
- Likewise, a smaller proportion were born before 1900: the figure for female Travellers is 26% (compared with 51% for core population females), and for male Travellers 28% (compared with 32% for core population males).
- In each group in SSSA, the largest repertoire size category is the single ballad. The biggest difference amongst the groups lies in the relative proportions of

---

the same as the Travellers'. However, the Travellers do still have a consistently higher percentage born before 1920. A dividing line c. 1930 might produce a more valid comparison (see below §9.5). However, this would exclude those with unknown d.o.bs: for these the recording date (before or after 1960) provides an alternative metric.

26   See Table A5c.

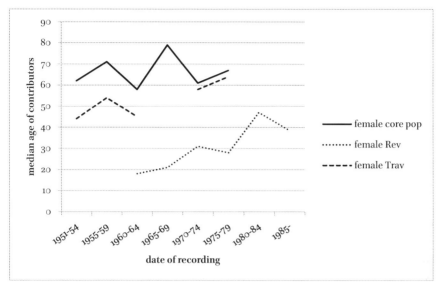

FIGURE 6.8 Median ages of female SSSA Child ballad contributors by half decade of first recording (known and estimated dates of birth). Figures based on 43 core population females, 29 Revival females, and 42 female Travellers.

contributors with only fragments and those with two or more whole ballads. The core population, and especially the females, tend towards fragments, but the proportions are reversed for female Travellers (see Figure 5.9 above).
– As noted above (§6.6), between G-D and the Travellers, the decline in the numbers of Child ballad types and tokens collected is smaller than the decline in contributor numbers, if the distorting effect of Bell Robertson's contribution in G-D is taken into account.[27]

However, within the more robust figures for the Travellers there are nevertheless signs of a decline over time:
– Contributor numbers decrease after the 1950s recording period.[28]
– Female Travellers also decrease very substantially in the types of Child ballads recorded. (Male Travellers, despite a decrease in the number of contributors, show an increase in tokens and especially in types, which is attributable to two very prolific contributors, Duncan Williamson and Stanley Robertson.)
– The median ages of the Traveller Child ballad contributors (52 for females, 50 for males), while lower than those of the core population, are still

---

27 See Table A11c.
28 See Table A11d.

considerably higher than those of the Traveller contributors overall (41 for both sexes).[29]
- After the 1900s birth cohort, Child ballad contributors as a percentage of all Traveller contributors fall with later decades of birth (until a small increase in the 1940s).[30]

6.9 The Cultural Context of Ballad Singing

The discovery that the big ballads were still part of the everyday repertoire of Traveller singers established the reputation of the Travellers as bearers of the folk song tradition, even to the extent of its being claimed that this tradition had devolved almost entirely to them:

> The fact that the greater part of this traditional repertory was made originally by *gorgios* is unimportant, since the *gorgios* have, on the whole, abandoned it. As with the scrap cars, obsolete sewing machines and old radios which litter their sites, the Travellers have taken whatever was retrievable of that abandoned repertory and made it their own.... In our view, a significant part of our national heritage has passed into the hands of the Travellers and is dependent upon them for its survival. We are not saying that there are no traditional singers left in Britain other than those who are Travellers.... But most of them are old and nearly all of them live in communities which have, for the most part, relegated the old songs ... to the lumbershed ...
>
> MACCOLL and SEEGER, 1977: 15

Without falling into the fallacy of identifying the Scots song tradition with the Travellers, we can say that the present study bears out the prominence of the Traveller contributors in the SSSA collection, so far as it has been catalogued in the TaD database. In trying to explain the persistence of ballad singing amongst the Travellers in the 1950s and later, Hamish Henderson posits a particular affinity for the pre-modern imaginative world of the big ballads: he describes Traveller society as 'representing the actual world of the ballad singers, a shared sensibility still artistically vital and fertile' (1980: 86). Hall (1975: 43–4) writes in a similar vein about a tragic view of life in the group of ballads he discusses that accords with the vulnerability of the Travellers to natural and

---

29   See Table A12.
30   See Figure 6.3.

societal forces beyond their control. If there is anything in these ideas they must, of course, also explain the appeal of the ballads to their original and much wider audiences.

Lyle writes, 'The world of the classical ballads ... already seemed old in the late eighteenth century. Nearly all of the classical ballads were known by 1820' (2013: 17). Buchan similarly regards Child 225 'Rob Roy', which refers to an event of 1750, as the last datable 'historical ballad' (1985: 446). Like Henderson's idea of a certain ballad 'sensibility', these judgements are aesthetic in character, and thus difficult to pin down. Songs did continue to be written in ballad form,[31] but they are not accepted by folk song experts as belonging to the classical ballad canon. At base, the idea of a bygone era of balladry is linked to the idea of a bygone period of history. Thus for Buchan the decline of the historical ballads is coterminous with the enormously disruptive agricultural developments of the eighteenth century (1972, 1997: 177 ff.). This was the beginning of the end of what Laslett (1983) memorably calls the 'world we have lost': a feudal, unlettered, materially poor but time-rich, kin-centred, pre-industrial world, in which people lived close to the elements, and relied heavily on natural light and local raw materials – a world, moreover, permeated by the supernatural. The historical processes that created the modern world – the Enclosure of the commons, the Agricultural Revolution, the Industrial Revolution – also converted the mass of the general population into wage labourers (see below, §7.2). The Travellers, with their preference for self-employment and living by their wits, were, like the crofters and small farmers of the North-East, but for rather longer, resistant to this conversion, and thus, perhaps, both these groups remained more in touch with the pre-modern sensibility of the old ballads. The rural population, however, went through further disruptive changes in the last quarter of the nineteenth century, which are discussed below (§7.6).

The idea of the Traveller way of life as essentially pre-modern is memorably embodied in Hamish Henderson's description of first hearing Jeannie Robertson sing, 'when she rose up like the Middle Ages in person' (paraphrased by Calder, 1992: xv). This is an allusion to Frederico García Lorca:

> Then La Niña de Los Peines got up like a madwoman, trembling like a medieval mourner, and drank, in one gulp, a huge glass of fiery spirits, and began to sing with a scorched throat, without voice, breath, colour, but ... with duende. She managed to tear down the scaffolding of the song,

---

31   A fairly recent ballad that gained popularity in the 1970s was Archie Fisher's 'The Witch of the West-Mer-Lands', also known as 'The Witch of the Westmorlands'.

> but allow through a furious, burning duende ... because she knew experts
> were listening, who demanded not form but the marrow of form ...
>
> G. L. LORCA, trans. A. S. KLINE, 2007

In his review of a volume in which this essay of Lorca's appeared in English translation, Henderson compared Lorca's description of *duende* with the Traveller concept of *conyach* (1987, 1992: 314).

Modern scholars tend to dismiss the romanticism of the late nineteenth century Gypsy lorists, such as John Sampson and Charles Leland, who 'mourned an age that was passing and imagined the Gypsies as a lasting but endangered remnant of that age. Their fantasy of an Edenic Romany existence, [was] the result of projection and an ultimately self-regarding nostalgia ...' (Nord, 2006: 126). However, these Victorian observers, who were serious scholars notwithstanding their flights of fancy, were not necessarily wrong about the inherently pre-industrial character of the Gypsy or Traveller lifestyle, of which its non-viability in industrialised societies may indeed be the measure.

The travelling way of life became barely viable with a reduced rural population and improved communications, which did away with the need for itinerants' trades and services. Despite their traditional contempt for those who worked for others (W. Simson ed. J. Simson, 1866: 225; Rehfisch, 1975: 275–6), the Travellers were to be found doing seasonal agricultural work by the late nineteenth century, and Col. Williamson of Lawers (born 1830),[32] giving evidence to an 1895 committee, stated that this was something that had changed since his young days (Dawson ed., 2005). The Departmental Committee on Vagrancy in Scotland (1936: 42) finds that the itinerants were by the 1930s mainly reliant on agricultural work, as their hereditary occupations, such as making tinware and peddling, had ceased to be profitable.

Another factor was the loss of the patronage of landowners. MacRitchie (1894: 111) describes how, in the lawless seventeenth century, noblemen took Gypsy bands under their protection, thus securing them as adherents. By contrast, Gentleman and Swift (1971: 16) refer to a 1925 report[33] that notes how on many estates the old gentry and nobility who used to give Travellers camping grounds, often on a hereditary basis, had been replaced by *nouveaux riches* who moved them on mercilessly. The Departmental Committee on Vagrancy in Scotland (1936: 41) comments that conditions had deteriorated since the Departmental Committee on Tinkers (Scotland)'s 1918 report, with

---

32   A Col. David R. Williamson (1830–1913), resident at Lawers, is listed by Lundy (2019).
33   By the Central Committee on the Welfare of Tinkers, apparently an initiative of the Perth branch of the Scottish National Society for the Prevention of Cruelty to Children.

the systematic demolition of the condemned buildings that had formerly been used in winter by Travellers. Landlords and factors were also becoming less inclined to give permission to camp. As mentioned above, this was partly owing to changes of land ownership, but it also coincided with a move to collecting scrap and rags, which made different demands on camping sites (pp. 41, 43). It was also becoming difficult to remain settled long enough to meet the requirements of schooling for Traveller children (p. 41), without settling permanently in houses, as the Border Gypsies had largely done by 1918 (Departmental Committee on Tinkers (Scotland), 1918: 11).

It is not actually necessary to explain the retention of traditional singing by the Travellers, since its corollary, the decline of traditional singing, is already well explained by the advance of a commercial music culture borne by new technology: we need only observe that there was a delay in the assimilation of the Travellers to this new consumer culture (see further below, §8.4). It may be that the real difference between the Traveller singers and the general population, by the time the SSSA began collecting in the 1950s, was that the Travellers, more readily than the population at large, found – or had earlier in their lifetimes found – listeners for traditional songs within the family circle, including the big ballads, but that this was not long to continue.[34]

6.10   The Performance Context of Ballad Singing

In the past, when singing to oneself was a pervasive accompaniment to routine tasks, singers might be overheard who were not performing to an audience as such. Listeners who regularly shared a domestic or work space with a person who sang in this way would hardly be able to avoid picking up fragments of the person's favourite songs, and would have the opportunity to learn them, if they cared to. Martha Johnstone (born 1901) comments that '... the people sung them ... they were easy picked up, the young people easy picked them up, if ye were willin tae learn, ken?' (quoted by L. Williamson, 1985: 31).

This is particularly relevant to the big ballads, as they may in reality be better suited to such contexts than to platform performance. Greig comments on the physical demands of singing at length if the voice has to be projected:

---

34   A practical factor is that camping in the open air is obviously more hospitable to music-making and singing than the crowded living conditions of towns and cities. Betsy Whyte recalls that playing the pipes was impossible after moving into a council house: 'Even singing could be heard through the thin walls as plainly as if the singing was in the same room' (1979, 2001: 150).

> As we have before remarked, this kind of thing is dying out. For one thing, there is hardly sufficient leisure nowadays for recitals of this length. Another reason is found in the fact that no modern vocalist singing with a pianoforte accompaniment could well stand the strain of singing half a hundred verses on end. Lilting lightly by the fireside the singer of a bygone day could get through a long ballad of this kind without undue fatigue.
>
> G-D, note to Song 1062

Similarly, a G-D contributor, Mrs Harper, recalls her mother (born 1846) describing how she and her friends entertained themselves in their youth, gathering at someone's house in the evening, the women taking their knitting, and singing ballads, 'the whole assembly joining in or repeating the last line of each verse in order to give the singer time to get breath for his next verse' (Lyle, 2002b: 565). McCormick (1907: 14) likewise describes a Gypsy singing or chanting a song with 'a great many stanzas' and others joining in the chorus (see above, §3.3).

As a performance, the big ballads also make demands on the attention of the listener, as Rev. Duncan observes (quoted above, §6.3), but the audience in a domestic setting need not give their undivided attention, in competition with the demands of other adults, children, animals, the fire, and the sudden urge to make a cup of tea. Evidencing the need for singers who desire the listeners' attention to counter this tendency are Linda Williamson's (1985: 99 ff.) photographs and descriptions of singers catching hands or otherwise making physical contact with a listener, in a way that is rather reminiscent of Coleridge's ancient mariner.

Our analysis confirms that the collecting effort was timely. Even amongst the Travellers the Child ballad contributors are older on average, at the time of first recording, than contributors in general, although still younger than the core population ballad contributors. After the first decade of SSSA recording, in the 1950s, there are smaller numbers of new Traveller ballad singers, and while the number of types and tokens increases amongst males, largely thanks to Duncan Williamson and Stanley Robertson, both decrease markedly amongst females. There is anecdotal evidence that tastes were changing amongst Lizzie Higgins' generation (see below, §8.4), although in the circle around Duncan Williamson (born 1928) ballad singing was still a regular activity in the 1970s (L. Williamson, 1985). As Petrie (1997: 269) observes, 'a community with shared values and regular singing opportunities' is necessary for the continuation of a song tradition.

CHAPTER 7

Social Change and Education *versus* Tradition

7.1 Demography of the Contributors

Greig often uses the term 'peasant(ry)' to describe the social milieu in which he believes the North-East folk song tradition to be grounded. This usage was general amongst folk song collectors at the time, including the English collector Cecil Sharp, whose idea of the English peasantry is discussed by Knevett and Gammon (2016). Carter likewise uses the term with reference to what he alternatively calls 'pre-capitalist agriculture'. Carter acknowledges that 'peasant' is derogatory in everyday usage (1979: 4), and mentions that Sandy Fenton[1] objected to it (p. 8), as does Olson (1989: 85, n. 52).[2] The word's connotations of ignorance are at odds with the North-East's reputation for high educational standards (see below, §7.3). The negative connotations of a stagnant, inward-looking society – or alternatively the romantic image of an unchanging, unspoilt society, insulated from outside influences – are likewise at odds with the ferment of change that went on in the North-East, as in other rural areas, in the second half of the nineteenth century, with the arrival of steamships, the building of the railways, population movement into the growing industrial centres, the ongoing mechanisation of agriculture, and the consolidation of farms into large commercial holdings.

As well as objections to the negative connotations of the term 'peasant(ry)', there is also, as Bearman (2000) explains, a theoretical objection by Marxist writers to Cecil Sharp's claim to have collected peasant song, at a time when the peasantry as an economic entity no longer existed. Others prefer to write of the 'rural working class'. However, Sharp is referring to individuals, mostly elderly when he was collecting in Somerset in 1903 and subsequent years, who bore the last remnants of a peasant culture. He observes, 'The English peasant still exists, although the peasantry as a class is extinct' (Sharp ed. Karpeles, 1965: 150).

The pre-industrial rural population of Scotland, brought up on presbyterianism, was much more bookish than the equivalent population in England,

---

[1] Alexander Fenton, the distinguished Scottish ethnologist, who was brought up in the North-East.
[2] Greig's observation is perhaps also vitiated by his lack of personal connection with the local song culture: he was unaware of the wealth of song in his area before he began his researches (Olson, 1989: 80; 2007c: 333).

and one would certainly not wish to import Sharp's ideas about English peasant culture into a discussion of Scottish folk song. There are, however, striking similarities between Sharp and G-D in the demography of their contributors. Sharp collected from a wide social range, including, as mentioned above (§1.6), clergymen, prosperous farmers and tradesmen, and their wives and daughters.

Similarly, Olson points out that G-D's contributors 'came from all walks of life, including the middle classes' (1989: 85, n. 52). It is difficult to put figures on the social background of the G-D contributors, as there is information of this kind for only about 40% of them, but certainly at least 10% come from professional backgrounds (Table 7.1). Many of these, like Duncan himself, would have come from the countryside, or had family links to it. Even in the 1970s, Carter (1979: 5) observed, 'Aberdeen is a very rural city: its inhabitants' links with the surrounding countryside are deep and abiding.' There is information about the geographical background of about 75% of the G-D contributors or their families, and on this basis it can be estimated that at least 49% are from rural backgrounds (Table 7.2).[3]

TABLE 7.1 Social background of G-D contributors. Note: data are based in some cases on contributors' family members.

	Contributors					
	Male		Female		All	
	n	%	n	%	n	%
(Farm)servant/crofter	23	8	21	11	44	9
Farmer	28	10	23	12	51	11
Traditional trades	18	6	5	3	23	5
Professions	31	11	17	9	48	10
Itinerant	1	0	3	2	4	1
Other	14	5	6	3	20	4
No information	165	59	123	62	288	60
TOTAL	280	100	198	100	478	100

---

3   This is probably a considerable under-estimate. Even when there is relevant information, it is often ambiguous between a parish and a village of the same name (e.g. Crimond or New Deer). These cases are counted here as villages.

TABLE 7.2 Geographical background of G-D contributors. Note: data are based in some cases on contributors' family members. Since Greig and Duncan did almost all of their collecting in the North-East, the great majority of the individuals for whom there is no specific information are likely to be North-Easterners.

	Contributors					
	Male		Female		All	
	n	%	n	%	n	%
Rural N-E	140	50	97	49	237	49
Village/town N-E	51	18	47	24	98	20
Aberdeen	9	3	5	3	14	3
Not N-E	8	3	9	5	17	4
No information	72	26	40	20	112	24
TOTAL	280	100	198	100	478	100

SSSA is an eclectic collection, but nevertheless is heavily biased towards rural contributors, as Munro (1991: 151–3) acknowledges. This study does not attempt to analyse the background of the SSSA *contributors*, but a rough impression can be gained from the fact that out of 366 general population *recipients* recorded by SSSA in the data,[4] at least 89 (i.e. 24%), are known to be from agricultural backgrounds, though we only have information for 42%. To put this figure in perspective, 17.1% of the Scottish population were resident in rural areas at the 1951 Census (General Registry Office, 1952: 8), and 7% of the economically active population were in agricultural occupations (broadly understood to include horticulture and forestry) (figure based on General Registry Office, 1956: vii, Table B).

Of the 89 from known agricultural backgrounds, 31, i.e. 35%, are from the North-East. By comparison, in 1950 Aberdeenshire and Moray together made up about 14% of the regular agricultural labour force of Scotland, and about 15% of the agricultural holdings (figures based on *Agricultural Statistics 1950 and 1951 Scotland*, 1953: Tables 55 and 62). Rough as these comparisons are, they do seem to indicate that the rural North-East is significantly over-represented in SSSA.

---

[4] I.e. not including those for whom we have transmission data only at second hand.

7.2 The 1840s Birth Cohort

Sharp considered that the last generation of Somerset folk singers worth collecting from were those born in the 1840s (Sharp ed. Karpeles, 1965: 157).[5] As we have seen, this is also the modal decade of birth of G-D's contributors.[6] Sharp does not pinpoint any single reason for the perceived change after this birth cohort, but suggests, amongst other things, the opening up of communications with the coming of the railways in the middle decades of the century. The Bristol to Exeter line was built in the early 1840s, somewhat earlier than the line south from Aberdeen, opened in 1850, and the Great North of Scotland line, opened from Aberdeen as far as Huntly in 1854. He also mentions the political turmoil of the time, which pitted the interests of landowners against the bulk of the population. The First Reform Act of 1832 enlarged the franchise in England and Wales and did away with rotten boroughs; the repeal of the Corn Laws in 1846 reduced the price of imported food in the British Isles, also against the interests of large producers. Likewise in Scotland, there was a Reform Act in 1832; and 1843 saw the Disruption, a schism in the Church of Scotland over the issue of landowners' power to appoint ministers, and thus to exert social control over the parishioners.

The opposing class interests that were crystallised by these political struggles went back to the Enclosure Movement of the eighteenth century, which created large commercial farms and reduced to the status of wage labourers the sub-tenants (*cottars* in Scotland, *cottagers* in England), who were now deprived of the resources of the commons (*commonties* in Scotland). The importance of these resources for subsistence – pasture for a cow, fuel, materials for thatching and for animal bedding – is described by Bourne (1912, 1984: 77 ff.) and by Jones (1964: 30 ff.). Jones also describes the myriad small *ferae naturae* that could be gathered for use or sale. Sharp saw the Enclosure Acts as having deprived the country people of their culture ('their spiritual birthright') as well as of the land (Knevett and Gammon, 2016: 51, quoting a 1918 letter of Sharp). In the Scottish context, Devine writes of 'Lowland Clearances' (1999: 147 and *passim*). Most of the displaced left the land, whether to emigrate or find work in urban centres. Some were absorbed by new industrial villages. In the North-East, where there was still a frontier of cultivation, some were able,

---

5 He had a few younger contributors whose particular circumstances of life explained their being out of step with their contemporaries. Cf. Rev. Duncan (1908, 1974: 7–8), quoted above, §6.3.
6 See Figure 2.13 and Table A13.

with great labour, to break in small crofts from the waste, perhaps to be evicted when the landowner took back the now cultivated land (Carter, 1979: 74–5).

James Hogg, 'the Ettrick Shepherd', wrote that, whereas in his youth (he was born in 1770), singing was almost the sole amusement in the countryside, for the last twenty years he had been unable to persuade people to sing at kirns (harvest home feasts) (1831–2: 257), and in general he observed (pp. 258–9) that in Ettrick and Yarrow:[7]

> ... there is a change from gay to grave, from cheerfulness to severity; and it is not easy to trace the source from which it has sprung. The diet of the menials and workmen is uniformly much better than it was when I went first to service half a century ago. The tasks of labour are not more severe, but ... in general less oppressive. But with regard to the intercourse between master and servant, there is a mighty change indeed, and to this I am disposed principally to attribute the manifest change in the buoyant spirit and gaiety of our peasantry. Formerly every master sat at the head of his kitchen table, and shared the meal with his servants.... Every night the master performed family worship... The consequence of all this familiarity and exchange of kind offices was, that every individual family formed a little community of its own, of which each member was conscious of bearing an important part....
>
> But ever since the ruinous war prices [i.e. during the Napoleonic Wars, 1803–15] made every farmer for the time a fine gentleman, how the relative situations of master and servant are changed! Before that time every farmer was first up in the morning, conversed with all his servants familiarly, and consulted what was best to be done for the day. Now the foreman, or chief shepherd, waits on his master, and, receiving his instructions, goes forth and gives the orders as his own, generally in a peremptory and offensive manner. The menial of course feels that he is no more a member of a community, but a slave; ... a mere tool of labour ..., and the joy of his spirit is mildewed. He is a moping, sullen, melancholy man, flitting from one master to another ... and now all the best and most independent of that valuable class of our community are leaving the country.

In the North-East between 1750 and 1830, 'Society was remodelled, and people's ways of working, thinking, and relaxing all recast' (Buchan, 1972, 1997: 177). With the displacement of the small sub-tenants, the agricultural population of

---

[7] Parishes in the Central Borders.

the region fell by more than a third (from 38,610 to 25,224) between 1801 and 1841 (p. 186). Social class differentiation did away with the convivial winter evenings in farm kitchens when the farmer, his family, and his servants entertained each other 'telling stories, singing, making music, playing games and … posing riddles' and '[n]eighbours would drop in and various itinerants … would also enliven proceedings' (Buchan, 1984, 2013: 381).

The well-to-do evidently participated in the folk tradition in the past, but perhaps their most important role was to provide spaces and host occasions for singing and music making to take place. To what extent can we generalise about the decline of social singing and of occasions for social singing? If there were periods and regions where the spirit of communities was embittered or depressed – the Borders in the early years of the nineteenth century, the countryside in the last quarter of the nineteenth century (see §7.6 below), everywhere after the First World War (see §8.2 below) – was this a temporary phenomenon from which the folk tradition rebounded, or a permanent lowering of its vitality?

Clearly it was not the case that everybody ceased to sing, particularly at work or for their own entertainment (cf. §8.3 below). Singers from the Borders are not lacking in the SSSA collection, for instance Wat Thomson (born 1882) and, most notably, Willie Scott (born 1897)[8] and members of his family. Nevertheless, by the 1950s the SSSA fieldworkers looked to the North-East and not to the Borders for classical ballads. As always, we are dealing with tendencies and relativities, not with absolutes. The birth cohort of the 1840s was not the last generation of folk singers, though this generation does stand out in terms of the numbers recruited by both G-D and Sharp, reflecting their ability to supply the type of by then old-fashioned traditional material that these collectors were seeking.

Nor had the professional class or the large farmers and merchants all divested themselves of the folk culture, as the demography of the collections attests. Nevertheless, by the end of the nineteenth century, the rural entertainments that might be attended by all classes were typically concerts in village halls with platform performances, of the kind described, in an English context, by Bourne (1912, 1984: 141 ff.). Similarly, Greig comments that, in contrast to the uncritical fireside audiences of the past:

> Now-a-days we cultivate singing as an art, till as a rule in a company nobody will sing at all unless they can do it fairly well. And singers are

---

8   TaD ID 2894.

taking up a different class of song – songs of more pretension and usually with a pianoforte accompaniment'.

GREIG ed. GOLDSTEIN and ARGO, 1963: 10

7.3 Education and the Regional Culture of the North-East

The rural population of Lowland Scotland was not reduced to the state of demoralisation, deracinated from the old peasant culture without being educated in the new, that Bourne describes in his Surrey village: this may well be relevant to the contrast between them in the preservation of folk song, of which Bourne could detect no traces amongst his neighbours (1912, 1984: 142–3). The rural North-Easterners described for instance by Cameron (1978, 1987) and Ogston (1986), and earlier by William Alexander in his novel, *Johnny Gibb of Gushetneuk*,[9] are dour, abrasive, and self-reliant, not notable for *joie de vivre*, but, even at the bottom of the social hierarchy, not cowed by their social superiors, though their spirits might sometimes be broken by the losing battle to make a living from a croft (Cameron, 1980, 1995: 31). This part of Scotland continued to be particularly rich in folk song, including the big ballads. It also produced the songs known as bothy ballads, which describe the work and the people on specific farms, sometimes in celebration, sometimes in complaint. (Although Carter believed the bothy ballad was unique to the North-East, there are a few examples, listed by Olson, 2007c: 335, Table 20.2, from elsewhere in the Lowlands.)

The North-East enjoyed a particularly high standard of education in the nineteenth century, supported by the Dick Bequest, an endowment left by James Dick in 1828 that subsidised schoolmasters' salaries and thus attracted graduates to schools throughout the region (Cruickshank, 1965). However, most children attended only for a few years, and thereafter spent their time in the company of adults, learning the skills they needed for work. The Education Act of 1872 made schooling compulsory up to the age of thirteen, raised to fourteen in 1883.[10] The effect of the Act would thus have been felt by children born from 1859 onwards. However, we see no particular pattern in G-D in the 1860s birth cohort. For females the fall from the 1840s peak is interrupted by a small rise in the 1870s (see Figure 2.13 above), but this is attributable to family

---

9   First published in serial form in 1869–70.
10 With the possibility of exemptions (see above, §6.6).

relationships.[11] For males there is a small rise in the 1860s. These men who were in their forties when they contributed to G-D include Rev. Duncan's brother George, and the poets Charles Murray, George Bruce Thomson, and David Rorie,[12] individuals who represent a response at an intellectual level to the cultural changes of the time.

There was a contemporary recognition that the education system as it had developed in the second half of the nineteenth century was detrimental to the distinctive traditional culture of the region. Milton (1983: 85) points out that the 1872 Education Act was the culmination of a process of centralisation and anglicisation of schooling that began much earlier. An important development was national inspection from 1845 onwards. It was at this stage that pressure began to be placed on rural schoolteachers to speak English (as opposed to local Scots dialects) in the classroom (K. Williamson, 1983: 54). By the 1860s and 1870s a movement had emerged 'to resist the standardising, rationalising pressures of the age and in favour of the local, the idiosyncratic, the dialectal' (Milton, 1983: 88). Milton suggests (p. 91) that it was not a coincidence that so many North-Eastern vernacular poets were born in the 1860s. In addition to the three G-D contributors mentioned above, Violet Jacob, Mary Symon and Marion Angus all belong to this birth cohort.

The attachment of a significant portion of the middle classes to the local region and its culture may well have contributed to the strength of folk song in the North-East, along with the commitment of the many crofters to remaining on the land, and the cherished independence of the small farmers that Carter (1979: 162) points to as a reason for the strength of the local dialect of Scots, known as the Doric, up to the First World War. Holmquist, in his study of the Cantabrian dialect of Spain, likewise regards loyalty to the local dialect as 'a measure of integration into the traditional way of life in the Cantabrian region' (1988: 1). Some of the factors that he identifies (p. 25) as contributing to the maintenance of the traditional dialect would also apply to the North-East of Scotland at the period we are concerned with:

> a historic tradition of independence and self determination; an agrarian economy which limited the spheres of activity and the resources of the majority of the people; an inward orientation which, although a source of strength, could also be a source of weakness in dealings with the outside

---

11 Six of these women (out of fifteen with known or estimated d.o.bs in the 1870s) are the daughters of other contributors.
12 Rorie's parents were from the North-East and he spent much of his working life there (Milton, 2002).

SOCIAL CHANGE AND EDUCATION *VERSUS* TRADITION 125

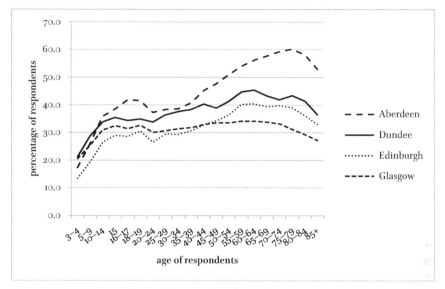

FIGURE 7.1   Percentage of respondents aged 3 and over claiming 'some skills' in Scots by age, 2011 Census: cities. (Figure from Macafee, 2017: fig.12; data from 'Table DC2121SC – Scots language skills by sex by age', in 'Scotland's Census', n.d.)

world; and finally, a tradition of marital endogamy, which limited intercourse with the outside world and produced a homogeneous society in which the slightest deviation from normal behavior [sic] could be considered an aberration.

If we can take the Scots language as an indicator of the strength of regional culture, it is worth observing that of the four cities in Scotland, Aberdeen even now has the highest percentage of self-identified Scots speakers, according to the 2011 Census (the only Census so far to include this question) (Figure 7.1). The North-East council areas – Aberdeen, Aberdeenshire and Moray – all have higher percentages than the Scots-speaking areas of the country taken as a whole (Figure 7.2).[13]

However, if the North-Eastern traditional culture had some resistance to the direct impact of a centralised, anglicised education system, it was no less

---

13   The Scots-speaking areas are identified as the council areas in the Census that approximate to the traditional dialect areas, as mapped in SND (see Chapter 6, n. 2), with the addition of Caithness and Nairn, where 2007 electoral ward figures have been taken in order to extract these two largely Scots-speaking areas from the Highland council area. For discussion, see Macafee (2017).

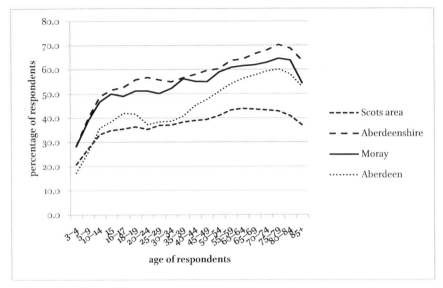

FIGURE 7.2 Percentage of respondents aged 3 and over claiming 'some skills' in Scots by age, 2011 Census: North-East (Aberdeenshire, Moray and Aberdeen) compared with the Scots-speaking area of Scotland overall. (Based on 'Table DC2121SC – Scots language skills by sex by age', in 'Scotland's Census', n.d.)

vulnerable than other regions to the more profound effects on the social structure of compulsory schooling into the teenage years, through the role of education in what is known as the demographic transition.[14]

7.4   The Demographic Transition Model

It has been suggested that there is an inherently antagonistic relationship between education and the traditional rural extended family, with the birth rate being the battlefield over which this is most clearly played out. It is difficult to obtain any hard data on how family life was structured in the past. Different generations or branches of a family could be closely involved in each other's lives without living under the same roof (Laslett, 1983: 93). As Teitelbaum (1984: 226) observes, in relation to his statistical study of fertility from 1851–1931, 'Some potentially important variables, such as the true extent

---

14   Also known as the 'first demographic transition'; the second being the shift to below-replacement fertility rates in developed countries.

of extended versus nuclear family structure, cannot even be approximated.' He nevertheless accords the extended family an important theoretical role in the maintenance of high fertility.

In its simplest form, the demographic transition model posits three historical stages:
- In stage I there is high mortality, requiring high fertility to maintain the population. The extended family is a major source of pressure enforcing the social norms of early marriage and large families.
- In Stage II mortality declines and there is a population explosion.
- In Stage III there is a decline in fertility. However, this last can only happen once the social and economic institutions traditionally favouring high fertility have been weakened, the extended family being one of these institutions (Teitelbaum, 1984: 3–4).

The role played by formal education is that it counters the pressures towards fertility and the conservation of a traditional way of life – which for societies before the demographic transition is generally a rural way of life – with an individualist and rationalist point of view, and inculcates 'the belief that life chances might be improved through individual action' (p. 213). The decline in fertility in Scotland does seem to follow soon after the introduction of compulsory education to age thirteen in 1872. The decrease in the birth rate begins in the late 1870s and declines steadily after 1880 (apart from small increases after each of the two World Wars) (Kyd ed., 1952: Plate A, p. xxxiv; Teitelbaum, 1984: 76).

Compulsory schooling has the immediate effect of reducing the economic value of children and increasing the costs of raising them. The effect on the children themselves is to influence expectations, and it was for this very reason that education was not always welcomed. The equivalent Education Act in England was passed in 1870. Evans (1970: 21) describes the resistance of East Anglian farm workers to formal education:

> There was no surge towards book-learning: on the contrary, there is strong evidence that there was a resistance towards it. I myself have been told by a number of the older people that reading was not encouraged in their homes; and in any case there were few books available for them to read; ... many parents discouraged reading; and three East Anglians who were born in different districts between 1880 and 1905 have told me that reading was frowned on at home as it would tend to make them dissatisfied and would take them 'out of their station in life'. The older generation, therefore, in spite of compulsory education persevered in the old culture which was almost entirely oral.

The Travellers long maintained the same attitude. Rehfisch (1975: 282) writes that 'education above the rudimentary level is not seen to be of any great value in the society, as indeed it is not. Far more useful is for the child to learn the ways and means whereby he will be earning a living.' Similarly, Bancroft et al. (1996: 13–14) observe that 'Traveller culture emphasises the application of oral/dexteral ability ... they emphasise the transfer of skills across generations which will enable them to create the potential for self-employment.' By the same token, Traveller children were expected to contribute to the family's earnings from an early age.

Wood's (1991) account of the parish of Forgue[15] would suggest that any resistance of the North-Eastern rural population to schooling their children was based more on the children's indispensability, even if only to free adults for other work by minding younger children, and the problem, in the more remote parts, of getting them safely to school and home again, when they had to wade burns, cross ditches on planks of wood, and trace snow-covered tracks through heather and whins. With the prolonged agricultural depression of the late 1870s–1914, the children of North-Eastern crofters and small farmers proved ready to make use of the wider sphere of employment opportunities for which their formal education had prepared them:

> The difficulties of 'the great depression' bore on all classes, but they had a particularly serious effect on the peasantry. Small farmers and crofters were forced to screw yet more labour out of their family workers ... ... increasing numbers of peasant children refused to suffer the burden of family labour any longer, and escaped to the towns or the colonies, often through the escape-hatch offered by the new state education system.
> CARTER, 1979: 177.

Especially large numbers left the land in the 1890s (Carter, 1979: 95; cf. Kyd ed., 1952: Plate B, p. xxxv). The North-East was not included in the Crofters' Holdings Act of 1886, and without that protection the crofting way of life did not long remain viable.[16] Also, as Devine points out, another driver of the rural exodus was the replacement of local craft work by cheap factory-made goods transported by rail (1999: 464).

---

15   In the old county of Aberdeenshire, east of Huntly and west of Turriff.
16   Sharp may also be registering the effects of the agricultural depression when he writes, in 1907, 'The evidence is overwhelming that, as recently as thirty or forty years ago, every country village in England was a nest of singing birds' (Sharp ed. Karpeles, 1965: 133).

The Travellers appear to have lagged behind the trend. Even in 1866, when family sizes were larger in general, J. Simson (in W. Simson ed. J. Simson, 1866: 10–11) remarks on the large families that Gypsies (the term he uses for Scottish Travellers) had. More recent observers agree that large families were the rule (Departmental Committee on Tinkers (Scotland), 1918: 10; Gentleman and Swift, 1971: 27, 29). A study of Welsh Travellers carried out in 1965–66 found that marriage usually took place when both partners were in their teens (Ministry of Housing and Local Government, Welsh Office, 1967: 28). Rehfisch (1975: 280) gives a somewhat later age for Scottish Travellers in his study, commenting that girls are usually married by twenty, young men by twenty-two.

Traveller community organisations both in Britain and in Ireland emphasise the importance of the extended family in Traveller culture and society (The Traveller Movement, 2019; Pavee Point Travellers Centre, 2010). The Traveller household is characterised by the Ministry of Housing and Local Government, Welsh Office (1967: 4) as a family unit with communal housekeeping and cooking; it 'might consist of more than two generations, might comprise more distantly related members than is usual in the settled community and might occupy more than one caravan or other dwelling.' Group camping is obviously conducive to an extended family structure, provided of course that suitable sites exist. The success of the Travellers – or at least that segment of them who continued to be itinerant[17] – in remaining on the margins of the capitalist economy enabled them to retain this family structure, along with the preference for keeping children out of school beyond a very basic level, integrating them instead into the family's livelihood.

It is not a coincidence, then, that the Travellers in the 1950s, and even later, exhibited a constellation of social and economic characteristics that favoured the continuity of traditional culture. Early marriage and high fertility, the early withdrawal of children from formal education, low levels of literacy,[18]

---

17 J. Simson (in W. Simson ed. J. Simson, 1866: 10–11) points out that, given the large families that 'Gypsies' had, and the limited capacity of their lifestyle to support them, it was inevitable that a proportion of each generation would have to seek their livelihood amongst the settled population. He attempts to use a knowledge of Romany words (or at least some kind of reaction to hearing them) as a measure, and comes up with an estimate of 100,000 people in Scotland having some Gypsy heritage (1866: 417), in contrast to W. Simson's estimate of 5,000 (W. Simson ed. J. Simson, 1866: 367) (c. 1846? – the book remained unpublished for twenty years). The latter figure is more in line with the estimates of numbers on the roads in the late nineteenth century and early twentieth century (see above, §3.4).

18 Illiteracy shows a significant correlation with fertility in Teitelbaum's statistical analysis of data for 1851–1931, where the variable used is the proportion of males signing the marriage register by mark (1984: 213).

family-centred economic activity in which children are involved from an early age, extended family living and childcare arrangements, and a traditional structure of authority within the family – these are the norms of a society that has not undergone the demographic transition.

7.5   Extended Family Song Transmission

We see this conservative family structure of the Travellers reflected in song transmission patterns. The generally high levels of family transmission for both sexes of the Travellers, and the contrast in this respect between male Travellers and other male groups, were discussed above (§4.4.5). The contrast is even greater in extended family transmission:

– 32% of male Traveller *recipients* participate in extended family transmission, in comparison with just 13% each of general population and G-D males.[19]
– The figure for female Travellers is 42%, in comparison with 17% of general population and 25% of G-D females.
– For all groups, the set of recipients who participate in extended family transmission is smaller than those who participate in nuclear family transmission; for the SSSA general population it is much smaller, especially in comparison with the Travellers. This can be seen most clearly when the two sets are compared in terms of ratios (Table 7.3). For the general population females, the ratio of recipients in nuclear to recipients in extended family transmission is 3.2 to 1, for the males 2.6 to 1; while for the Travellers the equivalent figures are 1.5 to 1 for females and 1.8 to 1 for males.
– The pattern for *pairs* is similar, with the Travellers of both sexes, and also the G-D females, having higher percentages of pairs sourced to the extended family than do other groups (Figure 7.3).
– With the SSSA general population we are reaching further back into the past to find individuals who learned songs from members of their extended families. The general population of both sexes have appreciably larger percentages born before 1900 for extended than for nuclear family *recipients* – 34% as against 27% for males, and 45% as against 36% for females – whereas the Travellers' figures for both family categories are very similar: 26% as against 24% for males, and 21% as against 20% for females.[20]
– Female Travellers have a relatively high percentage of family transmission *pairs* sourced to Generation 2 (the grandparental generation), in marked

---

19   See Table A9a.
20   See Table A7.

contrast to the low percentage of the general population females (see Figure 6.4 above).
- Female Travellers are notable for the relatively high proportion of *pairs* sourced to the same generation, Generation 0. Consequently, while Generation 1 (the parental generation) still dominates for female Travellers, as it does for all groups, it does not do so to the same extent. It is the larger number of pairs sourced to Generation 0 – which includes cousins and in-laws[21] – that puts the female Travellers slightly ahead of G-D females in terms of the extended family (Figure 7.3), despite the latter having a higher percentage of pairs sourced to Generation 2 (cf. Figure 6.4).

The high proportion of extended family transmission in the Traveller group, and the large range of relatives mentioned by the female Travellers in particular, together with their high percentage of same generation sources, are probably all related to the tendency of the Travellers to have large families, and thus large numbers of siblings, cousins, aunts and uncles.

TABLE 7.3 Ratios of nuclear to extended family recipients for all recipients and for Child ballad recipients

	Ratio of nuclear to extended family recipients	
	All recipients	Child recipients
Male core pop		1.9
Female core pop		2.0
Male Revival		n/a
Female Revival		1.0
Male Trav	1.8	1.5
Female Trav	1.5	1.4
Male gen pop	2.6	2.0
Female gen pop	3.2	1.9
ALL SSSA	2.3	1.6
Male G-D	2.2	4.0
Female G-D	2.3	2.3
ALL G-D	2.3	2.7

---

21   For details see Table A16a.

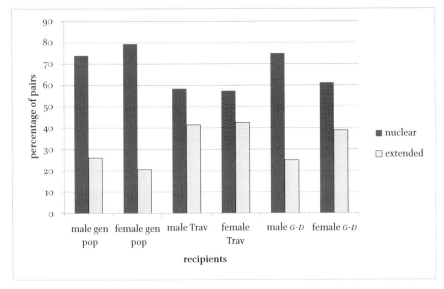

FIGURE 7.3 Percentages of SSSA and G-D family transmission pairs with nuclear and extended family sources
Note: figures based on 151 SSSA pairs with general population male recipients, 133 with general population females, 85 with male Travellers, and 131 with female Travellers; and 60 G-D pairs with male recipients and 104 with females.

7.6 Rural Society in Flux

The last quarter of the nineteenth century saw the exhaustion of the crofting way of life in the North-East and in general the demise in Scotland, as in England, of what George Ewart Evans calls 'the old prior culture' (1970: 17) based on local resources, traditional local practices, hand tools, and manual labour assisted only by horses and oxen. It is this way of life that is the background setting for much of the traditional folk repertoire, since 'Not so long ago the countryman was the ordinary man' (Jones, 1964: 29). As Evans remarks, 'There is ... hardly an object linked with the old prior culture, either through the work or the home-life, that is without some celebration either in literature or the oral tradition' (1971: 164).

The late nineteenth century is perhaps too close to G-D's period of collection to be reflected in the data: as we have seen, the peak decade of birth of the G-D contributors is the 1840s. On the other hand, the peak decade of the SSSA general population is the 1900s. Neither collection gives us a very clear view of the birth cohorts of the period in between.[22] There are, however, two findings that are perhaps to be seen in this context. The first relates to the 1880s–1890s birth cohorts, and the second to childhood song acquisition.

There is a small decline or dip in the numbers born in the 1880s or 1890s in some sub-sets of the data. This would be too small and inconsistent to take into consideration were it not for its recurrence:

– Figures 7.4, 7.5 and 7.6 show the percentages of *recipients* who participate in nuclear family, extended family, or non-family transmission. The pattern is particularly clear in extended family transmission (Figure 7.5).
– The Child ballad numbers are too small for nuclear and extended family transmission to be tabulated separately, but the 1880s dip does appear for most groups in the percentage who participate in family transmission in general (Figure 7.7);
– Combining the G-D and SSSA general population data, the percentage of male-sourced family *pairs* oscillates, but again there is a dip, for both male and female recipients, in the 1890s (see Figure 4.9 above).

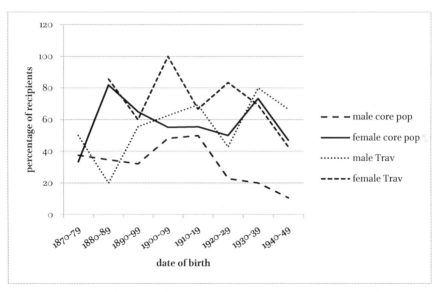

FIGURE 7.4 SSSA recipients in nuclear family song transmission as a percentage of all SSSA recipients, by decade of birth, 1870–1949 (known and estimated dates of birth, outliers omitted). For numbers, see Figure 4.1.

---

22 Cf. Figure 6.1. A similar analysis of the Carpenter collection ('The James Madison Carpenter Collection', n.d.) would perhaps fill this gap.

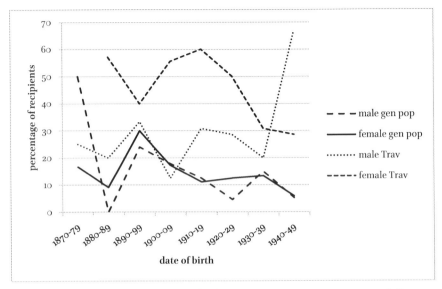

FIGURE 7.5   SSSA recipients in extended family song transmission as a percentage of all SSSA recipients, by decade of birth, 1870–1949 (known and estimated dates of birth, outliers omitted). For numbers, see Figure 4.1.

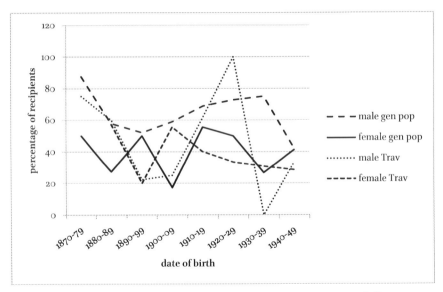

FIGURE 7.6   SSSA recipients in non-family song transmission as a percentage of all SSSA recipients, by decade of birth, 1870–1949 (known and estimated dates of birth, outliers omitted). For numbers, see Figure 4.1.

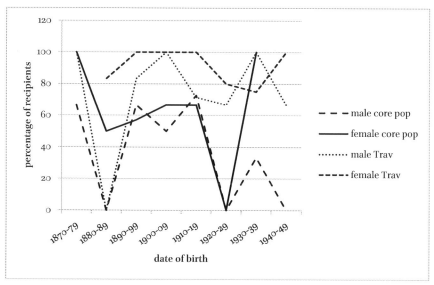

FIGURE 7.7   SSSA Child ballad recipients in family song transmission as a percentage of all SSSA Child ballad recipients, by decade of birth, 1870–1949 (known and estimated dates of birth, Revival recipients omitted, outliers omitted). Figures based on 46 male core population Child ballad recipients, 22 female core population, 26 male Travellers, and 34 female Travellers.

This dip in the 1880s or 1890s birth cohorts perhaps reflects the rural population flux of this period. It is particularly interesting in view of the relationship between (extended) family transmission and the persistence of traditional singing, in particular the Child ballads (see above, §6.7).

The second finding relates to the learning of songs in childhood (i.e. under the age of fourteen).[23] The childhood data have to be treated tentatively, as the numbers are small – 142 individuals in SSSA.[24] Also, this was not a question that was systematically asked in fieldwork, and being less salient, it might also be less regularly captured in the TaD summaries, although the person's age at the time of learning can sometimes be worked out from other information. It is fairly obvious that *family* childhood transmission, in particular, is subject to under-reporting; and indeed, if songs were learned from parents, grandparents, or other older family members, it would generally be redundant to state that they were learned while growing up at home. These data are also subject to the qualification that a contributor may have made a general statement

---

23   See above, §2.2.
24   See Table A3c.

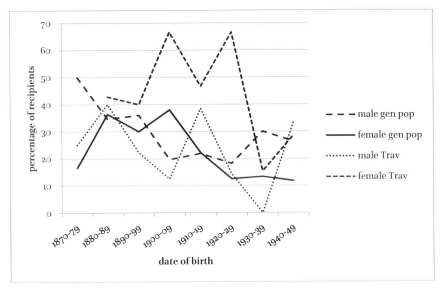

FIGURE 7.8 SSSA recipients for whom there is information that they acquired songs in childhood as a percentage of all SSSA recipients, by decade of birth, 1870–1949 (known and estimated dates of birth, outliers omitted). For numbers, see Figure 4.1.

(along the lines of 'I learned most of my songs from my grandmother') that makes it unnecessary to give sources for specific songs subsequently – and the data used here are based only on information attached to specific songs.

These reservations notwithstanding, it is curious that there is a consistent downward trend for general population males between the 1870s and the 1920s in the percentage of recipients who mention childhood song acquisition (Figure 7.8), whereas the other groups are more erratic.[25] This unusual patterning of general population males is particularly interesting because their non-family pairs are overwhelmingly male-sourced;[26] and even within the family, male-sourced pairs are in the majority for this group.[27]

The North-East is particularly prominent: so far as the geographical background of the recipients can be identified, at least 18% of the general population males are from the North-East, and 29% of the corresponding childhood recipients. Hunter (2002: 549), in his biography of G-D's contributor Robert

---

25   The numbers in G-D are too small to break down by d.o.b.
26   See Figure 4.3.
27   See Figure 4.6.

Alexander (born 1835 or 1836),[28] remarks on the 'curious feature' of Alexander's repertoire that it was all learned over a short period of time in his youth, as a farmer's son. Some of his songs from non-family sources were identifiably learned when he was a child. These sources include a man from Aberlour (Song 92E), a Highland farmservant (Song 130B), an old neighbour (Song 1024A), an Irishman (Song 1088A), and a tramp called Charles Farquharson. We do not know how typical Alexander was in having acquired his repertoire so exclusively in his childhood and youth, but if there was a disruptive effect on song transmission from the developments of the late nineteenth century – perhaps even from the 1872 Education Act – we should look for it especially amongst general population males, who in previous decades would have been joining the male workforce, or working alongside male family members on the land, at an early age.

---

28   Hunter (p. 594, n. 1) identifies a Robert Alexander who died in 1917 aged 82.

CHAPTER 8

The Missing Singers of the 1920s

8.1 A Bimodal Distribution

If the SSSA contributors were evenly distributed by age, the resulting graph of their decades of birth would look something like Figure 8.1. The numbers of the elderly and of young people would be expected to be lower, so the graph retains the actual figures for those at the extremes.[1] A large number of under-twenties were recorded in the 1950s, especially the second half of the decade, when recordings were made of the pupils in Morris Blythman's school folk club. Hence the slight peak in the 1940s decade of birth. Otherwise, the hypothetical graph is constructed by taking each half-decade of recording, counting the adults with the relevant decades of birth (i.e. those in the central age range, approximately 20–69) and evenly redistributing them across those decades of birth. The numbers in each decade of birth are then added together from the different periods of recording. The result is a fairly even spread across the decades of birth in the central part of the graph, with smaller numbers at either end.

In reality, however, the distributions of both sexes of the general population come to a peak in 1900–09, instead of holding up into the 1940s (see Figure 2.10 above). There is then a second peak, giving a bimodal distribution. This is much less marked for the Travellers, but they also have a slight dip, and at the same point as the general population females, the 1920s. The general population males continue to decline in numbers, taking their low point between the two peaks into the 1930s. As explained above (§2.6), the second peak of the general population represents the Folk Revival, which can be distinguished for the Child ballads sub-set of the data, where the contributors are better documented.

The 1900s peak, then, is produced by the uneven distribution of the age groups recorded. To some extent, this is a problem that all fieldwork-based research faces: older people simply have more leisure to engage with projects proposed by others. However, there is more than this at work. The general population are on average (using median values) older than the Travellers, suggesting that the fieldworkers were reaching further back in time with this group in

---

[1] Amounting to 9% of the data counted as elderly and 10% counted as children or teenagers (on the basis of known and estimated dates of birth).

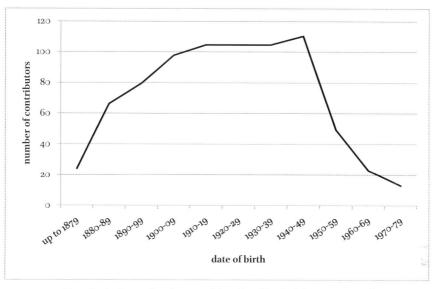

FIGURE 8.1 Hypothetical SSSA distribution of decades of birth if there were equal representation of adults in each age group, from 20s to 60s, at the time of first recording

particular, and there is actually a tendency for the median age of the general population to increase over the period of recording.[2] Even as late as the early 1970s a not inconsiderable proportion of the general population contributors were born before 1900.[3]

8.2 Is the 1920s Dip Merely a Coincidence?

There could be various explanations for the apparent dearth of contributors born in the 1920s, but one possible explanation that we can dismiss is any drop in population after the First World War. Births in Scotland were actually at a particularly high level in 1920 after lowered figures during and after the war. For the remainder of the 1920s they did not reach pre-war levels, but they were higher than in the 1930s ('Births time series data', 2017). It may, however, be a factor that the generation born in the 1920s grew up in communities devastated by their losses. An indication of the dampening of folk culture at the time is the cessation of seasonal celebrations in various towns and villages,

---

2 See Figures 2.3 and 2.4.
3 See Tables A6c and A6d.

where these were suspended during the war and not resumed afterwards. For instance, the Galoshins play ended in Darnick[4] and in Kippen,[5] and the Fastern's E'en ba' game (Shrove Tuesday handball scrum) in Kirk Yetholm.[6] Rob Watt, from the North-East, recalled that he learned many of his songs from farmservants in the stable or chaumer when he was a schoolboy, but some only later as 'the waar was on, the '14 waar – that stoppit aa the singin there'.[7] Bruford recounts how Ethel Findlater took him to meet a man who, c. 1914, was her source for a song:

> Not only had he totally forgotten the song, but his wife told us that she had never heard him sing in fifty years of marriage. How much this was due to a changed atmosphere in Orkney after 1918 ... is hard to tell, but there is no doubt that many others who had been singers ceased to be....
> BRUFORD, 1986: 111

Another possibility is that the dip is an artefact of the collection: contributors born in this decade might have been born too late to have emerged as notable singers by the 1950s, but born too early to have participated in large numbers in the Folk Revival. The 1920s low point may simply reflect the steepness of the downward trend from the 1900s peak. There might also be an element of antiquarianism. It is notable that the SSSA and G-D collections, at their different periods of time, both drew heavily upon the older age groups in the general population. Greig makes it explicit in various writings that he sought out older contributors primarily, in the belief that the traditional songs that he and Duncan were interested in were becoming moribund:

> The older people have pretty much ceased to sing the folk-songs of their youth, having long been taught to regard them as semi-barbarous compared with modern songs; while the younger generation hardly know the old-time minstrelsy at all.
> GREIG ed. GOLDSTEIN and ARGO, 1963: 10

---

4 SA1977.205.B3, TaD 42784; SA1979.91, TaD 87872. The Galoshins play was performed by groups of boys going door-to-door on New Year's Eve or Hallowe'en (see *SND* s.v. *Galatian*). Lyle's interviews on this subject are published in Lyle ed. (2011).
5 SA1982.113.
6 SA1956.134.B5–6, TaD 78665.
7 SA1960.249.A9, TaD 80209.

THE MISSING SINGERS OF THE 1920S

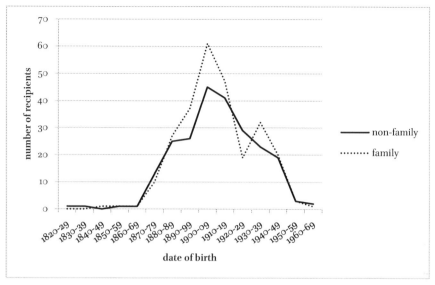

FIGURE 8.2 Numbers of SSSA recipients in family and non-family song transmission by decade of birth (known and estimated dates of birth)

The SSSA were not deliberately seeking older contributors, and their Traveller contributors have a d.o.b distribution pattern closer to the hypothetical one.[8] The SSSA were, however, seeking particular types of song, especially the big ballads, that were 'old'. The collection and preservation of antiquities was an intellectual framework that potential contributors could readily understand, and such a perception – that the motivation was essentially antiquarian – might have nudged the recruitment of contributors towards older people. As we saw above (§5.2), there is an association between the Child ballads and older women, in particular. Such an antiquarian bias – amongst the potential contributors, even in not amongst the fieldworkers themselves – would have had the effect of skewing the age groups.

The finding of a peak around the 1900s for the general population and around the 1910s for the Travellers, falling to a low point, usually in the 1920s, before the numbers recover again in the Folk Revival, is a robust one, and is largely maintained when the data are subdivided.[9] Surprisingly, even amongst

---

8 See Figure 2.10.
9 Cf. Figures 2.5, 2.6 and 2.8 for Child ballad contributors, Figure 4.1 for recipients, and Figure 8.2 for family recipients. The dip is not in evidence for recipients in non-family transmission in Figure 8.2, which is dominated by general population males, and accordingly reflects their more continuous downward trend.

the sources – to whom many of the explanations considered above would not apply – there is a slight dip for the general population in the 1920s, though this is only really apparent when the estimated d.o.bs are added.[10]

8.3   Singing at Work and Play *versus* Recorded and Broadcast Music

Buchan describes how, in the nineteenth century, the company gathered in a farm kitchen, shoemaker's shop or smithy in the evenings would engage in crafts and odd jobs while singing, story-telling and so on (1985, 2013). Until quite recently, singing was a habitual accompaniment to routine activities. Both Travellers and others recall singing, or hearing members of the older generation sing, while passing time in the evening around the fire, going from one place to another, going about everyday tasks, or minding children or animals. Douglas quotes Jim Wallace from Fife (born 1928) talking about his father (a farm worker?): 'People used tae sing quite a lot. In thae days, they didn't need much excuse tae sing. Even the old man – there wasn't a note o' music in him – but he was aye gaun aboot hummin away tae hissel' (Douglas ed., 1992: 92).

Bruford says of Peter Pratt from Orkney (aged 86 in 1966) that people who knew him well did not even know he could sing: '[I]t seems likely that he sang these songs to himself, at the plough' (1986: 113). Betsy Whyte (a Traveller born in 1919) mentions her mother singing while working.[11] John Argo (a North-East farmer born in 1912)[12] likewise recalls that his mother sang about the house, for instance while spinning, nursing his baby brother, or milking[13] Andrew Gibson (a Peeblesshire shepherd born in 1889) comments, 'Herds whistled and sang a lot. They were a happy band of men.'[14] John Strachan (a North-East farmer born in 1875) mentions singing while harrowing.[15] Annie Forbes from Caithness (born c. 1890?[16]) recalls that her father and another fisherman sang while mending nets.[17] Mary Smith describes how she learned 'Mormond Braes' from a man singing as he walked down the street.[18] Bell Robertson gives

---

10   Cf. Figures 5.12 and 5.13.
11   SA1974.243.B4–6.
12   Father of the song collector, Arthur Argo.
13   SA1952.22.A8, TaD 9359; SA1952.21.A5, TaD 19665; SA1952.21.A9, TaD 19673.
14   SA1969.187.B15, TaD 4177, quoted from the Summary.
15   SA1952.27.B13 (B22), TaD 10709.
16   She was married in 1913. SA1968.323.A13, TaD 24852.
17   SA1968.323.A13, TaD 24852.
18   There is no information about Mary Smith, except that she was a mother when recorded in 1961 (SA1961.38.B4–B5). Since the other contributors on the tape are Travellers, she may also have been a Traveller.

a description of how she learned songs as a child from her mother's servant, Meggie Johnston: 'She was very fond of me and took me with her everywhere. I liked her and liked to go but refused unless she sang and every night we went to the byre I made her sing the whole time of milking ...' (G-D, note to Song 987B).

Singing was also habitual in other workplaces besides domestic and agricultural ones. For instance, Minnie McPake (born 1908), who worked in a woollen mill in Peebles, describes learning a song from a weaver as she worked alongside her.[19] Douglas tells us of Dick Cowan from Liddesdale (born 1892): 'As a tailoring apprentice, he learned songs from his boss who sang as he worked. In the days when people had repetitive tasks and worked long hours, singing helped the work along and cheered the worker' (1992: 20).

Additionally, singing at work was often, as Korczynski (2003: 317) puts it, a tool, serving to set the pace of the work. Sea shanties and waulking songs are, of course, the prime examples of songs specifically adapted to this purpose. Korczynski writes, 'Like other tools in this [i.e. the pre-industrial] period, the songs and the singing voice were self-fashioned or maintained, self-owned, non-standardized, and cherished by their owners' (p. 318). As industry became increasingly mechanised after the late 1890s, and craft work was replaced by assembly-line production, it was the machines, micro-managed from above, that set the pace (Whitston, 1997: 214–5). In 1903 the American Frederick Taylor published *Shop Management* and in 1911 *The Principles of Scientific Management*. His time-and-motion approach (satirised by Charlie Chaplin in his 1936 film, *Modern Times*) also influenced management in Britain. Korczynski writes of a 'big split' at this stage between work and singing. Singing and whistling were not only removed from the workplace under this management regime, but might be forbidden and penalised (p. 320 ff.), though to what extent this applied in Scotland remains to be investigated.[20] When radio became available, the workforce were instead provided with piped broadcasts to relieve the tedium (p. 325). In the 1920s dip, and perhaps also in the over-representation of rural contributors, we may be seeing an effect of this silencing of singers in the industrial workplace.

More clearly related to the specific timing of the 1920s dip, however, is the advent of broadcast music itself. The birth cohort born in the 1920s was the first to be exposed to it in childhood (see above, §4.1). It is perhaps in the nature of broadcast music to be even more disruptive than the gramophone. The listeners' choice of what to hear is limited to the selection of a channel (amongst a

---

19   SA1969.187.B3, TaD 4161.
20   Korczynski (p. 321) gives examples from English factories.

very small number initially and for a long time); or in the case of piped music, there is no choice at all.

8.4   The Decline of Traditional Singing amongst the Travellers

Anecdotal evidence exists that even amongst the Travellers, tastes were changing in the mid-twentieth century. For instance Betsy Whyte talks about how being recorded by the SSSA led to her sons having 'more tolerance for the old songs that she sings'.[21] Lizzie Higgins (born 1929), the daughter of Jeannie Robertson (born 1908), also found herself regarded as an anachronism within her family. She says that her maternal grandmother Maria Stewart's eighty-six grandchildren were all beautiful singers, but preferred pop songs: Lizzie was the only one who knew folk songs. She was shy of singing the old-fashioned songs amongst her more 'with-it' relatives, but would sing along with her grandmother, while the others smiled mockingly. By contrast, she says, in her mother Jeannie's generation, the men and the women were all good folksingers.[22]

Similarly, Linda Williamson recounts a conversation with Martha Johnstone (born 1901) about the latter's attempts to interest her grandchildren in old songs:

> Mrs Martha Johnstone made an effort to teach her grandchildren her old songs but she was not optimistic about holding their attention. When I first visited her in 1975 she told me she had been trying to teach her youngest son's children, who were living in the same house with her, 'The Golden Vanity' (CH. 286).... she explained why she thought they were not interested in the song. 'Aye, I was trying to learn the wee yins but they would rather hae something ... they see too much o this carry-on on the television.'
>
> L. WILLIAMSON, 1985: 44

On the other hand, the group of Travellers recorded by Williamson in the 1970s seem to have been more retentive of traditional singing than Lizzie Higgins' extended family. Williamson (1985: xii) writes, 'Of the 136 travellers recorded, 102 recorded songs. Of these, 50 sang ballads.'

There is a very striking divergence of the male Travellers from other groups over time when we take the extended family recipients as a percentage of all recipients (see Figure 7.5 above) (though the figures are very small, so the

---

21   SA1978.122, TaD 64239, quoted from the Summary.
22   Summarised from SA1973.152, TaD 82324.

finding must be treated cautiously). The four male Travellers who constitute the surprisingly strong 1940s cohort all come from families who have produced notable singers:[23]
- John MacDonald, first recorded at the age of ten, is the grandson of Martha Johnstone (a prolific contributor of Child ballads).
- John MacPhee, first recorded at the age of fourteen, is probably related to Betsy Johnston, as he was recorded along with her.[24] Betsy Johnston was specifically sought out by Hamish Henderson as a singer (sleeve note, *The Muckle Sangs*, 1975; [Henderson], 1975: 11).
- Donald Campbell is the grandson of Hugh (Auld Hughie) Whyte (born c. 1889?), a source named by several SSSA contributors, including the tramp Blin Jimmie Bowie,[25] as well as members of Whyte's own family.[26]
- Stanley Robertson is the nephew of Jeannie Robertson.

This centrality of a few families who produced well-known singers is another hint that the Traveller singing tradition was not necessarily universal amongst this population, but was particularly associated with certain families, at least latterly.

Various comments by Travellers in the SSSA recordings mention a succession of developments in popular culture and media technology that were incrementally important in the penetration of consumerism into Travellers' – as into others' – everyday lives. Lucy Stewart (born 1901) remarks, 'After about 1910 American jazz became popular and the old songs were forgotten about, except in Ireland.'[27] Bryce Whyte (born 1914) recalls that his family 'took an old-fashioned gramophone with them while travelling' from which he learned Harry Lauder and Will Fyffe songs.[28] Stanley Robertson (born 1940) opines, 'Once Traveller families got television, the get-togethers dwindled away, except when they were out in the country.'[29] Small battery televisions were common amongst Travellers by the end of the 1960s (Gentleman and Swift, 1971: 58), and Gentleman and Swift state that traditional song had declined in consequence. MacColl and Seeger (1986: 34 ff.) likewise mention the negative effect of television on family get-togethers amongst the Stewarts of Blairgowrie, and

---

23   However, it is not necessarily these notable individuals who are mentioned as their sources.
24   On tape SA1956.169.
25   SA1952.30.B1 (B11).
26   Bella Whyte on SA1954.95.B7 and SA1954.95.B9; Donald Campbell on SA1961.38.B9; and Ina Allanson on SA1961.38.A1, TaD 37309, and SA1961.38.A9, TaD 37317.
27   SA1975.148.A2, TaD 39941, quoted from the Summary.
28   SA1987.10.2–3, TaD 78717, quoted from the Summary.
29   SA1983.47.3, TaD 70052, quoted from the Summary.

Clement (1981: 25) observes that 'Portable televisions in caravans have begun to supplant the campfire singsongs and storytelling sessions.' The bohemian lifestyle of the Travellers may have postponed – but only for a generation or so – the impact of recorded and broadcast music.

8.5   The Folk Revival

The efforts of song collectors in the 1950s and later were directed towards finding people who remembered the pre-mass-consumption song culture or, resisting changing fashions, still maintained it. The emphasis on the Travellers naturally followed, as their way of life delayed their assimilation into the consumer culture, if only for a generation or so. Similarly, in Gaelic-speaking communities, the language served to insulate the culture somewhat from external influences. Those external influences had two main effects: the over-shadowing, and to a large extent replacement, of self-made entertainment by commercial recordings; and the creation of a range of musical choices and associated sub-cultural identities.

From the 1920s on, youth groups, church groups and other civic organizations, joined periodically by the BBC, attempted to promote singing for pleasure, to compensate for the decline in home music making (Munro, 1996: 25). However, the best was the enemy of the good. Munro writes of the skiffle movement of the 1950s, which she suggests was killed by its own success, 'Young folk enthusiasts felt that there was no point in doing themselves what they could hear professionals doing much better' (p. 35). Commercial popularity also has a selective effect on what survives in the singing repertoire (Olson, 2007c: 328), and professionally-rendered versions of individual songs tend to eclipse other versions. Bob Lewis, a Sussex singer born in 1936, learned 'The Spotted Cow' from his mother. He described the effect of hearing Steeleye Span's version:

> I heard them live in concert on a couple of occasions ... After that, any attempt of mine to perform the song was assumed to be a copy of Steeleye Span which seems to have become the definitive version. Even now I am not totally happy that my performance is exactly the way I learnt it from my mother and may have become something of a hybrid.
> BURNS, 2004: 121

Folk songs were 'for ages the favorites [sic] of Nature's Judges – the Common People', as Johnson puts it in the Preface to vol. II of *The Scots Musical Museum*. That naïveté is not possible when a taste for folk song is only one musical choice amongst many, especially in the context of youth sub-cultures defined by musical tastes (MacKinnon, 1993). Even singers who come from families with a folk singing tradition must make a conscious choice to align themselves with the tradition. The Folk Revival attempts to perpetuate, but cannot reproduce, the pervasive, communally dispersed song tradition of the past. There has been a great deal of discussion in the literature of the issues of deracination and cultural appropriation that this raises (for instance Brocken, 2003; O'Reilly, 2004; Atkinson, 2004), and a great deal of division within the folk community about which aspects of the tradition are essential (MacKinnon, 1993; Brocken, 2003) – the corpus of songs, the line of transmission, participation as opposed to passive consumption, the style of singing (unaccompanied or self-accompanied on the one hand, hybridised with rock music on the other), or the political and social orientation (towards the underdog). By-passing the idea of authenticity, Burnett *et al.* (2017: 66–7) make an analogy with the business world, where a major change in the knowledge base can lead to a new company being formed. The spinning-off of the Folk Revival is similar to the formation of a new company out of an old one. The situational context and personnel of the folk scene are different from the old milieu of self-made entertainment, and the links with the old 'company' are historical, rather than constitutive. The new company has a life of its own.

The present study has attempted to separate out, as Revival singers, some SSSA contributors who are clearly associated with the folk scene. However, the distinction between Revival singers and others is not a hard and fast one, and with the advent of folk clubs and commercial recordings it became, as Munro points out, 'less meaningful with each decade' (1996: 51). Singers who grew up in the 1950s and after had the Folk Revival as part of their cultural milieu. In future work it would be more objective, and perhaps actually more valid, simply to contrast the more recent birth cohorts with the earlier ones. The bimodal distibution that has emerged in this study points to c. 1930 as the appropriate dividing line between the two groups, before and after being a 'folk singer' or a consumer of folk song became a deliberate choice.

CHAPTER 9

Conclusions

9.1 Issues and Themes

The findings of a quantitative analysis of singers and their sources have been deployed in this work to address a variety of issues and themes in relation to Scots folk song. Chapter 3 examined the question of whether Greig and Duncan somehow fell short in their collection efforts by not seeking out Travellers – as the SSSA later did –, concluding that no support was found for the idea that the Travellers at that time would have produced a significant body of song over and above the general repertoire. Chapter 4 looked at song transmission, including the role of literacy, and compared the results for the different groups in the study, particularly with regard to the balance of family and non-family inter-personal transmission. Chapter 5 addressed the question of whether women, especially young women, were more reticent in the past as singers in public settings. It first considered the possibility that the collections could have been skewed towards older women because they were more likely to contribute the sought-after Child ballads. While this did seem to be a possibility, an examination of the contributors in relation to their sources confirmed that men were much more prominent as singers outside of the family context. The role of women as domestic servants and as farmservants was discussed, and it was suggested that in practice the domestic, rather than specifically the family, context might be more relevant to understanding in what contexts (young) women felt free to sing unselfconsciously.

Chapter 6 charted the decline in popularity of the Child ballads over time, taking G-D as a baseline against which to compare the SSSA data in terms of repertoire and the chronological distribution of contributors and their sources. It found that the Travellers continued to sing the long narrative ballads for their own entertainment for only one or two generations longer than the general population. The cultural context of ballad singing was discussed in terms of the advance of modernity and the insulation against it provided by the Traveller lifestyle. The performance context was touched upon, and it was suggested that the long ballads were more suited to singing while passing the time than to platform performance.

A commonality was suggested between the Travellers and the rural population of the North-East: both were notable for the richness of their traditional song culture, which continued to transmit older songs as well as embracing newer ones. Both these populations clung to their independence and resisted the historical forces that generally transformed small craftsmen and peasants (if the term may be used) into wage-labourers. Chapter 7 considered the survival of traditional singing against the background of social change in the late eighteenth and early nineteenth centuries, and the effect of extended compulsory education in the late nineteenth century. It contrasted the conservative family structure of the Travellers, and their resistance to formal education, with the demographic transition that took place in the wider society. Chapter 8 identified a dip in the numbers of contributors born in the 1920s, marking the transition from the core population to the Folk Revival, and suggested that the most likely explanation was that this birth cohort was the first to grow up with broadcast music.

In general this work has inclined to a broad sweep, setting the results against the background of a dynamic struggle between the forces of modernity and those of tradition, with modernity always advancing but being slowed to a greater or less extent by the degree of resistance offered by different groups. On this analysis, the distinctiveness of the Travellers is mainly that they are time-shifted relative to the general population. Also, although this study has not attempted to make systematic comparisons between rural and urban populations, or between different parts of the Lowlands, the operation of stronger traditional forces in the countryside can be seen in the rural bias of the two collections, and in the over-representation of the North-East.

9.2 Summary of Main Findings

Even when some of the findings of this study are already well known, for instance the strong association of the Travellers, especially the female Travellers, with the Child ballads and with family song transmission, it is important that they are manifest in the catalogued material: the School of Scottish Studies Archives demonstrably constitute a permanent record of the basis on which the collectors formed their own general impressions at the time. However, this study has also revealed patterns that are not, as it were, visible to the naked eye:

- If the estimated d.o.bs can be relied upon, the modal decade of birth of the G-D contributors and recipients falls in the 1840s, and this is also the modal decade of birth of female sources, with males only slightly earlier, in the 1830s. This suggests a high degree of transmission amongst people in the same birth cohorts.
- The distribution of the SSSA general population contributors over decades of birth is bimodal, and the second peak is attributable to the Folk Revival,

with the trough falling in most cases – perhaps not by chance – in the 1920s, the first decade of wide exposure to broadcast music. A small dip at this point is also visible for the Travellers and for various groups of song sources.
- The general population contributors tend to be older when recorded than the Travellers.
- The Travellers are over-represented in SSSA not only in terms of numbers, but in terms of the amount of transmission information collected in proportion to their numbers.
- Although the family is the largest category of song transmission instances for the Travellers, instances from written or audio sources are not entirely lacking.
- Female servants are an important non-family (but nevertheless domestic) song source for both sexes in G-D.
- General population and G-D males agree in participating more in non-family than family transmission pairs, in sharp contrast to Traveller males. This preference is not so strong with regard to the Child ballads.
- The female Travellers are the most restricted to their own family circle. They are also the only group who have more female than male sources in non-family transmission pairs. In particular, there is very little transmission between female Travellers and general population males, in either direction (despite the latter being the main non-family source for all other SSSA groups), until the involvement of prominent female Traveller singers in the Folk Revival.
- Within the family, the parental generation is the main source for all groups, but less so for the Travellers, presumably reflecting the larger numbers of relatives and in-laws that come with their typically larger family size. Female Travellers, in particular, are unusual in their high proportion of transmission from family members in the same generation.
- In the general population, the percentage of recipients who participate in extended family transmission declines after the 1890s birth cohort.
- There appears to be a small dip in numbers in the 1880s or 1890s birth cohorts, particularly in the percentage of recipients who participate in family transmission. These individuals were born at a time of major disruption in the rural economy and rural society. The number of general population males who acquire songs in childhood also falls after this time.
- There is support for the idea that women, especially young women, were more reticent as singers in mixed company, until the emergence of young female singers in the Folk Revival. The general population females are on average older when first recorded. In non-family transmission, males predominate as sources for the G-D and general population groups. While

CONCLUSIONS 151

female Travellers are the largest source for male Travellers within the family, they are the smallest outside the family.
- G-D has a larger number of Child ballad types than any of the SSSA groups in the data (even if the very prolific Bell Robertson is excluded), but the biggest difference is between the G-D and core population females, with a 47% decrease in the number of contributors, but a 113% decrease in the number of ballad types.
- In G-D, the Child ballads are not associated with older contributors, or with transmission from the extended family more than the nuclear family, unlike either the SSSA general population or the Travellers.
- The Child ballads are more family-oriented in terms of transmission. Across G-D and SSSA, there is a very strong positive correlation between participation in Child ballad transmission and participation in family transmission. The family orientation means that there is less transmission, in either direction, between the Travellers and the core population (for Child ballads) than there is between the Travellers and the general population (for songs overall).
- The association often claimed in the literature between women and the Child ballads is not borne out by the number of core population contributors in SSSA, or the numbers of ballad types that they contribute in the data, but there are indications that this had changed over time. The core population females have their modal decade of birth two decades earlier than the males, in contrast to G-D, where there is no such gap. Combining the core population and G-D data into a single time series, the percentage of Child ballad *contributors* who are female falls sharply in the 1900s birth decade. The percentage of Child ballad *sources* who are female is 75% or over up to 1800–09 but falls to 33% by 1900–09.

9.3 Group Portraits

9.3.1 *Greig-Duncan*

A large proportion of the G-D contributors have unknown d.o.bs, which limits what can be done with the data. Fortunately, a fair amount of confidence can be placed on the estimated dates: 43 of the 109 are based on family relationships; several are based on knowing that a person was either a schoolchild or a elderly person at a particular date; and several others are based on information such as the learning of a song fifty or more years previously, meaning that when twenty years is added to allow for the person being an adult at that time, he or she cannot be many decades older than that estimate. (In other cases, where, for instance, the learning of a song is not so far back in time, the d.o.bs are treated as unknown.)

Amongst the G-D contributors in the data, there is a very similar sex ratio to the SSSA material, 59% male to 41% female, despite the difference in collection methods. G-D's contributors are from all walks of life, with at least 10% coming from professional family backgrounds, so far can be told from the limited information, and at least 49% from rural family backgrounds. G-D's focus on older contributors is reflected in the modal decade of birth, which falls in the 1840s. The G-D Child ballad contributors have the same modal decade of birth (in contrast to the SSSA core population of Child ballad contributors, who tend to have earlier d.o.bs than the general population). However, the percentage of contributors who provide Child ballads declines from the 1850s birth cohort on. Females, although slightly out-numbered as Child ballad *contributors* in G-D, provide more types and tokens, and more often provide two or more ballads. They heavily out-number males as Child ballad *sources*, the more so the further back in time. These findings give support to the idea that the ballads were particularly popular amongst women in the past, while not implying that male contributors or sources are lacking.

Turning to song transmission, G-D recipients and sources have the same or almost the same modal decade of birth (the 1840s or 1830s), again in contrast to the SSSA general population, where the modal value of the sources is at least a generation earlier. The G-D females agree with other female groups in having a higher level of participation as *recipients* in family than in non-family transmission, and in sourcing more *instances* of song transmission to the family.

While males are the most numerous non-family source for both sexes, female servants are a small but important category in G-D that does not figure in SSSA, apart from some women working on farms. This difference between the two collections reflects the earlier prevalence of domestic service, even in households that were not particularly well-to-do, before the decline in average family size.

Within the family there is a striking preponderance of female sources for females in G-D, perhaps reflecting the division of labour in agricultural households (and others similarly engaged in a family trade or business), which gave younger children of both sexes equal time with their mothers and grandmothers, but more time, as they grew older, working alongside their same-sex family members. The G-D recipients, of all groups, have the narrowest range of relatives as sources. While in all groups vertical relationships (with the parental or grandparental generations) far out-number horizontal relationships (with siblings, cousins or spouses), horizontal relationships form a particularly low proportion of the G-D data at 11%, in comparison with 16% for the general

CONCLUSIONS   153

population in SSSA and 20% for the Travellers.[1] On the other hand, the percentage of sources in Generation 2 (the grandparental generation) is particularly high. In extended family childhood transmission, female *recipients* are very much over-represented (though the numbers are very small at this level of sub-division).[2] Taken together with the unusually large proportion of non-family-sourced *pairs* identified by G-D females, these findings suggests a pattern of song circulation different from either SSSA group.

A disproportionately large percentage of Child ballad transmission information comes from females in G-D,[3] but the G-D females do not form so large a proportion of the individual *recipients* who contribute this data,[4] indicating that the picture is distorted by the large amount of information provided by a few individuals, especially Bell Robertson, Bell Robertson's mother (at second hand), Mrs Gillespie, Annie Shirer and Mrs Lyall.[5] The G-D males have a slightly higher level of participation, as recipients, in family transmission for Child ballads than they do for song transmission overall, but at 41% this is still well below the female figure of 71%.[6]

9.3.2   The Travellers

Chapter 3 examined all of the evidence for Traveller and other itinerant or vagrant contributors and sources in G-D and argued that the Travellers are not under-represented there. The findings do not support the idea that because the Travellers were a richer source of traditional material than the general population in the mid-twentieth century, they would also have been a richer source before the First World War. Two small exercises in comparison between the G-D and SSSA repertoires were conducted (based on Child ballads and on fragmentary material in G-D) and it was argued that this tends to confirm that the Traveller repertoire is largely the same as that of the general population.

Reason was found to doubt, also, the idea that the Travellers were the custodians of an oral tradition that was necessarily of great time depth. Embedded as they were in a literate society, and with literate individuals amongst them,

---

1   For numbers, see Table A16a.
2   See Table A3c.
3   See Table 1.2 above.
4   See Table A3b.
5   On the male side, there is only one recipient with a comparable number of instances, George Duncan, the Rev. James Duncan's brother. However, his data for song transmission instances are often in duplicate, as he frequently sources his songs to both his father and mother: both are counted here.
6   Cf. Tables A9a and A9b.

the Travellers recorded by the SSSA in the 1950s–70s were just as likely as any other contributors to have a printed text not far back in the line of transmission. Where they differed from the general population is that they by-passed what was described in Chapter 4 as the third stage in the history of song transmission: dependence on literacy to acquire and remember the words of songs.

At 22% the Travellers are present in the data out of all proportion to their numbers in the Scottish population. The Traveller contributors also appear to be rather better documented in terms of biographies, but this may be to some extent an artefact, as individuals about whom there is not even contextual information would be classified here as 'general population' by default. However, we do see the same pattern again for the Child ballad contributors, who are better documented.[7]

Although the male and female Traveller contributors have the same modal decade of birth, in 1910–19, a smaller proportion of the women were born before 1920 or before 1900. In this respect the female Travellers stand out as the group in the SSSA data with the most recent d.o.bs. However, the number of new Traveller contributors falls away steeply over time (both overall and for Child ballads). Together with anecdotal evidence of changing tastes, this suggests that the Travellers maintained traditional singing for their own entertainment – at least in some family circles and in some contexts, such as the berry-picking – only for a generation or so longer than the general population.

The Travellers comprise 29% of the Child ballad contributors. The proportions of males and females, both as contributors and as sources, are much more nearly equal than those of the core population, as are their ages at the time of recording. However, the numbers of ballad types and tokens recorded from female Travellers greatly outnumbers those recorded from males in the first decade of recording, the 1950s. In the later phase of recording, the balance is shifted by two prolific contributors, Duncan Williamson and Stanley Robertson. At the time of recording, the Traveller Child ballad contributors are younger on average than those from other groups (though still older than the Traveller contributors overall), and they more often produce versions with at least five verses, and have more than one Child ballad in their repertoires. This confirms the perception of fieldworkers at the time, that the Travellers were a particularly rich source for this sought-after type of song material. However, the percentage who provide Child ballads declines after the 1900s birth cohort.

The Travellers, especially the women, are very much over-represented in the song transmission data, in proportion to the numbers recorded. This

---

7   See Tables 1.1 and 1.2.

is especially the case with respect to family transmission, childhood transmission, and the Child ballads. The majority of Travellers' song transmission instances (especially the Child ballads) are sourced to the family. Male Travellers, in particular, differ from other male groups in this respect. However, a small number of individuals, mostly women, do also mention some written and recorded sources. The dip in d.o.bs in the 1920s, which may be attributable to the advent of broadcast music, is also present, though to a smaller extent than for the general population, in the Traveller data.

Female Travellers are an important source for male Travellers only within the family. This tends to confirm that the women were reticent about singing in mixed company (despite the success of the SSSA in recruiting female Traveller contributors in roughly the same numbers as men). Travelling in extended family groups would have meant that female Travellers nevertheless had ample opportunities to transmit songs. Outside of the community, however, their role as sources was negligible until a few notable singers were introduced to a wider audience in the Folk Revival. The Travellers who figure as sources for the general population prior to this are mainly hawkers, casual agricultural workers (in the case of men), and street singers (in the case of women and children).

The limited singing contact between female Travellers and the general population is reciprocal: whereas general population males are the most numerous non-family source for male Travellers (as they are for both sexes of the general population), the small proportion of non-family sources for the female Travellers are mostly other Travellers (prior to the involvement of prominent Traveller singers in the Folk Revival). They are also mostly female.

The distinctive characteristic of the Travellers' singing culture that this study has been able to substantiate – at least on the basis of the data used, with all the issues of representativeness, selection bias, and self-reporting that attend it – is the centrality of family transmission, for both sexes. The extent of song transmission within the extended family is the most striking difference between the Travellers and the general population in the data, especially for female recipients. It is, moreover, sustained to later d.o.bs, in contrast to the general population's downward trend after the 1890s birth cohort.[8] It is also reflected in the relationships of the sources, with Generation 1 (the parental generation) being less dominant for female Travellers than for other groups. In addition to Generation 2 (the grandparental generation), this group has a higher percentage than other groups from Generation 0. This no doubt reflects the larger families that Travellers had and the opportunities their way of life

---

8   See Figure 7.5.

provided to live in family groups. Transmission from Generation 0, i.e. horizontal transmission, contributes to the relatively late modal decade of birth of male Traveller sources, in the 1900s, only one decade earlier than male Traveller contributors.

There is a strong correlation between the percentages of *recipients* in Child ballad and in family – especially extended family – transmission. The Travellers participate at a high level in both. Additionally, for the Travellers, especially the women, Child ballads comprise a very high percentage of the *instances* of family transmission, reaching 48% for female Travellers in extended family transmission. The Child ballads also form a high percentage (38%) of the childhood transmission instances that are identifiable for this group.

9.3.3   *The General (Including Core) Population*

The general population, as defined here, comprises the Folk Revival contributors and what has been termed here the 'core population'. A distinction is made between the two groups only in the Child ballad data, where there is more biographical information. The presence of the Revival singers is, however, visible in the second peak of the bimodal distribution of d.o.bs. The first modal value is in the 1900s, a decade earlier than the Travellers. Numbers decline to a trough in the 1920s for women, and continue to decline into the 1930s for men. In Chapter 8 this decline was associated with the advent of broadcast music.

The North-East provides at least 16% of the general population contributors overall and at least a third of the core population Child ballad contributors. No attempt is made to ascertain the occupational background of all of the *contributors*, but over a third (31 out of 89) of those *recipients* who are identifiably from farming backgrounds are from the North-East.

There are indications that females in the general population are under-represented as contributors, especially in the first decade of SSSA recording: in addition to the large sex difference in numbers, higher numbers of new female contributors are recorded in the early 1960s than in the 1950s. Since females are similarly under-represented as sources, this appears to confirm a degree of female reticence in mixed company. The greater age of the women recorded (up to the mid-1970s recording period, when the Folk Revival reverses the trend) further appears to confirm that this reticence is especially characteristic of younger women. Female *sources* in this group likewise have earlier d.o.bs, in terms of the percentages born before 1900 or 1880, than the corresponding males.

The association often made in the literature between female singers and the Child ballads is not borne out by the contributors from the SSSA core population. Females from this group are outnumbered by males (though not to the same extent as the general population figures for songs overall), and they do not reach the same level of types or tokens as males. However, there are some indications that ballad singing had been more prevalent amongst the female core population in the past: as contributors they have a higher median age when recorded than males, and they have an earlier modal d.o.b both as contributors and as sources. Comparison with the G-D data also supports the idea that this is something that has changed over time.

Turning to song transmission, the modal decade of birth of general population sources is three decades (males) or four decades (females) earlier than that of recipients, suggesting less peer-to-peer transmission than in G-D. There is a strong association between Child ballads and family song transmission, but, like the G-D males, the core population males still participate as recipients in Child ballad family transmission in smaller proportion than the females, 49% in comparison with 69%. The long-term trend of the decreasing popularity of the ballads also continues with the males from the core population, who have fewer types and tokens in the recording period after the 1950s, despite the number of contributors being larger.

General population females are the only group who have a measurable percentage of song transmission instances from school or church groups. The general population males, like the G-D males, participate as *recipients* much more in non-family than in family transmission, and have a preponderance of male-sourced pairs. This population group is also the largest *source* in non-family pairs for other groups except female Travellers, suggesting that general population men were much more prominent as singers in mixed company than women.

As recipients, the general population participate far less in extended than in nuclear family transmission. In transmission pairs, the women have a particularly high level of sources in Generation 1 (the parental generation) and a particularly low level in Generation 2 (the grandparental generation). Those who do participate in extended family transmission tend to come from earlier birth cohorts, having a higher proportion born before 1920 or before 1900 than those in family transmission overall.

The general population males are characterised by their preponderance of male sources in non-family song transmission pairs, and even in family transmission they differ from other groups in having more male-sourced pairs. They are also unusual in mentioning more fathers than mothers in family pairs. Even within the extended family, grandfathers and grandmothers figure in roughly equal numbers. The general population males are also distinctive in their downward trend as childhood recipients between the 1870s and the 1920s birth cohorts.

9.3.4 The Folk Revival Contributors

From the data examined in this study, it is apparent that the recording of Scots song by the SSSA could easily have turned out to be a merely antiquarian pursuit amongst an aging population, mostly born before the advent of the mass media in the 1920s, with many born in the nineteenth century. Although the Traveller contributors in the data have on average more recent d.o.bs than those from the general population, the number of Travellers being added to the body of recorded singers also falls away after the initial recording period of the 1950s. The success of the efforts of the SSSA and others to bring the singers they discovered into public view, and to inspire new performers and create new audiences for folk song, carries the tradition forward into the Folk Revival.

Folk Revival contributors are defined, for the purposes of this study, as singers who typically give performances in folk clubs or festivals, or are recording artists. The younger generations of Traveller singers are not counted as Revival singers, since they preferred to identify themselves as Travellers, but some well-known performing artists in this group should probably be counted in the Revival. The view of the Folk Revival singers obtained through the lens of this study is an incomplete one. When they had been recorded at festivals and competitions, the TaD cataloguing did not always succeed in matching names to the voices on tape. It is likely that further research would produce better data. In this study, we have only attempted to identify the Revival contributors in the Child ballad sub-set of the data.

Most of the individuals counted here as Folk Revival singers have d.o.bs from the 1930s on, producing a second peak in the distribution of Child ballad contributors by decade of birth, following the trough of the 1920s. Younger females are particularly characteristic of the Revival, with fifteen females (out of 29 with known or estimated d.o.bs) under the age of thirty at the time of recording. Some of the singers born in the 1940s and later were involved as children with the Revival. For instance, Andy Hunter was a pupil of Morris Blythman at Allan Glen's School.[9] Gordeanna McCulloch learned 'The Cruel Mither' (Child 20) at Norman Buchan's school folk club (Munro, 1996: 84). Isla St Clair, the daughter of folksinger Zetta Sinclair, was recorded as a child singing 'Lord Gregory' (Child 76), which she learned from her mother.[10] Pat Bowley, the daughter of folksinger Ella Ward, learned 'The Twa Brithers' (Child 49) from Hamish Henderson.[11]

---

9   SA1964.40.A1, TaD 50838.
10   SA1966.113.A10, TaD 57242.
11   SA1971.297.A1, TaD 66762.

Between G-D and the Revival contributors, the drop in the number of ballad types is much smaller, proportionately, than the drop in the number of contributors. Between those first recorded in the 1950s and those first recorded later, the contributed repertoire of the Revival singers increases in rough proportion to the increase in numbers of contributors. Their ballad repertoire in the data, with 80 types, is somewhat larger than either the core population (71 types) or the Travellers (69 types).

In terms of *instances*, the rate of family transmission is very low, and reference to written and audio or performance sources correspondingly high. In terms of *recipients*, family transmission is again very low. However, we must treat these findings cautiously, given the small numbers of Revival singers for whom there is transmission data via the TaD cataloguing. Although the Revival singers have not been separated out in the overall song material, several well-known names do appear as family song recipients in the full data set. The majority of the non-family Child ballad sources identified by Revival recipients are well-known singers, including Jeannie Robertson, Lizzie Higgins, Ewan MacColl, Robin Hall, and Hamish Henderson.

9.4 Timeline

Scottish Ethnology since the 1950s, concerned to perpetuate and renew the folk tradition, not to write its epitaph, has perhaps preferred not to dwell on the story of decline that was so obvious to earlier observers, and that is ineluctable in the quantitative findings reported in this work. There does seem to be a long-term decline of popular interest in the big historical ballads, as measured in terms of Child's ballad catalogue. Otherwise, the decline in folk song that is charted here – and the subsequent revival in a different performance context – has been observed in terms of the characteristics, especially the decades of birth, of the contributors to the collections, and the changing patterns of song transmission that they collectively report. The process of decline proceeds at different rates for either sex, and for the general population in comparison with the Travellers, but all SSSA groups show some effect of the disruptive period of the 1880s–90s in rural society, and of the initial impact of broadcast music in the 1920s–30s.

The timeline in Table 9.1 summarises the findings in relation to birth cohorts. Numerous estimates and assumptions had to be made in order to convert often fragmentary information into quantifiable data, and accordingly, as stated at the outset (§1.6), it is the patterns in the findings, rather than the actual figures, that are of interest. The decades of birth identified in Table 9.1 may err on one

TABLE 9.1 Timeline

Decade of birth	Contributors/recipients	Child ballad contributors/recipients	Sources	Child ballad sources
1780s–1810s				The proportion of Child ballad sources who are female is 75–80% (Fig. 5.5).
1820s				The proportion of Child ballad sources who are female is over 50% (Fig. 5.5).
1830s			Peak of male G-D sources (Fig. 5.15).	
1840s	Peak of G-D contributors of both sexes (Fig. 2.13).	Peak of G-D Child ballad contributors of both sexes (Fig. 5.7).	Peak of female G-D sources (Fig. 5.15).	Peak of G-D Child ballad sources of both sexes (Fig. 5.8).
1850s		The percentage of G-D contributors who contribute Child ballads drops after this high point (Fig. 6.2).		
1860s	(Small) second peak of male G-D contributors (including vernacular poets) (Fig. 2.13).		Peak of female gen. pop. sources (Fig. 5.13).	Peak of female core pop. Child ballad sources (Fig. 5.6).

CONCLUSIONS 161

TABLE 9.1 Timeline (cont.)

Decade of birth	Contributors/recipients	Child ballad contributors/recipients	Sources	Child ballad sources
1870s	(Small) second peak of female *G-D* contributors (family contacts) (Fig. 2.13). Percentage of male gen. pop. recipients who participate in childhood transmission falls from this starting point (Fig. 7.8).	The proportion of contributors who contribute Child ballads drops below 50% (Fig. 6.2); specifically for *G-D* and gen. pop. contributors (Fig. 6.3).	Peak of male gen. pop. sources (Fig. 5.13).	
1880s	Dip in family and non-family transmission for some SSSA groups (Figs. 7.4, 7.5, 7.6).	Dip in Child ballad family transmission for some SSSA groups (Fig. 7.7).		Peak of Child ballad sources for SSSA groups except female core pop. (1860s) (Fig. 5.6).
1890s	Dip in family and non-family transmission for some SSSA groups (Figs. 7.4, 7.5, 7.6).	Peak of female core pop. Child ballad contributors (Fig. 2.5).	Dip in the percentage of male sources in gen. pop. family pairs (Fig. 4.9).	
1900s	Peak of gen. pop. contributors of both sexes (Fig. 2.10).	The proportion of Trav. contributors who contribute Child ballads falls after this high point (Fig. 6.3). The proportion of non-Trav. Child ballad contributors who are female drops below 30% (Fig. 5.4).	(Small) peak of male Trav. sources (Fig. 5.13).	

TABLE 9.1 Timeline (cont.)

Decade of birth	Contributors/recipients	Child ballad contributors/recipients	Sources	Child ballad sources
1910s	(Small) peak of Trav. contributors of both sexes (Fig. 2.10).	Peak of most Child ballad contributors, but not female core pop. (1890s) (Figs. 2.5 and 2.6).		
1920s	Dip in SSSA contributors (Fig. 2.10) and recipients (Fig. 4.1), specifically recipients in family transmission (Fig. 8.2); gen. pop. females cross below female Travs. in terms of the percentage born before each date (Fig. 2.11).	Dip in Child ballad contributors (Fig. 2.8). The proportion of Trav. contributors who contribute Child ballads drops below 50% (Fig. 6.3).		
1930s	Low point of gen. pop. male contributors (Fig. 2.10).			
1940s	Second peak of gen. pop. contributors (Fig. 2.10).	Peak of Revival contributors (Fig. 2.7). (Small) second peak of male Trav. Child ballad contributors (Fig. 2.6).		

side or the other, but, importantly, any errors are no more likely to affect one group than another in the data, allowing comparisons to be made between the sexes, between the population groups, and over time. So, for instance, when it is stated that the proportion of Child ballad sources is 75–80% female for those born between 1780 and 1809, this may be deceptively precise, but it is probably safe to say that the female percentage is in the area of 75% or more in the cohorts born around the end of the eighteenth century and beginning of the nineteenth, with the proportion decreasing markedly over time.

9.5 Directions for Future Research

The present study illustrates the kind of quantitative research that is now possible, with the publication of *The Greig-Duncan Folk Song Collection* and the digitisation and re-cataloguing of much of the School of Scottish Studies Archives. The quantitative approach taken here is a new way of looking at the riches of the collections. As emphasised at the outset, this is merely a description of what is there: the collections were never intended to be representative. The SSSA fieldwork can be seen rather as a series of trawls for the biggest fish in a great uncharted sea. The results are nevertheless more varied, and therefore perhaps more representative, than this suggests, as they also include a substantial 'by-catch' of material recorded incidentally in domestic or group situations. Greig and Duncan were also very eclectic, and though they sometimes took down only tunes without lyrics, they did not subsequently discard anything that came their way.[12]

In applying quantitative methods to collections that were never designed to be surveys there is a risk of producing a distorted picture of the singing tradition, but at least these are different distortions from the ones produced by the usual focus on prominent individual singers. The reliance in this study on estimated dates of birth has no doubt introduced numerous small errors, but since many convincing patterns do emerge, the data appear to be voluminous enough for these to cancel each other out to some extent. This study has established methods for quantifying incomplete information by using certain assumptions to estimate dates of birth, and by incorporating contributors with unknown dates of birth into a loose chronology based on the time of recording. It has established that there is a good correspondence between figures obtained from known and from estimated d.o.bs, with any divergences being readily explicable. The additional numbers obtained by adding the

---

12 Though a few items seem to have been lost from the collection (see below, Appendix B).

estimated d.o.bs are useful to level out accidental skewing of the data, and also help to compensate to some extent for an under-representation of women. Another source of distortion is the handful of very prolific contributors. At the same time, it would appear that, as far back as the data reach, it was a genuine characteristic of the tradition that there were a few individuals – whom MacColl and Seeger (1977: 19) call 'Singers' with a capital S – who amassed large repertoires.

As the present author is not a folk song expert, analyses in this study that refer to repertoires are based on existing classifications, in particular Child's ballad catalogue. G-D itself – specifically the group of songs that appear only as fragments in G-D – is also used as a basis for comparison with the Traveller repertoire. There is ample scope for future quantitative studies to employ more refined definitions of specific song corpora and to track the transmission of these within and between groups over time. In general, the data used here could be expanded by reference to the SSSA's original cataloguing, but it would not be a simple matter to establish how much Scots song material, specifically, remains to be catalogued in TaD.

The Child ballad sub-set of the data is better documented, making it possible to distinguish, albeit roughly, between the core population and the Folk Revival singers. The data on the latter could probably be improved upon by reference to the SSSA original cataloguing and field notes, but the available data are sufficient to reveal that there is a second peak in dates of birth in the SSSA data, which is attributed here to the Folk Revival. Imperfect comparisons have sometimes been made above between the general population in the overall data and the core population in the Child data. It would, of course, be desirable in future work to extract a 'core population' sample from the overall SSSA material. Alternatively, as suggested above (§8.5), the contributors (including those with Traveller heritage) could simply be divided into those who grew up with the Folk Revival as part of their cultural milieu, and those who grew up before this, the dividing line being c. 1930.

The transmission data has inherent weaknesses and biases, as it depends almost entirely on self-reporting, and is subject to under- and possibly also over-reporting of particular types of information by different groups. Another likely source of error is the necessity, imposed by the methodology used here, of confining song transmission information to that associated with specific songs, in order to extract comparable data. This no doubt leads to an under-estimation of family transmission, especially. In addition, the size of the repertoires passed on from one person to another is not taken into account, only the existence of a contact involving at least one song or song fragment.

Nevertheless, with these caveats, the findings provide quite a nuanced view of song transmission within the family, between the sexes, and between the general population and the Travellers. It would be useful for future research to compare and reconcile the two types of information, i.e. quantitative data, as here, and generalisations made by the recipients. Childhood song transmission is another area that might benefit from more intensive research, in particular reference to audio rather than to the track summaries.

It was suggested above that a distinction between domestic and non-domestic relationships, rather than the family/non-family distinction, would more accurately capture the etiquette of singing so far as women are concerned. This question might be pursued further, though it might not be possible to extract enough pertinent information from the collections for quantitative analysis.

The SSSA general population has been treated in this study as though it were a homogeneous entity, which clearly it is not. However, it is hoped that the rough first approximations offered here will provide a context for more precise and specific studies in future. In some analyses the G-D data have been combined with the SSSA general or core population data in order to produce extended time series. It would, of course, be more valid to take only the North-Eastern component of the SSSA data. G-D's contributors are very largely from rural backgrounds, affording another basis of comparison with SSSA, which also has a high proportion of rural contributors. Reducing the amount of data would potentially increase the effect of random variation, making patterns harder to discern, but the present study provides some context for the future interpretation of smaller data sub-sets.

The antiquarian bias of the G-D collection is visible in the findings, with the modal decade of birth falling in the 1840s. Since the ages of 'old' contributors are probably under-estimated, at least some of these probably belong to even earlier decades. The picture that G-D gives us is therefore at least as much a picture of the first half of the nineteenth century as the second, i.e. before the massive upheavals brought about by the railways, extensive agricultural mechanisation, and, in some parts, before the enclosure of fields released the older children of small farmers and crofters to continue attending school. It would be interesting, in future research, to compare those born before the middle of the century and those born after. Including estimated d.o.bs, the d.o.bs of 105 of the G-D contributors in the data can be placed before 1850 (22% of the contributors). If the unknown d.o.bs are also included the figure rises to 120 (25%). The recipients are a smaller body, but with the inclusion of the second-hand recipients they reach back into the eighteenth century. Including estimated d.o.bs, there are 49 male and 48 female recipients in the data with d.o.bs before 1850 (43% of the recipients), or 60 males and 53 females if the unknown d.o.bs are also included (50%).

It would also be very interesting to analyse the relevant material in 'The James Madison Carpenter Collection' (n.d.) in the same way as is done here, since it falls between G-D and SSSA chronologically (and partly overlaps with both). This might give a clearer view of the 1880s–1890s birth cohorts, who are somewhat under-represented in the data here, though it is not clear whether this reflects a decline in the singing tradition at a time of rural upheaval, or is simply a coincidence. The fluctuating extent of same-sex family song transmission is another tentative (and unexplained) finding that might repay further investigation.

The study reported in this work errs in the opposite direction from previous studies of Scots folk song by taking into account all contributors, no matter how small their contribution. It has thus been possible to utilise materials that have been carefully preserved and curated, but that are of little interest individually. It is hoped that the present study will thereby contribute to a more detailed and nuanced picture of two major Scots folk song collections, and through the collections, the tradition itself.

APPENDIX A

Additional Tables

TABLE A1a Status of date-of-birth information of contributors

Contributors' date-of-birth status

	Known n	Known %	Estimated n	Estimated %	Unknown n	Unknown %	All n	All %
Male gen pop	265	46	98	17	208	36	571	100
Female gen pop	146	43	79	24	111	33	336	100
Male Trav	70	57	23	19	29	24	122	100
Female Trav	54	42	42	32	34	26	130	100
SSSA TOTAL	535	46	242	21	382	33	1159	100
Male G-D	53	19	51	18	176	63	280	100
Female G-D	48	24	57	29	93	47	198	100
G-D TOTAL	101	21	108	23	269	56	478	100

TABLE A1b Status of date-of-birth information of recipients

Recipients' date-of-birth status

	Known n	Known %	Estimated n	Estimated %	Unknown n	Unknown %	All n	All %
Male gen pop	146	56	65	25	51	19	262	100
Female gen pop	81	52	53	34	22	14	156	100
Male Trav	43	66	16	25	6	9	65	100
Female Trav	37	48	26	34	14	18	77	100
SSSA TOTAL	307	55	160	29	93	17	560	100
Male G-D	41	34	33	31	45	35	119	100
Female G-D	38	35	42	39	29	27	109	100
G-D TOTAL	79	35	75	33	74	32	228	100

TABLE A1c Status of date-of-birth information of sources

Sources' date-of-birth status

	Known n	Known %	Estimated n	Estimated %	Unknown n	Unknown %	All n	All %
male gen pop	36	7	189	36	294	57	519	100
female gen pop	18	8	142	60	75	32	235	100
male Trav	15	13	75	63	29	24	119	100
female Trav	19	17	87	76	9	8	115	100
SSSA TOTAL	88	9	493	50	407	41	988	100
male G-D	13	4	75	26	206	70	294	100
female G-D	20	9	100	45	101	46	221	100
G-D TOTAL	33	6	175	34	307	60	515	100

Note: SSSA data include 49 non-Scottish sources (of whom three, all female, appear to be Travellers, and the remainder consists of 12 females and 34 males); but exclude 73 sources too vague to classify (of whom 34 appear to be Travellers), e.g. 'old people'. The G-D data include 8 non-Scottish sources: four Irishmen in the non-family category, as well as three whalers who cannot be confirmed as Scottish, and an Irish grandmother in the family category.

TABLE A1d Status of date-of-birth information of Child ballad contributors

Child ballad contributors' date-of-birth status

	Known n	Known %	Estimated n	Estimated %	Unknown n	Unknown %	All n	All %
Male core pop	53	67	12	15	14	18	79	100
Female core pop	30	57	13	25	10	19	53	100
Male Revival	28	62	2	4	15	33	45	100
Female Revival	24	59	5	12	12	29	41	100
Male Trav	34	76	6	13	5	11	45	100
Female Trav	32	71	10	22	3	7	45	100
SSSA TOTAL	201	65	48	16	59	19	308	100
Male G-D	36	38	19	20	39	41	94	100
Female G-D	35	44	22	28	22	28	79	100
G-D TOTAL	71	41	41	24	61	35	173	100

ADDITIONAL TABLES

TABLE A2a Numbers of instances of song transmission, by context of transmission

Number of instances of song transmission

	Family	Non-family	Time or place	School or church	Written	Audio or performance	Forgotten or vague	All
Male gen pop	287	528	96	7	48	69	9	1044
Female gen pop	262	127	32	21	23	17	4	486
Male Trav	164	57	19	1	3	4	1	249
Female Trav	355	90	23	2	13	10	7	500
SSSA TOTAL	1068	802	170	31	87	100	21	2279
Male G-D	188	221	176	1	10	3	4	603
Female G-D	630	486	120	4	45	4	14	1303
G-D TOTAL	818	707	296	5	55	7	18	1906

TABLE A2b Percentages of instances of song transmission, by context of transmission

Percentage of instances of song transmission

	Family	Non-family	Time or place	School or church	Written	Audio or performance	Forgotten or vague	All
Male gen pop	27	51	9	1	5	7	1	100
Female gen pop	54	26	7	4	5	3	1	100
Male Trav	66	23	8	0	1	2	0	100
Female Trav	71	18	5	0	3	2	1	100
SSSA TOTAL	47	35	7	1	4	4	1	100
Male G-D	31	37	29	0	2	0	1	100
Female G-D	48	37	9	0	3	0	1	100
G-D TOTAL	43	37	16	0	3	0	1	100

Note: for numbers, see Table A2a.

TABLE A2C Numbers of instances of Child ballad transmission, by context of transmission

Number of instances of song transmission (Child ballads)

	Family	Non-family	Time or place	School or church	Written	Audio or performance	Forgotten/ vague	All
Male core pop	44	50	5	0	7	4	2	112
Female core pop	44	14	0	2	1	0	0	61
Male Revival	1	7	2	0	8	6	0	24
Female Revival	2	12	1	1	1	3	0	20
Male Trav	65	9	5	0	2	1	1	83
Female Trav	128	26	7	1	3	1	1	167
Male gen pop	45	57	7	0	15	10	2	136
Female gen pop	46	26	1	3	2	3	0	81
SSSA TOTAL	284	118	20	4	22	15	4	467
Male G-D	34	21	22	0	3	0	0	80
Female G-D	167	76	13	0	10	0	2	268
G-D TOTAL	201	97	35	0	13	0	2	348

TABLE A2d Percentages of instances of Child ballad transmission, by context of transmission

Percentage of instances of song transmission (Child ballads)

	Family	Non-family	Time or place	School or church	Written	Audio or performance	Forgotten/ vague	All
Male core pop	39	45	4	0	6	4	2	100
Female core pop	72	23	0	3	2	0	0	100
Male Revival	4	29	8	0	33	25	0	100
Female Revival	10	60	5	5	5	15	0	100
Male Trav	78	11	6	0	2	1	1	100
Female Trav	77	16	4	1	2	1	1	100

ADDITIONAL TABLES

TABLE A2d   Percentages of instances of Child ballad transmission, by context of transmission (*cont.*)

Percentage of instances of song transmission (Child ballads)

	Family	Non-family	Time or place	School or church	Written	Audio or performance	Forgotten/ vague	All
Male gen pop	33	42	5	0	11	7	1	100
Female gen pop	57	32	1	4	2	4	0	100
ALL SSSA	61	25	4	1	5	3	1	100
Male G-D	43	27	27	0	4	0	0	100
Female G-D	62	28	5	0	4	0	1	100
ALL G-D	58	28	10	0	4	0	1	100

Note: for numbers, see Table A2c.

TABLE A2e   Numbers of family, non-family, and childhood transmission instances

Number of instances of song transmission

	All	Non-family	Family	Nuclear	Extended	Childhood
Male gen pop	1044	528	287	223	61	138
Female gen pop	486	127	262	207	53	51
Male Trav	249	57	164	98	65	32
Female Trav	500	90	355	231	116	125
ALL SSSA	2279	802	1068	759	295	346
Male G-D a	603	221	188	167	21	103
Female G-D a	1303	486	630	522	107	153
ALL G-D a	1906	707	818	689	128	256
Male G-D b						103
Female G-D b						200
ALL G-D b						303

Note: G-D figures are given without (a) and with (b) the ambiguous 'girlhood' data (see text, §2.2). The numbers of nuclear and extended family instances do not add up to the numbers of family instances as a few are too vague to classify.

TABLE A2f Child ballad inter-personal transmission instances as percentages of all inter-personal transmission instances

Percentage of instances of song transmission

	All	Non-family	Family	Nuclear family	Extended family	Childhood
Male gen pop	13	11	16	13	25	17
Female gen pop	17	20	18	14	30	18
Male Trav	33	16	40	36	46	22
Female Trav	33	29	36	31	48	38
SSSA TOTAL	20	15	27	22	40	25
Male G-D a	13	10	18	18	14	18
Female G-D a	21	16	27	27	24	22
G-D TOTAL a	18	14	25	25	23	21
Male G-D b						18
Female G-D b						24
G-D TOTAL b						22

Note: since the distinction between the core population and the Revival contributors is only made for the Child ballads, percentages are calculated here for the combined category, the general population. For numbers, see Table A2e.

TABLE A3a Numbers and percentages of SSSA and G-D contributors and recipients as distributed across the demographic groups

	Contributors		Recipients									
	All		All		Non-family		Family		Nuclear family		Extended family	
	n	%	n	%	n	%	n	%	n	%	n	%
Male gen pop	571	49	262	47	155	58	108	35	87	34	34	30
Female gen pop	336	29	156	28	54	20	95	31	82	32	26	23
Male Trav	122	11	65	12	28	10	46	15	37	15	21	19
Female Trav	130	11	77	14	32	12	62	20	49	19	32	28
All males	693	60	327	58	183	68	154	50	124	49	55	49
All females	466	40	233	42	86	32	157	50	131	51	58	51
All gen pop	907	78	418	75	209	78	204	66	169	66	60	53

ADDITIONAL TABLES

TABLE A3a Numbers and percentages of SSSA and G-D contributors and recipients (*cont.*)

	Contributors		Recipients									
	All		All		Non-family		Family		Nuclear family		Extended family	
	n	%	n	%	n	%	n	%	n	%	n	%
All Trav	252	22	142	25	60	22	108	35	86	34	53	47
SSSA TOTAL	1159	100	560	100	269	100	311	100	255	100	113	100
Male G-D	280	59	119	52	67	60	46	42	35	36	16	37
Female G-D	198	41	109	48	44	40	63	58	63	64	27	63
G-D TOTAL	478	100	228	100	111	100	109	100	98	100	43	100

Note: categories are not mutually exclusive. In calculating the numbers of recipients in nuclear and extended family transmission, three individuals (one each of M gen pop, F gen pop, and F Trav) have been omitted, as the information available is too vague to identify which category or categories they belong to.

TABLE A3b Numbers and percentages of SSSA and G-D Child ballad contributors and recipients as distributed across the demographic groups

	Child contributors		Child recipients									
	All		All		Non-family		Family		Nuclear family		Extended family	
	n	%	n	%	n	%	n	%	n	%	n	%
Male core pop	79	26	51	31	19	40	25	25	17	22	9	19
Female core pop	53	17	29	18	6	13	20	20	16	21	8	17
Male Revival	45	15	8	5	5	11	1	1	1	1	0	0
Female Revival	41	13	13	8	10	21	2	2	1	1	1	2
Male Trav	45	15	27	16	3	6	22	22	15	20	10	21
Female Trav	45	15	37	22	4	9	32	31	26	34	19	40
Male gen pop	124	40	59	36	24	51	26	25	18	24	9	19
Female gen pop	94	31	42	25	16	34	22	22	17	22	9	19
All males	169	55	86	52	27	57	48	47	33	43	19	40
All females	139	45	79	48	20	43	54	53	43	57	28	60
All core pop	132	43	80	48	25	53	45	44	33	43	17	36

TABLE A3b Numbers and percentages of SSSA and G-D Child ballad contributors and recipients (cont.)

	Child contributors		Child recipients									
	All		All		Non-family		Family		Nuclear family		Extended family	
	n	%	n	%	n	%	n	%	n	%	n	%
All Revival	86	28	21	13	15	32	3	3	2	3	1	2
All gen pop	218	71	101	61	40	85	48	47	35	46	18	38
All Trav	90	29	64	39	7	15	54	53	41	54	29	62
SSSA TOTAL	308	100	165	100	47	100	102	100	76	100	47	100
Male G-D	94	54	34	45	15	54	14	32	12	34	3	23
Female G-D	79	46	42	55	13	46	30	68	23	66	10	77
G-D TOTAL	173	100	76	100	28	100	44	100	35	100	13	100

Note: categories are not mutually exclusive.

TABLE A3c Numbers and percentages of SSSA and G-D childhood recipients as distributed across the demographic groups

	Childhood recipients									
	All		Non-family		Family		Nuclear family		Extended family	
	n	%	n	%	n	%	n	%	n	%
Male gen pop	62	44	26	55	20	28	17	30	8	28
Female gen pop	37	26	9	19	18	25	16	29	2	7
Male Trav	16	11	5	11	10	14	7	13	7	24
Female Trav	27	19	7	15	23	32	16	29	12	41
All males	78	55	31	66	30	42	24	43	15	52
All females	64	45	16	34	41	58	32	57	14	48
All gen pop	99	70	35	74	38	54	33	59	10	34
All Trav	43	30	12	26	33	46	23	41	19	66
SSSA TOTAL	142	100	47	100	71	100	56	100	29	100
Male G-D a	32	60	12	52	10	50	8	53	2	17
Female G-D a	21	40	11	48	10	50	7	47	10	83

ADDITIONAL TABLES

TABLE A3C Numbers and percentages of SSSA and *G-D* childhood recipients (*cont.*)

	Childhood recipients									
	All		Non-family		Family		Nuclear family		Extended family	
	n	%	n	%	n	%	n	%	n	%
G-D TOTAL a	53	100	23	100	20	100	15	100	12	100
Male *G-D* b	32	52	12	48	10	48	8	50	2	17
Female *G-D* b	29	48	13	52	11	52	8	50	10	83
G-D TOTAL b	61	100	25	100	21	100	16	100	12	100

Note: *G-D* figures are given without (a) and with (b) the ambiguous 'girlhood' data (see text, §2.2).

TABLE A3d Numbers and percentages of SSSA and *G-D* childhood Child ballad recipients as distributed across the demographic groups

	Child childhood recipients	
	n	%
Male core pop	7	23
Female core pop	6	19
Male Revival	1	3
Female Revival	1	3
Male Trav	5	16
Female Trav	11	35
Male gen pop	8	26
Female gen pop	7	23
All males	13	42
All females	18	58
All core pop	13	42
All Revival	2	6
All gen pop	15	48
All Trav	16	52
SSSA TOTAL	31	100
Male *G-D* a	14	70
Female *G-D* a	6	30
G-D TOTAL a	20	100

TABLE A3d   Numbers and percentages of childhood Child ballad recipients (*cont.*)

	Child childhood recipients	
	n	%
Male G-D b	14	61
Female G-D b	9	39
G-D TOTAL b	23	100

Note: G-D figures are given without (a) and with (b) the ambiguous 'girlhood' data (see text, §2.2).

TABLE A4a   Numbers and percentages of SSSA and G-D inter-personal sources as distributed across the demographic groups

	Sources									
	All		Non-family		Family		Nuclear family		Extended family	
	n	%	n	%	n	%	n	%	n	%
Male gen pop	519	53	387	70	134	30	99	33	34	24
Female gen pop	235	24	102	18	136	31	101	34	37	26
Male Trav	119	12	41	7	80	18	49	16	31	22
Female Trav	115	12	26	5	92	21	51	17	39	28
All males	638	65	428	77	214	48	148	49	65	46
All females	350	35	128	23	228	52	152	51	76	54
All gen pop	754	76	489	88	270	61	200	67	71	50
All Trav	234	24	67	12	172	39	100	33	70	50
SSSA TOTAL	988	100	556	100	442	100	300	100	141	100
Male G-D	294	57	237	64	58	40	42	43	16	34
Female G-D	221	43	136	36	87	60	56	57	31	66
G-D TOTAL	515	100	373	100	145	100	98	100	47	100

Note: SSSA data include 49 non-Scottish sources, of whom three appear to be Travellers. They exclude 71 sources too vague to classify, of whom ten appear to be general population family sources, eleven Traveller family sources, 23 general population non-family sources, and six Traveller non-family sources, leaving 21 very vague such as 'old folk' or '(old) Travellers', of whom some of the 17 that are Traveller sources, in particular, are probably family sources. The G-D data include 8 non-Scottish sources: 7 males in the non-family category, and an Irish grandmother in the family category. Categories are not mutually exclusive, e.g. an individual can figure as a family source for one recipient and as a non-family source for another.

ADDITIONAL TABLES

TABLE A4b Numbers and percentages of SSSA and G-D Child ballad inter-personal sources as distributed across the demographic groups

	\multicolumn{10}{c}{Child ballad sources}
	\multicolumn{2}{c}{All}	\multicolumn{2}{c}{Non-family}	\multicolumn{2}{c}{Family}	\multicolumn{2}{c}{Nuclear family}	\multicolumn{2}{c}{Extended family}
	n	%	n	%	n	%	n	%	n	%
Male core pop	66	29	42	51	24	16	12	13	12	19
Female core pop	46	20	11	13	35	24	25	27	10	16
Male Revival	7	3	7	9	0	0	0	0	0	0
Female Revival	3	1	2	2	1	1	1	1	0	0
Male Trav	49	22	8	10	41	28	23	25	20	32
Female Trav	56	25	12	15	46	31	30	33	20	32
Male gen pop	73	32	49	60	24	16	12	13	12	19
Female gen pop	49	22	13	16	36	24	26	29	10	16
All males	122	54	57	70	65	44	35	38	32	52
All females	107	47	25	30	82	56	56	62	30	48
All core pop	112	49	53	65	59	40	37	41	22	35
All Revival	10	4	9	11	1	1	1	1	0	0
All gen pop	122	54	62	76	60	41	38	42	22	35
All Trav	105	46	20	24	87	59	53	58	40	65
SSSA TOTAL	227	100	82	100	147	100	91	100	62	100
Male G-D	40	36	26	41	12	26	10	29	2	15
Female G-D	72	64	38	59	35	74	25	71	11	85
G-D TOTAL	112	100	64	100	47	100	35	100	13	100

Note: the SSSA data include 16 non-Scottish sources (of whom one is a female Traveller, one a female Revival singer, and the remainder are male, including four song collectors and/or Revival singers); the data exclude 16 sources too vague to classify (of whom two appear to be core population family sources, two Traveller family sources, five core population non-family sources, and seven Traveller non-family sources). Categories are not mutually exclusive: see note to Table A4a.

TABLE A5a Percentages of SSSA contributors born before 1900 and before 1920 (known dates of birth only)

	All n	%	Percentage of contributors Pre-1900 %	Pre-1920 %
Male gen pop	265	100	22	54
Female gen pop	146	100	23	49
Male Trav	70	100	26	56
Female Trav	54	100	15	48
TOTAL	535	100	22	52

TABLE A5b Percentages of SSSA contributors born before 1900 and before 1920 (known and estimated dates of birth)

	All n	%	Percentage of contributors Pre-1900 %	Pre-1920 %
Male gen pop	363	100	20	54
Female gen pop	225	100	24	54
Male Trav	93	100	24	53
Female Trav	96	100	17	47
TOTAL	777	100	21	53

ADDITIONAL TABLES

TABLE A5C Percentages of SSSA Child ballad contributors born before 1900 and 1920 (known and estimated dates of birth)

	All		Percentage of Child ballad contributors	
			Pre-1900	Pre-1920
	n	%	%	%
Male core pop	65	100	32	85
Female core pop	43	100	51	79
Male Revival	30	100	3	13
Female Revival	29	100	0	14
Male Trav	40	100	28	65
Female Trav	42	100	26	69
Male gen pop	95	100	23	62
Female gen pop	72	100	31	53
TOTAL	249	100	27	61

TABLE A6a Percentages of SSSA contributors born before 1920, by date of first recording (known dates of birth only)

Contributors

Recording date	Male gen pop		Female gen pop		Male Trav		Female Trav		All	
	n	%	n	%	n	%	n	%	n	%
1951–54	51	63	15	40	20	75	10	60	96	61
1955–59	37	68	21	43	25	56	17	47	100	56
1960–64	56	55	35	57	11	64	11	45	113	56
1965–69	26	58	18	67	1	0	0		45	60
1970–74	52	56	19	68	2	50	3	100	76	61
1975–79	17	47	12	42	11	18	13	31	53	36
1980–84	4	25	4	0	0		0		8	13
1985–	22	9	22	27	0		0		44	18
TOTAL	265	54	146	49	70	56	54	48	535	52

Note: n is the overall population of that group, not the number born before 1920, thus e.g. 63% of the 51 general population males recorded in 1951–54 were born before 1920.

TABLE A6b Percentages of SSSA contributors born before 1920, by date of first recording (known and estimated dates of birth). See note to Table A6a.

Contributors

Recording date	Male gen pop n	%	Female gen pop n	%	Male Trav n	%	Female Trav n	%	All n	%
1951–54	66	68	27	67	26	73	20	70	139	69
1955–59	60	58	34	47	33	55	34	56	161	55
1960–64	66	56	45	64	14	57	15	33	140	56
1965–69	35	60	26	73	1	0	0		62	65
1970–74	66	56	29	62	3	33	5	60	103	57
1975–79	29	55	19	47	15	20	20	20	83	39
1980–84	7	29	10	40	1	0	2	0	20	30
1985–	34	9	35	23	0		0		69	16
TOTAL	363	54	225	54	93	53	96	47	777	53

TABLE A6c Percentages of SSSA contributors born before 1900, by date of first recording (known dates of birth only). See note to Table A6a.

Contributors

Recording date	Male gen pop n	%	Female gen pop n	%	Male Trav n	%	Female Trav n	%	All n	%
1951–54	51	29	15	20	20	30	10	20	96	27
1955–59	37	38	21	24	25	32	17	18	100	30
1960–64	56	25	35	31	11	36	11	27	113	28
1965–69	26	27	18	22	1	0	0		45	24
1970–74	52	13	19	42	2	0	3	0	76	20
1975–79	17	12	12	17	11	0	13	0	53	8
1980–84	4	0	4	0	0		0		8	0
1985–	22	0	22	5	0		0		44	2
TOTAL	265	22	146	23	70	26	54	15	535	22

TABLE A6d Percentages of SSSA contributors born before 1900, by date of first recording (known and estimated dates of birth). See note to Table A6a.

Contributors

Recording date	Male gen pop n	%	Female gen pop n	%	Male Trav n	%	Female Trav n	%	All n	%
1951–54	66	35	27	48	26	31	20	25	139	35
1955–59	60	30	34	26	33	27	34	24	161	27
1960–64	66	21	45	29	14	36	15	20	140	25
1965–69	35	20	26	23	1	0	0		62	21
1970–74	66	11	29	34	3	0	5	0	103	17
1975–79	29	7	19	11	15	0	20	0	83	5
1980–84	7	0	10	0	1	0	2	0	20	0
1985–	34	3	35	3	0		0		69	3
TOTAL	363	20	225	24	93	24	96	17	777	21

TABLE A6e Percentages of SSSA Child ballad contributors born before 1920 by date of first recording (known and estimated dates of birth). See note to Table A6a.

Contributors (Child ballads)

Recording date	Male core pop n	%	Female core pop n	%	Male Revival n	%	Female Revival n	%	Male Trav n	%	Female Trav n	%	All n	%
1951–54	16	94	8	88	4	25	3	67	14	86	12	75	57	81
1955–59	13	92	7	71	2	0	0		10	70	12	75	44	75
1960–64	12	92	14	79	2	50	5	0	5	80	9	56	47	68
1965–69	7	71	3	67	3	0	3	33	1	0	3	100	20	55
1970–74	9	78	6	83	13	8	5	0	2	50	6	50	41	41
1975–79	6	67	3	67	1	100	1	0	8	25	0		19	47
1980–84	2	50	0		1	0	2	50	0		0		5	40
1985–	0		2	100	4	0	10	0	0		0		16	13
TOTAL	65	85	43	79	30	13	29	14	40	65	42	69	249	61

TABLE A6f Percentages of SSSA Child ballad contributors born before 1900 by date of first recording (known and estimated dates of birth). See note to Table A6a.

Contributors (Child ballads)

Recording date	Male core pop n	%	Female core pop n	%	Male Revival n	%	Female Revival n	%	Male Trav n	%	Female Trav n	%	All n	%
1951–54	16	69	8	88	4	0	3	0	14	36	12	25	57	46
1955–59	13	31	7	71	2	0	0		10	40	12	42	44	41
1960–64	12	42	14	29	2	0	5	0	5	40	9	33	47	30
1965–69	7	0	3	67	3	0	3	0	1	0	3	0	20	10
1970–74	9	11	6	67	13	0	5	0	2	0	6	0	41	12
1975–79	6	0	3	0	1	100	1	0	8	0	0		19	5
1980–84	2	0	0		1	0	2	0	0		0		5	0
1985–	0		2	0	4	0	10	0	0		0		16	0
TOTAL	65	32	43	51	30	3	29	0	40	28	42	26	249	27

TABLE A7 Percentages of SSSA recipients in family transmission born before 1900 and before 1920 (known and estimated dates of birth)

Recipients

	Family n	Pre-1900 %	Pre-1920 %	Nuclear family n	Pre-1900 %	Pre-1920 %	Extended family n	Pre-1900 %	Pre-1920 %
Male gen pop	87	30	84	74	27	85	27	34	83
Female gen pop	78	37	67	72	36	65	19	45	75
Male Trav	40	28	65	34	24	65	18	26	53
Female Trav	55	20	62	45	20	62	29	21	69
TOTAL	260	30	71	225	28	71	93	31	71

Note: categories are not mutually exclusive.

ADDITIONAL TABLES

TABLE A8a Numbers and percentages of family and non-family recipient-source pairs

	Recipient-source pairs					
	Non-family		Family		All	
	n	%	n	%	n	%
Male gen pop	410	73	152	27	562	100
Female gen pop	104	43	136	57	240	100
Male Trav	51	37	87	63	138	100
Female Trav	84	38	138	62	222	100
SSSA TOTAL	649	56	513	44	1162	100
Male G-D	178	73	65	27	243	100
Female G-D	237	68	111	32	348	100
G-D TOTAL	415	70	176	30	591	100

Note: the numbers used below in more detailed analyses by generation or relationship are smaller, because of incomplete information (e.g. a source might be specified by relationship as 'a cousin', but without identifying the person's sex), and the exclusion of pairs where the source is a younger family member (as this category is too small for analysis).

TABLE A8b Numbers and percentages of family and non-family Child ballad recipient-source pairs, by sex and background of recipient. See note to Table A8a.

	Recipient-source pairs (Child ballads)					
	Non-family		Family		All	
	n	%	n	%	n	%
Male core pop	43	58	31	42	74	100
Female core pop	14	35	26	65	40	100
Male Revival	6	86	1	14	7	100
Female Revival	12	92	1	8	13	100
Male Trav	9	20	37	80	46	100
Female Trav	24	26	68	74	92	100
Male gen pop	49	60	32	40	81	100
Female gen pop	26	49	27	51	53	100
SSSA TOTAL	108	40	164	60	272	100
Male G-D	21	53	19	48	40	100

TABLE A8b Numbers and percentages of family and non-family Child pairs (*cont.*)

	Recipient-source pairs (Child ballads)					
	Non-family		Family		All	
	n	%	n	%	n	%
Female G-D	49	54	41	46	90	100
G-D TOTAL	70	54	60	46	130	100

TABLE A9a Recipients in family, non-family, and childhood transmission as a percentage of all recipients

	Recipients											
	All		Non-family		Family		Nuclear family		Extended family		Childhood	
	n	%	n	%	n	%	n	%	n	%	n	%
Male gen pop	262	100	155	59	108	41	87	33	34	13	62	24
Female gen pop	156	100	54	35	95	61	82	53	26	17	37	24
Male Trav	65	100	28	43	46	71	37	57	21	32	16	25
Female Trav	77	100	32	42	62	81	49	64	32	42	27	35
SSSA TOTAL	560	100	269	48	311	56	255	46	113	20	142	25
Male G-D a	119	100	67	56	46	39	35	29	16	13	32	27
Female G-D a	109	100	44	40	63	58	63	58	27	25	20	18
G-D TOTAL a	228	100	111	49	109	48	98	43	43	19	52	23
Male G-D b	119	100									32	27
Female G-D b	109	100									28	26
G-D TOTAL b	228	100									60	26

Note: categories are not mutually exclusive. G-D figures are given without (a) and with (b) the ambiguous 'girlhood' data (see text, §2.2).

ADDITIONAL TABLES

TABLE A9b Recipients in family, non-family, and childhood Child ballad transmission, as a percentage of all Child ballad recipients. See note to Table A9a.

Recipients (Child ballads)

	All n	All %	Non-family n	Non-family %	Family n	Family %	Nuclear family n	Nuclear family %	Extended family n	Extended family %	Childhood n	Childhood %
Male core pop	51	100	26	51	25	49	17	33	9	18	14	27
Female core pop	29	100	8	28	20	69	16	55	8	28	7	24
Male Revival	8	100	5	63	1	13	1	13	0	0	0	0
Female Revival	13	100	10	77	2	15	1	8	1	8	1	8
Male Trav	27	100	8	30	22	81	15	56	10	37	5	19
Female Trav	37	100	14	38	32	86	26	70	19	51	18	49
Male gen pop	59	100	31	53	26	44	18	31	9	15	14	24
Female gen pop	42	100	18	43	22	52	17	40	9	21	8	19
SSSA TOTAL	165	100	71	43	102	62	76	46	47	28	45	27
Male G-D a	34	100	15	44	14	41	12	35	3	9	14	41
Female G-D a	42	100	13	31	30	71	23	55	10	24	6	14
G-D TOTAL a	76	100	28	37	44	58	35	46	13	17	20	26
Male G-D b	34	100									14	41
Female G-D b	42	100									9	21
G-D TOTAL b	76	100									23	30

TABLE A10a Numbers and percentages of all contributors and Child ballad contributors that are male or female

All contributors | Child ballad contributors

	All n	All %	Male n	Male %	Female n	Female %	All n	All %	Male n	Male %	Female n	Female %
Core pop							132	100	79	60	53	40
Revival							86	100	45	52	41	48
Trav	252	100	122	48	130	52	90	100	45	50	45	50
Gen pop	907	100	571	63	336	37	218	100	124	57	94	43
G-D	478	100	280	59	198	41	173	100	94	54	79	46

TABLE A10b Numbers and percentages of all sources and Child ballad sources that are male or female

| | All sources |||||| Child ballad sources ||||||
| | All || Male || Female || All || Male || Female ||
	n	%	n	%	n	%	n	%	n	%	n	%
Core pop							111	100	65	59	46	41
Revival							10	100	7	70	3	30
Trav	234	100	119	51	115	49	105	100	49	47	56	53
Gen pop	754	100	519	69	235	31	121	100	72	60	49	40
G-D	515	100	294	57	221	43	112	100	40	36	72	64

TABLE A11a Percentage change in numbers of Child ballads and Child ballad contributors between G-D and SSSA core population

| | | | | Without Bell Robertson ||
	Males	Females	All	Females	All
G-D					
Contributors	94	79	173	78	172
Types	74	119	125	85	97
Tokens	248	378	626	286	534
SSSA core pop					
Contributors	79	53	132	53	132
Types	62	40	71	40	71
Tokens	202	107	309	107	309
% difference					
Contributors	−19	−49	−31	−47	−30
Types	−19	−198	−76	−113	−37
Tokens	−23	−253	−103	−167	−73

ADDITIONAL TABLES

TABLE A11b Percentage change in numbers of Child ballads and Child ballad contributors between G-D and SSSA Revival contributors

	Males	Females	All	Without Bell Robertson Females	All
G-D					
Contributors	94	79	173	78	172
Types	74	119	125	85	97
Tokens	248	378	626	286	534
SSSA Revival					
Contributors	45	41	86	41	86
Types	54	54	80	54	80
Tokens	94	92	186	92	186
% difference					
Contributors	−109	−93	−101	−90	−100
Types	−37	−120	−56	−57	−21
Tokens	−164	−311	−237	−211	−187

TABLE A11c Percentage change in numbers of Child ballads and Child ballad contributors between G-D and SSSA Travellers

	Males	Females	All	Without Bell Robertson Females	All
G-D					
Contributors	94	79	173	78	172
Types	74	119	125	85	97
Tokens	248	378	626	286	534
SSSA Travellers					
Contributors	45	44	89	44	89
Types	53	58	69	58	69
Tokens	128	197	325	197	325
% difference					
Contributors	−109	−80	−94	−77	−93
Types	−40	−105	−81	−47	−41
Tokens	−94	−92	−93	−45	−64

TABLE A11d Percentage change in numbers of Child ballads and Child ballad contributors recorded between the 1950s and subsequent decades

	Core pop			Revival			Trav		
	Males	Females	All	Males	Females	All	Males	Females	All
1950s									
Contributors	35	20	55	9	4	13	27	25	52
Types	48	19	53	14	15	27	35	54	60
Tokens	113	30	143	16	15	31	63	150	213
1960s–									
Contributors	44	33	77	36	37	73	18	19	37
Types	46	32	57	51	47	73	44	29	53
Tokens	89	77	166	78	76	154	65	47	112
% difference									
Contributors	20	39	29	75	89	82	–50	–32	–41
Types	–4	41	7	73	68	63	20	–86	–13
Tokens	–27	61	14	79	80	80	3	–219	–90

TABLE A12 Median ages at time of first recording of SSSA contributors and Child ballad contributors (known and estimated dates of birth)

	All contributors		Child contributors	
	n	Median age	n	Median age
Male core pop			65	57
Female core pop			43	62
Male Revival			30	30
Female Revival			29	29
Male Trav	93	41	40	50
Female Trav	96	41	42	52
Male gen pop	363	49	95	52
Female gen pop	225	52	72	48
TOTAL	777	47	249	52

TABLE A13 Modal (peak) decade of birth of contributors, recipients and sources (known and estimated dates of birth)

	Modal decade of birth							
	Contributors	Family recipients	Nuclear family recipients	Extended family recipients	Non-family recipients	Sources	Child contributors	Child sources
Male gen pop	1900–09	1900–09	1900–09	1900–09	1900–09	1870–79	1910–19	1880–89
Male Trav	1910–19	1910–19	1910–19	1910–19	1910–19	1900–09	1910–19	1880–89
Female gen pop	1900–09	1900–09	1900–09	1890–99	1890–99	1860–69	1890–99	1860–69
Female Trav	1910–19	1910–19	1910–19	1910–19	1910–19	1880–89	1910–19	1880–89
Male G-D	1840–49	1840–49	1840–49	1840–49/1850–59	1840–49	1830–39	1840–49	1840–49
Female G-D	1840–49	1840–49	1840–49	1840–49	1840–49	1840–49	1840–49	1840–49

TABLE A14a Percentages of SSSA sources born before 1880 and before 1900 (known and estimated dates of birth)

	All		Percentage of sources	
			Pre-1880	Pre-1900
	n	%	%	%
Male gen pop	225	100	46	70
Female gen pop	160	100	54	81
Male Trav	90	100	27	61
Female Trav	106	100	42	71
TOTAL	581	100	45	72

TABLE A14b Percentages of SSSA non-family sources born before 1880 and before 1900 (known and estimated dates of birth)

	All		Percentage of sources	
			Pre-1880	Pre-1900
	n	%	%	%
Male gen pop	110	100	30	59
Female gen pop	40	100	43	75
Male Trav	19	100	21	79
Female Trav	20	100	25	70
TOTAL	189	100	31	66

TABLE A15a Percentages of G-D sources born before 1800 and before 1840 (known and estimated dates of birth)

	All		Percentage of sources	
			Pre-1800	Pre-1840
	n	%	%	%
Males	88	100	19	63
Females	120	100	14	65
TOTAL	208	100	16	64

ADDITIONAL TABLES

TABLE A15b Percentages of G-D non-family sources born before 1800 and before 1840 (known and estimated dates of birth)

	All n	All %	Pre-1800 %	Pre-1840 %
Males	44	100	18	61
Females	58	100	5	50
TOTAL	102	100	11	55

TABLE A16a Numbers of family recipient-source pairs, broken down by relationship

Sources	Male gen pop	Female gen pop	Male Trav	Female Trav	Male G-D	Female G-D
Mother	38	49	21	33	22	41
Father	49	38	19	22	17	14
Brother	11	2	6	6	5	3
Sister	5	9	3	6	1	3
Wife	5		2			
Husband		6		6		2
Grandmother	10	10	7	17	5	17
Grandfather	11	3	6	7	2	8
Great aunt		1	2	1	1	
Great uncle	2				1	
Aunt	2	3	5	7	3	8
Uncle	5	5	3	8	3	3
Fo cousin		1	2	1		1
Mo cousin	1	1	1	2		1
F1 cousin			1	1		
M1 cousin	1		2			
Fo in-law	2	1		4		2
Mo in-law		1		3		

TABLE A16a Numbers of family recipient-source pairs, broken down by relationship *(cont.)*

	Recipients					
Sources	Male gen pop	Female gen pop	Male Trav	Female Trav	Male G-D	Female G-D
F1 in-law		2	2	2		1
M1 in-law	2		1	1		
All extended	36	28	32	54	15	41
All nuclear	108	104	51	73	45	63
All horizontal	24	21	14	28	6	12
All vertical	120	111	69	99	54	92
TOTAL	144	132	83	127	60	104

Notes: F0 = female in the same generation, M1 = male in the parental generation, etc. Vague relationships and pairs with younger generation sources are omitted. In the female Traveller sources, one great grandmother and one great grandfather have been counted as a grandmother and grandfather respectively. Non-Scottish sources are included.

TABLE A16b Numbers of family Child ballad recipient-source pairs, broken down by relationship. See note to Table A16a. In the female Traveller sources, one great grandfather has been counted as a grandfather. Revival recipients are omitted (one female and one male Revival recipient each have their mother as a source).

	Recipients					
Sources	Male core pop	Female core pop	Male Trav	Female Trav	Male G-D	Female G-D
Mother	12	10	11	17	10	20
Father	6	4	5	14	4	4
Brother			2	3		2
Sister			3	2		1
Wife	1					
Husband		2		2		1
Grandmother	2	4	3	9	1	7
Grandfather	5	1	3	5	1	
Great aunt			1			
Great uncle						

ADDITIONAL TABLES

TABLE A16b Numbers of family Child ballad recipient-source pairs (*cont.*)

	Recipients					
Sources	Male core pop	Female core pop	Male Trav	Female Trav	Male G-D	Female G-D
Aunt	1		2	3	1	3
Uncle	1	2	2	3		1
Fo cousin		1				
Mo cousin	1			2		
F1 cousin						
M1 cousin			2			
Fo in-law		1		2		
Mo in-law		1		2		
F1 in-law			1	2		
M1 in-law			1	1		
All nuclear	19	16	21	38	14	28
All extended	10	10	15	29	3	11
All horizontal	2	4	5	11	0	4
All vertical	27	21	31	54	17	35
TOTAL	29	26	36	67	17	39

APPENDIX B

Notes on the Selection of *Greig-Duncan* Data

The song notes compiled by the G-D editors from Greig's and Duncan's field notes and their correspondence with contributors can be quite cryptic, and there is no doubt a risk of misinterpretation on occasion. For example, the note to Song 1185 seems to say that Mrs Willox' mother is 86 (in 1911), but this would not allow for Mrs Willox herself to have heard Song 535A seventy years before. It has been assumed here that the wording is misleading and that it is Mrs Willox who is 86. It is probably a simple typographical error or poor legibility of the MS that accounts for Miss Michael's girlhood being dated c. 1870 at Song 1206A: the note at Song 992A clarifies that the date is actually 1810. (Miss Michael was a source of songs for Mrs Gillespie.)

A few discrepancies emerge when the biographical and song transmission data are compared. For example, in the note to Song 907B Mrs Lyall is quoted as saying that the song was '[l]earnt fifty to sixty years ago in Kincardine', i.e. c. 1848–58. We can be confident that Mrs Lyall's d.o.b is 1869, as stated in vol. 8 (Neilson, 2002: 566), as she is one of the contributors whose biography has been researched in detail. There is evidently some piece of information missing: probably she is passing on the song from her husband, David Lyall (born 1841), who learnt other songs in Kincardineshire around this time (Songs 22A, 1170).

It would have been possible, chronologically, for Mrs Gillespie to have collected Song 1054W from Mrs Johnston(e) (née Jane or Jean Sinclair) in 1908, when the latter was about 75, as the song note appears to say, in which case we would regard Mrs Gillespie as an intermediary rather than the recipient of song transmission. However, Mrs Gillespie was living in Glasgow at this time, so we follow Petrie's biography of Mrs Gillespie (2002a: 561) in assuming that this song, like others, was learned when she was in service together with Jean Sinclair in 1853–54.

It is occasionally unclear whether there are two different individuals of the same name. The address of William Watson is variously given as New Byth (FoC, p. 499) or New Deer (FoC, p. 509), but we have followed the Index in treating the different mentions as referring to the same person. There was an interval of time, during which he could have moved house.

Keith (in Greig ed. Keith, 1925, 'Index of contributors', pp. 281 ff.) suggests that Mrs Aitken is the same person as Mrs Clark, whose second husband was an Aitken. Mrs Clark moved to Edinburgh after her second marriage, and it is mentioned at the note to Song 277E that Mrs Aitken's address is Edinburgh. However, there is a separate version of the same song (277L) from Mrs Clark. Here the two contributors, Mrs Clark and Mrs Aitken, are taken to be different people.

Following FoC, the contributor identified as 'Kininmonth schoolgirl' is replaced in this study by her grandfather, for whom she appears to be acting as an amanuensis, and Mrs Anderson (D) is replaced by Katharine Duncan (see FoC, p. 522). G. Morrison is omitted, as there seems to be a misidentification (see FoC, p. 474).

There is a question mark over the relationship of G-D's contributors Alexander Robb and Annie Robb. Annie is thought to have been born c. 1872 and is said to be Alexander's sister (Porter and Campbell, 2002: 578; Campbell, 2009: 75), but the note at Song 197B states that Alexander's mother died aged 88 c. 1911. This would put the mother's date of birth c. 1823, making her about 49 when Annie was born. In addition, there is also a note at Song 160B that says Alexander Robb's grandmother was born c. 1780. This might of course be his paternal grandmother, but if it is his mother's mother, then his mother could indeed hardly have been born much after 1823. It is quite possible that Annie was brought up by her grandparents. Such arrangements were not uncommon at the time, whether because of illegitimacy or over-crowding in large families. Keith's identification of Annie as Alexander's niece (in Greig ed. Keith, 1925: 289) is therefore accepted here.

Identification of the contributors from record sources must be tentative, as the same names often recur in families. FoC tells us (p. 524 n. 14) that there is a sixty-year-old John Rae in the 1891 Census at the same address as the contributor John S. Rae; this may be the latter's father, since John S. Rae's d.o.b is given in FoC (p. 482) as 1859. Likewise the Kate (or Kirsty) Morrice born c. 1879 located by Campbell (2009) appears not to be the Kate (or Kirsty) Morrice who contributed to the collection via Annie Shirer, as the date is not compatible with Annie Shirer having learned Song 1055L around fifty years before 1910. Also, the c. 1879 Kate would only have been a child when Annie Shirer learned Song 1462A twenty years before 1910.

The Alexander Murison from whom Greig collected is unlikely to be the same Alexander Murison who was a source for Mrs Gillespie (*pace* Petrie, 2002a: 561), if the latter is the Mr Murison senior from whom she learned 1216A, amongst other songs, in the 1850s. (Mr Murison senior is named as A. Murison in the note to 831B, and as 'Alex. (?)' in the note to 1216A.) She and her brother, William Duncan, also learned songs around the same time from his son David (743B, 170A, 1273E). The designation 'senior' is taken here as meaning that the son was also an adult at the time, though this may be mistaken.

Also problematic is the identification of Mrs Lee with a woman who died in 1942 at the age of 89 and was the widow of a farmer named Lee (FoC, p. 525, n. 22). Mary Ann Crichton's information (cited on p. 493) is that Mrs Lee was married to a chemist named Lee, whom she left. She might, of course, have married a second husband who happened to have the same surname, but without any information linking her to Mr Lee the farmer, it seems safest to treat her (and therefore also Mr Lee the chemist, who is also a contributor) as d.o.b unknown.

Some individuals are included who are not indexed but who appear to be the contributors of songs collected or passed on by intermediaries. These are: Rothienorman correspondent (FoC, p. 503), Bell Robertson's girl source (Song 372D), Mormond man (Song 1925), old farmservant (Song 377A), old gentleman (Song 269), old lady (Song 214D), old woman (Song 968C), servant girl (Song 1098), wandering tramp (Song 951D), correspondent in Ayrshire (Song 878M), Jessie McDonald's father's cousin (Song 538F), John Anderson (Song 1262M and note at N), John Clark (Song 787B), Mrs Fyfe (Song 1256 supplementary note), Mrs Johnston (Song 1054W), Alex McDonald (Song 676 supplementary note), Mrs Mitchell (Song 213E), Mrs Murdoch (Song 307I), Mrs Meston (Song 277E), and Jeannie Brewer's sister (960A; see Petrie, 2002a: 562). However, we omit the following contributors of unknown sex: an Old Scot (Song 908C), Montgarrie mill worker (Song 853B), Annie Shirer's servants (Song 52F), former pupil (Song 1044S), friend of C. J. Yule (Song 228D), friend of Bell Robertson (Song 467C), and neighbour of Bell Robertson (Song 186J). In practice, individuals described as 'friends' are probably of the same sex as the named person, but this cannot be assumed.

Also included are the compilers of song MSS (sometimes obtained posthumously). These are: John Murray, John Garioch, James Walker, Mrs Thom, and an anonymous farmservant via Sam Davidson. Contributors writing from abroad who are included are: Miss Urquhart, R. D. Reid, Duncan Williams, James Scott and James Lawrence. The following contributors, mentioned in notes or in FoC, for whom there are no surviving texts, are included: Mrs Panton (FoC, p. 494), Maud old lady (supplementary note to Song 112), Miss McArthur (FoC, p. 494), and James Scott (FoC, p. 512). However, a friend of William Fraser in Burma (note at Song 912C) is omitted as being of unknown sex.

The following individuals have been omitted: James F. Dickie, William MacDonald, and C. J. Yule, who act only as intermediaries; girls in Durris, Miss Ella Boyd, Miss Mary Carle, James Cassie, Gavin Greig himself, Miss Isabella Harvey, Miss Katie Marwick, Mrs Moir, Miss Winnie Sabiston, Rev. John Strachan, Miss Eva Wards and J. A. Fairley, who contribute only children's songs, non-song material such as rhymes, or material from printed sources; John Murray and Gordon McQueen, who contribute only material of their own composition; New Leeds woman, Miss Alexa Brown, G. Cadger, C. Clark, Mr Coolle, Miss Dunbar, G. G. Farquhar, Mrs Forbes, Mrs Fowler, James Hardie, J. Lovie, K. N. MacDonald, James Macpherson, George Murray, J. C. Rennie, J. Scott Skinner, and George Wilson, for whom no lyrics are recorded. The two items from the Lucy Broadwood collection have also been omitted on the latter basis.

Bibliography

'1901 Census' (n.d.), National Records of Scotland, https://www.nrscotland.gov.uk/research/guides/census-records/1901-census (accessed 3 October 2019).

Agricultural Statistics 1950 and 1951 Scotland (1953) Department of Agriculture for Scotland (Edinburgh: HMSO), https://www.webarchive.org.uk/wayback/archive/20160106172313/http://www.gov.scot/Topics/Statistics/Browse/Agriculture-Fisheries/Publications/Agstats1950 (accessed 12 April 2021).

[Ainslie, Jock and Hamish Henderson] (1991) 'Jock Ainslie: a Stirlingshire horseman', *Tocher* 43, 51–8.

Alexander, William, ed. William Donaldson (1995) *Johnny Gibb of Gushetneuk in the Parish of Pyketillim* (East Linton: Tuckwell).

Anon. (1975) 'Gypsies in North Britain' in Rehfisch, ed., 85–121.

Anon. (2008) 'Scottish Gypsies are distinct ethnic group, rules judge', *The Herald*, 25 October 2008, http://www.heraldscotland.com/news/12372902.Scottish_gipsies_are_distinct_ethnic_group__rules_judge/ (accessed 3 October 2019).

Anon. (2011) 'Lost in translation: The mystery behind Scotland's travelling community', *The Scotsman*, 26 February 2011.

Atkinson, David (2002) *The English Traditional Ballad: Theory, Method, and Practice* (Aldershot and Burlington VT: Ashgate).

Atkinson, David (2004) 'Revival: genuine or spurious?' in Russell and Atkinson, eds., 143–62.

Atkinson, David (2010) 'Sound and writing: Complementary facets of the Anglo-Scottish ballad', *Twentieth-Century Music*, 7(2), 139–165, DOI: https://doi.org/10.1017/S1478572211000144 (accessed 11 December 2020).

Bancroft, A., M. Lloyd and R. Morran (1996) *The Right to Roam. Travellers in Scotland 1995/96* (Dunfermline: The Save the Children Fund).

Bearman, C. J. (2000) 'Who were the folk? The demography of Cecil Sharp's Somerset folk singers', *Historical Journal* 43, 751–5, https://www.jstor.org/stable/3020977 (accessed 3 October 2019).

Beech, John *et al.*, eds. (2007) *Oral Literature and Performance Culture*, vol. 10 of *Scottish Life and Society: A Compendium of Scottish Ethnology* (Edinburgh: Birlinn).

Bertie, David (2005) *John Skinner. Collected Poems* (Peterhead: Buchan Field Club).

'Births time series data' (updated 2017), National Records of Scotland, https://www.nrscotland.gov.uk/statistics-and-data/statistics/statistics-by-theme/vital-events/births/births-time-series-data (accessed 3 October 2019).

Bishop, Julia (2004) 'Bell Duncan: "The greatest ballad singer of all time"?' in Russell and Atkinson, eds., 393–421.

Bourne, George [*nom de plume* of George Sturt] (1912, 1984) *Change in the Village* (Harmondsworth: Penguin). Originally published 1912 (London: Duckworth).

'Broadside ballad entitled "The Tinker's Wedding"' (2004) National Library of Scotland, https://digital.nls.uk/broadsides/view/?id=19151 (accessed 9 October 2019).

Brocken, Michael (2003) *The British Folk Revival, 1944–2002* (Abingdon: Ashgate).

Brown, Mary Ellen (1997) 'Old singing women and the canons of Scottish balladry and song' in Gifford and McMillan, eds., 44–57.

[Bruford, Alan] (1975) '"Yowie wi the crooked horn"', *Tocher* 23, 264–5.

Bruford, Alan (1976) '"The Grey Selkie"' in Emily Lyle, ed., *Ballad Studies* (Cambridge: D. S. Brewer for the Folklore Society), 41–65.

Bruford, Alan (1986) 'Song manuscripts and the acquisition of song repertoires in Orkney and Shetland' in Ian Russell, ed., *Singer, Song and Scholar* (Sheffield Academic Press), 95–115.

Buchan, David (1972, 1997) *The Ballad and the Folk* (East Linton: Tuckwell Press). Originally published 1972 (London: Routledge and Kegan Paul).

Buchan, David (1984, 2013) 'The expressive culture of nineteenth century Scottish farm servants' in Buchan ed. Nicolaisen and Moreira (2013), 378–96. Originally published in T. M. Devine, ed., *Farm Servants and Labour in Lowland Scotland 1770–1914* (Edinburgh: John Donald, 1984), 226–42.

Buchan, David (1985) 'The historical ballads of the Northeast of Scotland' in *Lares* 51(4), 443–51, https://www.jstor.org/stable/44628673 (accessed 4 October 2019). Reproduced in Buchan ed. Nicolaisen and Moreira (2013), 148–56.

Buchan, David (1985, 2013) 'Performance contexts in historical perspective' in Buchan ed. Nicolaisen and Moreira (2013), 397–416. Originally published *New York Folklore* 11 (1985), 443–51.

Buchan, David, ed. W. F. H. Nicolaisen and James Moreira (2013) *The Ballad and the Folklorist. The Collected Papers of David Buchan* (St. John's: Memorial University of Newfoundland Folklore and Language Publications).

Burnett, Simon, Caroline Macafee and Dorothy Williamson (2017) 'Applying a knowledge conversion model to cultural history: Folk song from oral tradition to digital transformation', *The Electronic Journal of Knowledge Management* 15(2), 61–71, https://academic-publishing.org/index.php/ejkm (accessed 1 April 2021).

Burns, Robert (2004) 'British folk songs in popular music settings' in Russell and Atkinson, eds., 115–29.

Byrne, Steve (2010) 'Riches in the Kist: the living legacy of Hamish Henderson' in Eberhard Bort, ed., *Borne on the Carrying Stream. The Legacy of Hamish Henderson* (Ochtertyre: Grace Note Publications), 280–316.

Calder, Angus (1992) 'Introduction' in Henderson ed. Finlay, xiii–xv.

Cameron, David Kerr (1978, 1987) *The Ballad and the Plough* (London: Victor Gollancz).

BIBLIOGRAPHY

Cameron, David Kerr (1980, 1995) *Willie Gavin, Crofter Man* (Edinburgh: Birlinn). Originally published 1980 (London: Victor Gollancz).

Campbell, Katherine (2002) 'The music of the collection' in *The Greig-Duncan Folk Song Collection*, vol. 8, 447–63.

Campbell, Katherine (2003) 'Ballad singing in New Deer' in Thomas McKean, ed., *The Flowering Thorn. International Ballad Studies* (Utah State University Press and University Press of Colorado), 249–56. DOI: https://doi.org/10.2307/j.ctt46nrmo.3.

Campbell, Katherine (2007) 'Collectors of Scots song' in Beech *et al.*, eds., 427–439.

Campbell, Katherine, ed. (2009) *Songs from North-East Scotland. A Selection for Performers from the Greig-Duncan Folk-Song Collection* (Edinburgh: John Donald).

Carter, Ian (1979) *Farmlife in Northeast Scotland 1840–1914. The Poor Man's Country* (Edinburgh: John Donald).

'Census of Scotland, 1901 – Appendix Tables' (n.d.), Online Historical Population Reports, http://www.histpop.org (accessed 3 October 2019).

Child, Francis James (1882–98) *The English and Scottish Popular Ballads*, 5 vols. (Boston and New York: Houghton, Mifflin & Co.).

'Children Act, 1908' (1908) http://www.legislation.gov.uk/ukpga/1908/67/pdfs/ukpga_19080067_en.pdf (accessed 3 October 2019).

Clement, David (1981) 'The secret languages of the Scottish travelling people', *Grazer Linguistische Studien: Sprachliche Sonderformen* 15, 17–25.

The Concise Scots Dictionary (1985, 2017), ed.-in-chief Mairi Robinson (Aberdeen University Press, 1985); 2nd edition (Edinburgh University Press, 2017).

Cooke, Peter (2007) 'The music of Scottish Travellers' in Beech *et al.*, eds., 213–24.

Cowan, Edward, ed. (1980) *The People's Past: Scottish Folk, Scottish History* (Edinburgh University Student Publications Board).

Crofton, Henry Thomas (1880, 2001) *English Gypsies under the Tudors* (Paper read before the Manchester Literary Club, 12 January 1880). Reproduced as *Crofton's Tudor Gypsies*, ed. Robert Dawson (Blackwell, Derbyshire: privately published, 2001).

Cruickshank, Marjorie (1965) 'The Dick Bequest: The effect of a famous nineteenth-century endowment on parish schools of North East Scotland', *History of Education Quarterly* 5(3), 153–65. DOI: https://doi.org/10.2307/367114 (accessed 31 October 2019).

Dawson, Robert, ed. (2005) *The 1895 Scottish Traveller Report* (Blackwell, Derbyshire: privately published). Edited selections from the 'Report from the Departmental Committee on Habitual Offenders, Vagrants, Beggars, Inebriates and Juvenile Delinquents' (Edinburgh: HMSO, 1895).

Departmental Committee on Tinkers (Scotland) (1918) *Report of the Departmental Committee on Tinkers in Scotland* (Edinburgh: HMSO).

Departmental Committee on Vagrancy in Scotland, Department of Health for Scotland (1936) 'Report of the Departmental Committee on Vagrancy in Scotland' in *20th Century House of Commons Sessional Papers, 1935–36*, vol. XIV, 981–1072 [original page nos. 1–92].

Devine, T. M. (1999) *The Scottish Nation: 1700–2000* (London: Allen Lane).

Dick, James (1903) *The Songs of Robert Burns, Now First Printed with the Melodies for which they were Written. A Study in Tone-Poetry* (London: Henry Frowde).

Dictionary of the Older Scottish Tongue (DOST) (1937–2002), eds. W. Craigie *et al.*, 12 vols. (Oxford University Press). Online: Dictionary of the Scots Language http://www.dsl.ac.uk/ (accessed 3 October 2019).

[Douglas, Sheila] (1992) 'Willie MacPhee: Last of the travelling tinsmiths', *Tocher* 44, 78–83.

Douglas, Sheila (2002) 'Traveller Cant in Scotland' in John M. Kirk and Dónall Ó Baoill, eds., *Travellers and their Language* (Belfast: Queen's University), 125–31.

Douglas, Sheila (2004) 'Belle Stewart: "The Queen Amang the Heather"' in Russell and Atkinson, eds., 431–40.

Douglas, Sheila, ed. (1992) *The Sang's the Thing. Voices from Lowland Scotland* (Edinburgh: Polygon).

Douglas, Sheila, with Jo Miller, eds. (1995) *Come Gie's a Sang* (Edinburgh: The Hardie Press).

Duncan, P. S. (1966) 'James Bruce Duncan (1848–1917)', *Folk Music Journal* 1(2), 65–7, https://www.jstor.org/stable/4521741 (accessed 3 October 2019).

Evans, George Ewart (1970) *Where Beards Wag All* (London: Faber and Faber).

Evans, George Ewart (1971) *Tools of their Trades: An Oral History of Men at Work c. 1900* (New York: Taplinger Pub. Co.).

General Registry Office (1952) *Report on the Fifteenth Census of Scotland. Census 1951 Scotland*, vol. II *Population of Towns and Larger Villages (Excluding Burghs) and of Urban and Rural Areas* (Edinburgh: HMSO).

General Registry Office (1956) *Report on the Fifteenth Census of Scotland. Census 1951 Scotland*, vol. IV *Occupations and Industries* (Edinburgh: HMSO).

Gentleman, Hugh and Susan Swift (1971) *Scotland's Travelling People: Problems and Solutions* (Edinburgh: HMSO).

Gifford, Douglas and Dorothy McMillan, eds. (1997) *A History of Scottish Women's Writing* (Edinburgh University Press).

Glen, John (1900) *Early Scottish Melodies* (Edinburgh: J. & R. Glen), https://digital.nls.uk/special-collections-of-printed-music/archive/91347682 (accessed 18 October 2019).

Goffman, Erving (1959, 1969) *The Presentation of Self in Everyday Life* (Harmondsworth: Penguin, 1969). Originally published 1959.

Granovetter, Mark S. (1973) 'The strength of weak ties', *American Journal of Sociology* 78(6), 1360–80, https://www.jstor.org/stable/2776392 (accessed 3 October 2019).

BIBLIOGRAPHY

Gregory, E. David (2004) 'Roving Out: Peter Kennedy and the BBC Folk Music and Dialect Recording Scheme, 1952–1957' in Russell and Atkinson eds., 218–40.

The Greig-Duncan Folk Song Collection (G-D) (1981–2002), eds. Patrick Shuldham-Shaw *et al.*, 8 vols. (vols. 1–4 Aberdeen University Press; vols. 5–8 Edinburgh: Mercat Press).

Greig, Gavin, ed. Kenneth Goldstein and Arthur Argo (1963) *Folk-Song in Buchan and Folk-Song in the North-East* (Hatboro, Pennsylvania: Folklore Associates). 'Folk-song in Buchan' originally published *Transactions of the Buchan Field Club* 9 (1906–7), 1–76.

Greig, Gavin, ed. Alexander Keith (1925) *Last Leaves of Traditional Ballads and Ballad Airs* (University of Aberdeen).

Grellman, Heinrich, trans. Matthew Raper (1787) *Dissertation on the Gipsies ...* (London: privately printed).

Groom, Nicholas, ed. (1996) *Thomas Percy's Reliques of Ancient English Poetry* (London: Routledge).

Hall, Peter (1975) 'Scottish tinker songs', *Folk Music Journal* 3(1), 41–62, https://www.jstor.org/stable/4521964 (accessed 3 October 2019).

Heide, Eldar (2018) 'New perspectives on archival shortcomings. A note on self-perception, history and methodology within folkloristics, ethnology and cultural studies' in Lauri Harvilahti *et al.*, eds., *Visions and Traditions. Knowledge Production and Tradition Archives* (Folklore Fellows' Communications 315, Academia Scientiarum Fennica, Helsinki), https://www.researchgate.net/publication/329887560 (accessed 3 October 2019).

Henderson, Hamish (1962, 1992) 'Folk-song and music from the berryfields of Blair' in Henderson ed. Finlay, 101–3. Originally published as a sleeve note (Prestige/International 25016, 1962).

Henderson, Hamish (1963a, 1992) 'A plea for the sung ballad' in Henderson ed. Finlay, 44. Originally addressed to the BBC Scottish Home Service (1963).

Henderson, Hamish (1963b, 1992) 'The underground of song' in Henderson ed. Finlay, 31–6. Originally published *Scots Magazine* (February 1963).

Henderson, Hamish (1974, 1992) 'Davie Stewart' in Henderson ed. Finlay, 167–74. Originally published *Tocher* 15 (Autumn 1974).

[Henderson, Hamish] (1975) contributions in [Hamish Henderson and Ailie Munro] *The Muckle Sangs. Classic Scots Ballads* [booklet accompanying the LP of that name] (Edinburgh: School of Scottish Studies; now published by Greentrax).

Henderson, Hamish (1980) 'The ballad, the folk and the oral tradition' in Cowan, ed., 69–107.

Henderson, Hamish (1981a, 1992) 'The tinkers', in Henderson ed. Finlay, 229–30. Originally published in *A Companion to Scottish Culture*, ed. David Daiches (London, 1981).

Henderson, Hamish (1981b, 1992) 'The ballads' in Henderson ed. Finlay, 23–7. Originally published in *A Companion to Scottish Culture*, ed. David Daiches (London, 1981).

Henderson, Hamish (1986, 1992) 'The ballad and popular tradition to 1660' in Henderson ed. Finlay, 78–94. Originally published in R. D. S. Jack, ed., *History of Scottish Literature* vol. I, *Origins to 1660* (Aberdeen University Press, 1986).

Henderson, Hamish (1987, 1992) 'Lorca and cante jondo', review of Federico García Lorca, *Deep Song and Other Prose* (ed. and trans. C. Maurer, 1986), in Henderson ed. Finlay, 313–8. Originally published in *Cencrastus* 26 (1987).

Henderson, Hamish, ed. Alec Finlay (1992) *Alias MacAlias. Writings on Songs, Folk and Literature* (Edinburgh: Polygon).

Henderson, Hamish and Francis Collinson (1965) 'New Child ballad variants from oral tradition', *Scottish Studies* 9(1), 1–33.

[Henderson, Hamish and Adam McNaughton] (1991) 'Jean Elvin', *Tocher* 43, 40–1.

[Hogg, James] ('The Ettrick Shepherd') (1831–32) 'On the changes in the habits, amusements, and condition of the Scottish peasantry', *The Quarterly Journal of Agriculture* 3, 256–63.

Holmquist, Jonathan Carl (1988) *Language Loyalty and Linguistic Variation: A Study in Spanish Cantabria* (Dordrecht: Foris Publications).

Hughes, David W. (2008) *Traditional Folk Song in Modern Japan: Sources, Sentiment and Society* (Folkestone: Global Oriental).

Hunter, Andrew (2002) 'C1 Robert Alexander' in *The Greig-Duncan Folk Song Collection*, vol. 8, 549.

'The James Madison Carpenter Collection' (n.d.) Vaughan Williams Memorial Library https://www.vwml.org/archives-catalogue/JMC (accessed 3 October 2019).

Jeannie Robertson and 'The Gallowa' Hills' (1958) EP recording (London: Jazz Selection).

John MacDonald – The Singing Molecatcher of Morayshire (1975) LP recording (Topic Records 12TS263; CD now published by Greentrax CDTRAX 9053).

Jones, E. L. (1964) *Seasons and Prices. The Role of the Weather in English Agricultural History* (London: George Allen & Unwin).

Kelly, Christine (2016) 'Continuity and change in the history of Scottish juvenile justice', *Law, Crime and History* 6(1), 59–82, http://www.lawcrimehistory.org/journal/vol.6%20issue1%202016/kelly.pdf (accessed 3 October 2019).

Knevett, Arthur and Vic Gammon (2016) 'English folk song collectors and the idea of the peasant', *Folk Music Journal* 11(1), 44–66.

Knox, W. W. (n.d.) 'The Scottish educational system 1840–1940' in 'A History of the Scottish People', SCRAN, https://www.scran.ac.uk/scotland/pdf/SP2_1Education.pdf (accessed 3 October 2019).

Korczynski, Marek (2003) 'Music at work: Toward a historical overview', *Folk Music Journal* 8(3), 314–34, https://www.jstor.org/stable/4522689 (accessed 3 October 2019).

Kyd, J. G., ed. (1952) *Scottish Population Statistics including Webster's Analysis of Population 1755* (Edinburgh: Scottish History Society), https://www.nrscotland.gov.uk/files/research/census-records/websters-census-of-1755-scottish-population-statistics.pdf (accessed 3 October 2019).

Laslett, Peter (1983) *The World we have Lost – Further Explored* 3rd edn (London: Methuen & Co.).

Laws, G. Malcolm (1957) *American Balladry from British Broadsides* (Philadelphia: American Folklore Society).

Leitch, Roger, ed. (1988) *The Book of Sandy Stewart* (Edinburgh: Scottish Academic Press).

Liber Ecclesie de Scon (1843) ed. Bannatyne Club (Edinburgh: T. Constable for the Bannatyne Club).

Lorca, Federico García, trans. A. S. Kline (2007) 'Theory and play of the *duende*', Poetry in Translation http://www.poetryintranslation.com/PITBR/Spanish/LorcaDuende.php (accessed 3 October 2019).

Lundy, Darryl (2019) 'The Peerage', http://thepeerage.com/ (accessed 3 October 2019).

Lyle, Emily (2002a) 'The formation of the collection' in *The Greig-Duncan Folk Song Collection*, vol. 8, 465–529.

Lyle, Emily (2002b) 'C10 Mrs Harper and Mrs Greig' in *The Greig-Duncan Folk Song Collection*, vol. 8, 565.

Lyle, Emily, ed. (2011) *Galoshins Remembered: 'A Penny Was a Lot in These Days'* (Edinburgh: NMSE Publishing).

Lyle, Emily (2013) 'Ballad' in Sarah Dunnigan and Suzanne Gilbert eds., *The Edinburgh Companion to Scottish Traditional Literature* (Edinburgh University Press), 14–18.

Macafee, Caroline (2012, 2014) 'The language of the "Ramsay" ballad', Appendix 2 in Ian Olson, 'The battle of Harlaw, its Lowland histories and their balladry: historical confirmation or confabulation?', *Review of Scottish Culture* 24 (2012) 1–33. Reprinted as 'The orthography the "Ramsay" ballad' in Ian Olson, *Bludie Harlaw. Realities, Myths, Ballads* (Edinburgh: John Donald, 2014), 152–4.

Macafee, Caroline (2017) 'Scots in the Census: validity and reliability', in Janet Cruickshank and Robert Millar, eds., *Before the Storm: Papers from the Forum for Research on the Languages of Scotland and Ulster Triennial Meeting, Ayr 2015* (Aberdeen: Forum for Research on the Languages of Scotland and Ireland), 33–67, https://www.abdn.ac.uk/pfrlsu/documents/PFRLSU/Macafee_Scots_in_the_Census.pdf (accessed 3 October 2019).

Macafee, Caroline (2019) 'Gypsies, pedlars, beggars and other itinerants in the Scots dictionary record', *Scottish Language* 38, 1–54.

McCleery, Alison *et al.* (2008) 'Scoping and Mapping Intangible Cultural Heritage in Scotland. Final Report' (Edinburgh: Napier University Centre for Cultural and

Creative Industries), https://www.napier.ac.uk/~/media/worktribe/output-229389/ichinscotlandfullreportjuly08pdf.pdf (accessed 3 October 2019).

MacColl, Ewan and Peggy Seeger (1977) *Travellers' Songs from England and Scotland* (London: Routledge & Kegan Paul).

MacColl, Ewan and Seeger, Peggy (1986) *Till Doomsday in the Afternoon* (Manchester University Press).

McCormick, Andrew (1907) *The Tinkler-Gypsies of Galloway*, revised edn (Dumfries: J. Maxwell & Son).

McDiarmid, Carron and Graham Watson (2015) 'The Cultural Contribution of Gypsy/Travellers in the Highlands' (Report No. CPE 8/15 to the Highland Council, Community Safety, Public Engagement and Equalities Committee), https://www.highland.gov.uk/news/article/8687/cultural_contribution_of_gypsytravellers_in_the_highlands (accessed 3 October 2019).

McDiarmid, Matthew and J. A. C. Stevenson, eds. (1981) *Barbour's Bruce*, vol. III (Edinburgh: The Scottish Text Society).

McKean, Thomas (2002) 'C23 J. W. Spence and John Quirrie' in *The Greig-Duncan Folk Song Collection*, vol. 8, 590–1.

McKean, Thomas (2018) 'Willie Mathieson and the primary audience for traditional song', *Tautosakos darbai – Folklore Studies* 55(1), 36–59, http://www.llti.lt/failai/TD55_internetui-36-59.pdf (accessed 3 October 2019).

MacKinnon, Niall (1993) *The British Folk Scene: Musical Performance and Social Identity* (Milton Keynes: Open University Press).

MacRitchie, David (1894) *Scottish Gypsies under the Stewarts* (Edinburgh: David Douglas).

Milton, Colin (1983) 'From Charles Murray to Hugh MacDiarmid: Vernacular Revival and Scottish Renaissance' in David Hewitt and Michael Spiller, eds., *Literature of the North* (Aberdeen University Press), 82–108.

Milton, Colin (2002) 'C15 Charles Murray and David Rorie' in *The Greig-Duncan Folk Song Collection*, vol. 8, 571–2.

Ministry of Housing and Local Government, Welsh Office (1967) *Gypsies and Other Travellers. A Report of a Study Carried out in 1965 and 1966 by a Sociological Research Section of the Ministry of Housing and Local Government* (London: HMSO).

The Muckle Sangs. Classic Scots Ballads (1975) LP recording (Scottish Tradition 5, Edinburgh: School of Scottish Studies; CD now published by Greentrax, CDTRAX9005).

Munro, Ailie (1970) 'Lizzie Higgins and the oral transmission of ten Child ballads', *Scottish Studies* 14, 155–88.

Munro, Ailie (1984) *The Folk Music Revival in Scotland* (London: Kahn & Averill).

Munro, Ailie (1991) 'The role of the School of Scottish Studies in the Folk Music Revival', *Folk Music Journal* 6(2), 132–68.

Munro, Ailie (1996) *The Democratic Muse. Folk Music Revival in Scotland* (Aberdeen: Scottish Cultural Press). Revised edition of Munro (1984).

Neat, Timothy (2009) *Hamish Henderson: A Biography*, vol. 2 *Poetry Becomes People* (Edinburgh: Polygon).

Neilson, Anne (2002) 'C11 Mrs Lyall' in *The Greig-Duncan Folk Song Collection*, vol. 8, 566–7.

The New (or Second) Statistical Account of Scotland (NSA) (1834–45) The Statistical Accounts of Scotland 1791–1845, http://stataccscot.edina.ac.uk/static/statacc/dist/home (accessed 3 October 2019).

Niles, J. D. (1995) 'The role of the strong tradition bearer in the making of an oral culture' in Porter, ed., 231–40.

Nord, Deborah (2006) *Gypsies and the British Imagination, 1807–1930* (New York: Columbia University Press).

Ogston, David D. (1986) *White Stone Country. Growing up in Buchan* (Edinburgh: Ramsay Head Press).

Olson, Ian (1989) 'The Greig-Duncan Folk Song Collection: Last leaves of a local culture?', *Review of Scottish Culture* 5, 79–85.

Olson, Ian (1992) 'Some songs of place and ballads of name' in Simon Bronner, ed., *Creativity and Tradition in Folklore* (Logan, Utah: Utah State University Press), 41–55.

Olson, Ian (1995–96) 'The influence of nineteenth-century migrant workers on *The Greig-Duncan Folk Song Collection*', *Review of Scottish Culture* 9, 113–27.

Olson, Ian (1996–97) Review of N. Wursbach and S. M. Salz, *Motif Index of the Child Corpus. The English and Scottish Popular Ballad* (Berlin and New York, 1995), *Review of Scottish Culture* 10, 163.

Olson, Ian (1998) 'Scottish song in the James Madison Carpenter Collection', *Folk Music Journal* 7(4), 421–33, https://www.jstor.org/stable/4522608 (accessed 3 October 2019).

Olson, Ian (2002a) 'James Bruce Duncan' in *The Greig-Duncan Folk Song Collection*, vol. 8, 541–6.

Olson, Ian (2002b) 'Gavin Greig' in *The Greig-Duncan Folk Song Collection*, vol. 8, 531–9.

Olson, Ian (2003–4) '*The Greig-Duncan Folk Song Collection*' [review article], *Review of Scottish Culture* 16, 161–6.

Olson, Ian (2007a) 'Scottish contemporary traditional music and song' in Beech *et al.*, eds., 379–404.

Olson, Ian (2007b) 'Lizzie Higgins [Mrs Elizabeth Ann Youlden] 1929–1993', booklet accompanying *In Memory of Lizzie Higgins* (Musical Traditions CD MTCD337–8).

Olson, Ian (2007c) 'Bothy ballads and song' in Beech *et al.*, eds., 322–59.

Ong, Walter (2002) *Orality and Literacy: The Technologizing of the Word*, 2nd edn (London: Routledge).

Opie, Iona and Peter Opie (1959) *The Lore and Language of Schoolchildren* (London: Oxford University Press).

O'Reilly, Edmund (2004) 'Transformations of tradition in the Folkways Anthology' in Russell and Atkinson, eds., 79–94.

Oxford Dictionary of National Biography (updated 2019) (Oxford University Press) https://www.oxforddnb.com/ (accessed 3 October 2019).

The Oxford English Dictionary (OED) (1884–1928) Sir James Murray *et al.*, eds., 12 vols. (Oxford University Press). Second edn 1989, 20 vols. Third edn online: http://www.oed.com/ (accessed 3 October 2019).

Palmer, Neil (2002) 'C25 Mrs Walker and Mrs Beaton' in *The Greig-Duncan Folk Song Collection*, vol. 8, 593.

Pavee Point Travellers' Centre (2010) 'Profile of the Traveller Family', www.paveepoint.ie/wp-content/uploads/2010/07/Profile-of-the-Traveller-Family.pdf (accessed 3 October 2019).

'Pedlars Act 1871' (1871) 'legislation.gov.uk', http://www.legislation.gov.uk/ukpga/Vict/34-35/96 (accessed 3 October 2019).

Petrie, Elaine (1997) 'What a voice: women, repertoire and loss in the singing tradition' in Gifford and McMillan, eds., 262–73.

Petrie, Elaine (2002a) 'C9 Mrs Margaret Gillespie' in *The Greig-Duncan Folk Song Collection*, vol. 8, 559–64.

Petrie, Elaine (2002b) 'C20 Miss Bell Robertson' in *The Greig-Duncan Folk Song Collection*, vol. 8, 579–85.

Pitcairn, Robert (1833) 'Appendix V. Documents Relative to the "Egyptianis," or Gipsies' in *Criminal Trials in Scotland*, vol. III *From A.D. M.CCCC.LXXXVIII to A.D. M.DC. XXIV* (Edinburgh: William Tait; London: Longman *et al.*), 590–5.

Porter, James, ed. (1995) *Ballads and Boundaries: Narrative Singing in an Intercultural Context. Proceedings of the 23rd International Ballad Conference of the Commission for Folk Poetry (Société International d'Ethnologie et de Folklore) University of California, Los Angeles, June 21–24, 1993* (Department of Ethnomusicology & Systematic Musicology, UCLA).

Porter, James and Katherine Campbell (2002) 'C19 Alexander Robb' in *The Greig-Duncan Folk Song Collection*, vol. 8, 577–8.

Porter, James and Herschel Gower (1995) *Jeannie Robertson. Emergent Singer, Transformative Voice* (Knoxville: University of Tennessee Press).

'Records of the Parliaments of Scotland to 1707' (n.d.) http://www.rps.ac.uk (accessed 3 October 2019).

Rehfisch, Farnham (1975) 'Scottish Travellers or tinkers' in Rehfisch, ed., 271–83.

Rehfisch, Farnham, ed. (1975) *Gypsies, Tinkers and Other Travellers* (London: Academic Press).

Rice, Timothy (1994) *May It Fill Your Soul: Experiencing Bulgarian Music* (University of Chicago Press).

Rieuwerts, Sigrid (1995) 'Boundaries of cultural experience: singer and scholar' in Porter, ed., 374–6.

Rieuwerts, Sigrid (2002) 'Women as the chief preservers of traditional ballad poetry', *Acta Ethnographica Hungarica* 47(1–2), 149–59. DOI: https://doi.org/10.1556/AEthn.47.2002.1-2.16 (accessed 3 October 2019).

The Roud Folk Song Index (n.d.), compiled by Steve Roud (Vaughan Williams Memorial Library) https://www.vwml.org/search/search-roud-indexes (accessed 3 October 2019).

Russell, Ian and David Atkinson, eds. (2004) *Folk Song: Tradition, Revival and Re-creation*. (Elphinstone Institute, University of Aberdeen).

'Scotland's Census' (n.d.) 'National Records of Scotland', http://www.scotlandscensus.gov.uk/ (accessed 3 October 2019).

The Scots Musical Museum (1787–1803), ed. James Johnson, 6 vols. (Edinburgh: James Johnson), https://digital.nls.uk/special-collections-of-printed-music/archive/91519813 (accessed 19 October 2019). Second edn 1839, with additional notes and illustrations by William Stenhouse (Edinburgh and London: William Blackwood and Thomas Cadell). Third edn 1853, ed. David Laing, 4 vols. (Edinburgh and London: William Blackwood and Sons).

A Scots Reader Book II – Senior [c. 1937] (n.a.) (Edinburgh and London: Oliver and Boyd).

The Scottish National Dictionary (SND) (1931–75), eds. William Grant *et al.*, 10 vols. (Edinburgh: Scottish National Dictionary Association). Online: 'Dictionary of the Scots Language' http://www.dsl.ac.uk/ (accessed 3 October 2019).

Sharp, Cecil J., ed. Maud Karpeles (1965) *English Folk Song. Some Conclusions*, 4th edn (London: Simpkin & Novello). Originally published 1907.

Shoolbraid, Murray, ed. (2010) *The High-Kilted Muse: Peter Buchan and his* Secret Songs of Silence (Jackson: University of Mississippi Press, in association with the Elphinstone Institute, University of Aberdeen).

Shuldham-Shaw, Patrick (1973, 1981) 'The Greig-Duncan Folk Song Collection', *New Edinburgh Review* (August, 1973), 3–5. Reprinted in *The Greig-Duncan Folk Song Collection*, vol. 1, vii–xiv.

Shuldham-Shaw, Patrick and Emily Lyle, eds. (1974) 'J. B. Duncan's lecture to the Aberdeen Wagner Society, 1908', *Scottish Studies* 18, 1–37.

Simson, James (1866) 'Disquisition on the past, present and future of Gipsydom', in W. Simson ed. J. Simson, 371–542.

Simson, Walter, ed. James Simson (1866) *A History of the Gipsies with Specimens of the Gipsy Language* (New York: M. Doolady; London: Sampson Low, Son and Marston).

Spence, Lewis (1920) *An Encyclopaedia of Occultism* (London: G. Routledge & Sons).
Spence, Lewis (1955) 'The Scottish Tinkler Gypsies', *Scotland's Magazine* 51(2), 20–4.
Stewart, Elizabeth, ed. Alison McMorland (2012) *Up Yon Wide and Lonely Glen* (Jackson: University Press of Mississippi).
Stewart, Sheila (2006) *Queen amang the Heather: The Life of Belle Stewart* (Edinburgh: Birlinn).
Teitelbaum, Michael (1984) *The British Fertility Decline: Demographic Transition in the Crucible of the Industrial Revolution* (Princeton University Press).
Tobar an Dualchais/Kist o Riches (n.d.) http://www.tobarandualchais.co.uk/ (accessed 3 October 2019).
The Traveller Movement (2019) 'Values and culture of GRT communities', https://travellermovement.org.uk/about/gypsy-roma-traveller-history-and-culture#values (accessed 3 October 2019).
Turbett, Colin (2009) 'Issues close to home – Scottish Traveller community marginalised', Taycoast Scottish Socialist Party, https://taycoastssp.blogspot.com/2009/07/issues-close-to-home-scottish-traveller.html (accessed 3 October 2019).
Verrier, Michael (2004) 'Folk club or epic theatre: Brecht's influence on the performance practice of Ewan MacColl' in Russell and Atkinson, eds., 108–14.
Walker, William (1883) *The Life and Times of the Rev. John Skinner M.A.* (London: W. Skeffington & Son).
Walker, William (1915) *Peter Buchan and Other Papers on Scottish and English Ballads and Songs* (Aberdeen: D. Wyllie & Son).
Watson, William (1937) *Scottish Verse from the Book of the Dean of Lismore* (Edinburgh: Oliver & Boyd for the Scottish Gaelic Texts Society).
Wedderburn, Robert, ed. Alasdair Stewart (1979) *The Complaynt of Scotland* (c. 1550), (Edinburgh: Scottish Text Society).
'Whalsay's Heritage of Song' (2015) School of Scottish Studies Archives, University of Edinburgh, http://www.sssa.llc.ed.ac.uk/whalsay/about/ (accessed 3 October 2019).
Whitston, Kevin (1997) 'The reception of scientific management by British engineers, 1890–1914', *The Business History Review*, 71(2), 207–29. DOI: https://doi.org/10.2307/3116158 (accessed 31 October 2019).
Whyte, Betsy (1979, 2001) *The Yellow on the Broom* (Edinburgh: Birlinn). Originally published 1979.
Williamson, Keith (1983) 'Lowland Scots in education: an historical survey. Part II', *Scottish Language*, 2, 52–87.
Williamson, Linda (1985) 'Narrative Singing among the Scots Travellers: A Study of Strophic Variation in Ballad Performance' (University of Edinburgh PhD thesis), https://www.era.lib.ed.ac.uk/handle/1842/8223 (accessed 3 October 2019).

Williamson, Linda (2020) 'Clàr na Seachdain/Recording of the Week', Tobar an Dualchais ~ Kist o Riches Facebook Page, 13 November at 07:18, https://www.facebook.com/TobaranDualchaisKistoRiches/posts/3668291823233507 (accessed 13 November 2020).

'Willie, we have Missed You' (n.d.) Duke University Libraries Digital Repository, https://idn.duke.edu/ark:/87924/r4zg6kg81 (accessed 9 October 2019).

Wood, Sydney (1991) 'Education in nineteenth-century rural Scotland – an Aberdeenshire case study', *Review of Scottish Culture* 7, 25–33.

Index

agricultural depression   1, 22, 128, **132**–**7**, 150, 159, 166
agricultural or rural background   19, 118–9, 123, 143, 149, 152, 156
Agricultural Revolution   113, 120–2
Alexander, Robert   46, 136–7
antiquarianism   140–1, 158
assembly line production   18, 143
Atkinson, David   4, 11, 23, 54
audiences   3–4, 10, 53, 78, 92, 115–6, 122
audio *see* broadcast music; gramophones

bawdy songs   23, 50
Bearman, C. J.   19, 117
'The Birks of Aberfeldy'   48, 51
birth cohorts
    1840s   37, 101, 120–2, 149, 152, 165
    1860s   123–4
    1880s–1890s   70, **133–5**, 150, 159, 166
    1920s   19, 33, 59, **138–44**, 147, 149, 150, 155, 156, 158, 159
    1940s   61, 138, 158
birth rates *see* demographic transition; Travellers
Bishop, Julia   105–6
Blythman, Morris   138, 158
'The Bonnie Banks o' Airdrie'   44, 51
Borders   40, 97, 115, 121–2
bothy ballads   123
bothy singing *see* contexts of singing
Bourne, George   120, 122–3
broadcast music   57–8, **143**–**4**, 149, 156
broadsides   49, 56, 62, 106
Bruford, Alan   48, 54, 56, 58, 140, 142
Buchan, David   105–6, 113, 121–2, 142
Buchan, Norman   158
burker stories   16
buskers *see* street singers
Byrne, Steve   11, 15, 22n, 23, 56–7

Campbell, Katherine   43, 47, 56, 66, 195
    see also Porter, James
cant *see* Travellers
carding *see* contexts of singing

Carpenter, James Madison   77, 105–6, 133n, 166
Carter, Ian   7, 62, 91, 107, 117, 118, 121, 123, 124, 128
Child, Francis James   48n17, 77, 95, *et passim*
childhood
    definition   24–5
    song transmission   92, **135**–**7**, 143, 156
    see also demographic transition; education
Children Act 1908 *see* education
children's songs   23, 196
Clement, David   146
Collinson, Francis *see* Henderson, Hamish
contexts of singing
    domestic work   77–8, 115, 142
    farm work   63, 67, **93**–**4**, 115, 142
    fireside/farm kitchens/bothies/smithies   58, 61, 91, 116, 122, 142, 146
    platform concerts   9, 115–6, 122–3
    work-associated social gatherings   8, 63, 93, 121
    workplaces (other than farms)   63, 93, 115, **142**–**3**
Cooke, Peter   3, 41n5, 47, 49, 52
crofting *see* North-East
Crofton, Henry Thomas   40–1

demographic transition   126–30, 152
Departmental Committee on Tinkers (Scotland)   45, 66, 114–5, 129
Departmental Committee on Vagrancy in Scotland   45–6, 114–5
dependence on literacy *see* literacy
Devine, T. M.   120, 128
dialect *see* Scots language
domestic servants   66, 91, 92, 143, 152
Doric *see* Scots language
Douglas, Sheila   11, 53, 68, 71–2, 143
Duncan, Bell   77–8, 105–6
Duncan, George   49, 56, 106, 124
Duncan, Rev. James   43, 49, 98, 106, 118, *et passim*

INDEX

education
    and Travellers   24n5, 42, 73, 115, 129–30
    Children Act 1908   42, 73
    Education Act 1872   4, 123–4, 127, 137
    in the North-East   107, 117, **123–6**, 128
    Reformatory Schools (Scotland) Act 1854   42
    school leaving age   4, 24, 107, 123
    versus tradition   19, **126–30**
Enclosure Movement *see* Agricultural Revolution
Evans, George Ewart   127, 132
'The Ewie wi' the Crookit Horn'   48–9, 73n63
extended family structure   126–30

family size *see* demographic transition; Travellers
farming *see* agricultural or rural background; North-East
farmservants   61, 62, 91, 92–4, 121, 137
fertility *see* demographic transition
fieldwork *see The Greig-Duncan Folk Song Collection*; School of Scottish Studies
Findlater, Ethel   56, 57
First World War   124, **139–40**
Folk Revival   *passim*
    and Travellers   9, 11, 92, 104
    and young female singers   75, 76, 158
    definition   2, 9
    see also source singers; Henderson, Hamish
'The formation of the collection' (FoC)   5–6, 22, 58, 194–6

Gaelic   23, 146
Gammon, Vic *see* Knevett, Arthur and Vic Gammon
generations, average length of   7
Gentleman, Hugh and Susan Swift   39, 41, 46, 72–3, 114, 129, 145
geographical background *see* regional background
Gillespie, Mrs Margaret   5, 55, 66, 92, 105, 106, 194, 195
girlhood *see* childhood
Gower, Herschel *see* Porter, James

gramophones   57–8, 62
Greig, Gavin   43, 48n18, 57, 115–6, 117, 122–3, 140, *et passim*
The Greig-Duncan Folk Song Collection (G-D) *passim*
    biases   6, 43, 51, 77
    fieldwork   4, 25, 163
    intermediaries   4, 5, 22, 52–3
Gypsies *see* Travellers

Hall, Peter   47–8, 112–3
handwritten lyrics   56–7, 62
    see also song manuscripts
harvest home *see* contexts of singing
hawkers   41–2, 44, 46–7, 65, 92
    see also itinerants
Henderson, Hamish
    and the Folk Revival   2, 11, 15–6, 24, 72, 104, 158, 159
    and Francis Collinson   43, 98
    as author   20, 39, 41, 42–3, 48n16, 55, 73n63, 98n, 104, 112, 113–4
    as collector   3, 8, 42, 77, 95, 145
Higgins, Lizzie   11, 72, 87, 92, 104, 106, 144, 159
Hogg, James   121
Holmquist, Jonathan Carl   124–5
Hunter, Andrew (Andy)   87, 96, 136–7, 158

illiteracy *see* literacy
Irish itinerants   41–2, 47, 137
Irish migrant labour   23
itinerants   122
    see also Irish itinerants; hawkers; tramps; Travellers; vagrants

'Jock o' Hazeldean' (Child 293)   48, 55
Johnstone, Martha (Martha Reid)   45, 104–6, 115, 144, 145
Jones, E. L.   120, 132

Keith, Alexander   98, 194, 195
Kennedy, Mary   45, 49, 65
kindly relations *see* social relations
kirn *see* contexts of singing
Knevett, Arthur and Vic Gammon   117, 120
Korczynski, Marek   143

Laslett, Peter   66, 113, 126
Leitch, Roger   15, 41
literacy   54
  dependence on literacy   56–7, 74
  non-literacy   72–4, 129
  see also handwritten lyrics; print; song manuscripts
Lyall, Mrs   7, 66n45, 107, 153, 194
Lyle, Emily   4, 22, 25, 43, 52, 113, 140n4
  see also 'The formation of the collection' (FoC)

MacColl, Ewan   11, 53, 159
  and Peggy Seeger   4, 9, 43, 53, 72n55, 112, 145
McCormick, Andrew   42, 45, 49, 65, 116
McKean, Thomas   25, 92n43, 104, 107
MacKinnon, Niall   147
MacRitchie, David   40–1, 42, 114
manuscripts see song manuscripts
Mathieson, Willie   5, 17, 56, 63, 87, 93, 104, 107
meal-and-ale see contexts of singing
memory
  memorisation   54–5
  failure of memory   3, 10, 17, 85
  see also literacy
Milton, Colin   124
Mitchell, Willie   56, 87
modernity versus tradition see tradition versus modernity
Munro, Ailie   3, 9, 43, 119, 146

Napoleonic Wars   40, 121
network theory see social network theory
Niles, J. D.   104
non-literacy see literacy
Nord, Deborah   114
North-East
  crofting and farming   7, 62, 107, 113, 120–1, 124, 128, 132, 165
  in School of Scottish Studies data   96, 119, 122, 136, 156
  poets   124
  regional culture   23, 51–2, 83, 88, 96, 101, 105, 117, **123**–6, 148–9
  see also education

Olson, Ian
  on Greig-Duncan   43, 118
  on the North-East   23, 96
  on songs   48–9, 123, 146
  on terminology and methodology   2, 9, 95, 98n
  on Traveller singers   3, 11, 15, 47, 51–2, 55–6, 62, 65, 73
oral tradition   9, 11, 49, 54, 71–4, 95, 153–4
Ord, John   22
Orkney   58, 97, 140

pedlars see hawkers
Percy, Bishop Thomas   55, 56, 98
performance   10–12, 53, 75, 91, 115–6
  see also audiences; contexts of singing
Petrie, Elaine   78, 93, 107, 116, 194
platform concerts see contexts of singing
Porter, James   43
  and Herschel Gower   11, 75, 91
  and Katherine Campbell   195
print   55–6, 61, 72, 73–4, 106, 150
  see also broadsides

'The Queen amang the Heather'   72n55, 93

recorded music see broadcast music; gramophones
Reformatory Schools (Scotland) Act 1854 see education
regional background   118, 136
  see also North-East
Rehfisch, Farnham   43, 114, 128, 129
Reid, Martha see Johnstone, Martha
Revival see Folk Revival
Rieuwerts, Sigrid   10
Robertson, Bell   17, 24, 44–5, 55, 66, 103, 105, 107, 142–3
Robertson, Jeannie
  and Child ballads   48, 72, 95, 104, 106
  as source singer   2, 26, 87, 92, 106, 113, 159
  sources of repertoire   11, 54–5, 72, 73, 96, 106
Robertson, Stanley   16, 55, 72, 104, 106, 111, 145
Romany see Travellers
rural background see agricultural or rural background

INDEX

school *see* education
school leaving age *see* education
School of Scottish Studies (SSSA) *passim*
   biases 3, 11–16, 43, 52, 77–85, 91, 119, 141, 146
   fieldwork 1, 3, 6, 8, 9, 10, 30, 61, 95, 103, 135, 163
   see also Bruford, Alan; Cooke, Peter; Henderson, Hamish; Munro, Ailie; North-East
Scots language 124–5
The Scots Musical Museum 48–9, 73, 146
Scott, Sir Walter 10, 55
Scott, Willie 93, 122
second-hand recipients 2, 22, 26, 59, 165–6
Seeger, Peggy *see* MacColl, Ewan
self collection *see* song manuscripts
servants *see* domestic servants; farmservants
Sharp, Cecil 19, 117–8, 120, 122, 128n16
Shelta *see* Travellers
Shepheard, Pete 47
Shetland 7, 40, 63, 97
Shirer, Annie 66, 105, 106, 153, 195
Shuldham-Shaw, Patrick 4
Simson, James 40, 129
Simson, Walter 40, 42, 45, 114
'Singers' with a capital S 9, 17, 104, 145, 163, 164
   see also source singers
singing styles *see* Travellers
Skinner, Rev. John 48–9
smithies *see* contexts of singing
social class 19, 118, 120–3, 152
social network theory 72
social relations 92, 121–2
   see also Travellers
song manuscripts 56–7, 196
   see also handwritten lyrics
source singers 2, 9, 15, 53, 87
   see also Higgins, Lizzie; Robertson, Jeannie; Stewart, Belle; Stewart, Sheila; Whyte, Betsy
Spence, Lewis 41
Stewart, Belle 2, 11, 50, 55, 72, 73, 92, 145
Stewart, Sheila 43n, 55, 72, 92, 145
street singers 42, 44, 46–7, 50, 62n35, 65, 92

Teitelbaum, Michael 126–7, 129n18
'Thomas the Rhymer' 10, 55
threshing *see* contexts of singing
'The Tinker's Wedding' 49, 51n31
Tobar an Dualchais/Kist o Riches (TaD) 1, 6, 9, 20, 21, 50, 58, 63, 135, 144
tradition *versus* modernity 18, 112–5, 117, 120–3, 126–30, 132, 143–6, 148–9, 165
tramps 42, 44, 46, 92n41, 137
   see also itinerants
Travellers *passim*
   age of marriage 129
   family size 7n17, 129–30, 131
   family structure 24n5, 128, 129–30, 155–6
   history 40–2
   language 41, 45, 49, 129n17
   occupations 8, 41–2, 44, 67, 91, 114–5, 128
   population numbers **45–6**, 129n17
   repertoire 47–52, 62, 80
   singing styles 44–5, 47
   social relations 65–6, 91, 92, 114–5, 155
   terminology 39–42
   see also education; demographic transition; itinerants; tradition *versus* modernity

vagrants 42, 45–6
   see also Departmental Committee on Vagrancy in Scotland; itinerants

Walker, William 22, 48n20
Whyte, Betsy 23n3, 50, 52, 55, 105n10, 115n, 142, 144
Whyte, Bryce 3, 145
Williamson, Duncan 10, 45, 55, 104, 105n10, 111, 116
Williamson, Linda 10, 41n5, 45, 50, 75, 104–5, 109, 116, 144
'Willie's Fatal Visit' (Child 255) 50, 72
Wood, Sydney 128
World War I *see* First World War
writing *see* handwritten lyrics; print; song manuscripts

'Yowie wi the Crooked Horn' *see* 'The Ewie wi' the Crookit Horn'

Printed in the United States
by Baker & Taylor Publisher Services